COMMITTEE ON
POPULATION AND DEMOGRAPHY　　　　　　　Report No. 23

The Determinants of Brazil's Recent Rapid Decline in Fertility

Thomas W. Merrick
Elza Berquo

Panel on Fertility Determinants
Committee on Population and Demography
Commission on Behavioral and
　Social Sciences and Education
National Research Council

NATIONAL ACADEMY PRESS
Washington, D.C.　1983

NOTICE: The project that is the subject of this report was approved by the Governing Board of the National Research Council, whose members are drawn from the councils of the National Academy of Sciences, the National Academy of Engineering, and the Institute of Medicine. The members of the committee responsible for the report were chosen for their special competences and with regard for appropriate balance.

This report has been reviewed by a group other than the authors according to procedures approved by a Report Review Committee consisting of members of the National Academy of Sciences, the National Academy of Engineering, and the Institute of Medicine.

The National Research Council was established by the National Academy of Sciences in 1916 to associate the broad community of science and technology with the Academy's purposes of furthering knowledge and of advising the federal government. The Council operates in accordance with general policies determined by the Academy under the authority of its congressional charter of 1863, which establishes the Academy as a private, nonprofit, self-governing membership corporation. The Council has become the principal operating agency of both the National Academy of Sciences and the National Academy of Engineering in the conduct of their services to the government, the public, and the scientific and engineering communities. It is administered jointly by both Academies and the Institute of Medicine. The National Academy of Engineering and the Institute of Medicine were established in 1964 and 1970, respectively, under the charter of the National Academy of Sciences.

Available from

NATIONAL ACADEMY PRESS
2101 Constitution Avenue, N.W.
Washington, D.C. 20418

Printed in the United States of America

PANEL ON FERTILITY DETERMINANTS

W. PARKER MAULDIN (Chair), The Rockefeller Foundation, New York
ELZA BERQUO, Centro Brasileiro de Analise e Planejamento, Sao Paulo, Brazil
WILLIAM BRASS, Centre for Population Studies, London School of Hygiene and Tropical Medicine
DAVID R. BRILLINGER, Department of Statistics, University of California, Berkeley
V.C. CHIDAMBARAM, World Fertility Survey, London
JULIE DAVANZO, Rand Corporation, Santa Monica
RICHARD A. EASTERLIN, Department of Economics, University of Southern California, Los Angeles
JAMES T. FAWCETT, East-West Population Institute, East-West Center, Honolulu
RONALD FREEDMAN, Population Studies Center, University of Michigan
DAVID GOLDBERG, Population Studies Center, University of Michigan
RONALD GRAY, School of Hygiene and Public Health, The Johns Hopkins University, Baltimore
PAULA E. HOLLERBACH, Center for Policy Studies, The Population Council, New York
RONALD LEE, Graduate Group in Demography, University of California, Berkeley
ROBERT A. LEVINE, Graduate School of Education, Harvard University
SUSAN C.M. SCRIMSHAW, School of Public Health, University of California, Los Angeles
ROBERT WILLIS, Department of Economics, State University of New York, Stony Brook

ROBERT J. LAPHAM, Study Director

COMMITTEE ON POPULATION AND DEMOGRAPHY

ANSLEY J. COALE (Chair), Office of Population Research, Princeton University
WILLIAM BRASS, Centre for Population Studies, London School of Hygiene and Tropical Medicine
LEE-JAY CHO, East-West Population Institute, East-West Center, Honolulu
RONALD FREEDMAN, Population Studies Center, University of Michigan
NATHAN KEYFITZ, Department of Sociology, Harvard University
LESLIE KISH, Institute for Social Research, University of Michigan
W. PARKER MAULDIN, Population Division, The Rockefeller Foundation, New York
JANE MENKEN, Office of Population Research, Princeton University
SAMUEL PRESTON, Population Studies Center, University of Pennsylvania
WILLIAM SELTZER, Statistical Office, United Nations
CONRAD TAEUBER, Kennedy Institute, Center for Population Research, Georgetown University
ETIENNE VAN DE WALLE, Population Studies Center, University of Pennsylvania

ROBERT J. LAPHAM, Study Director

NOTE: Members of the Committee and its panels and working groups participated in this project in their individual capacities; the listing of their organizational affiliation is for identification purposes only, and the views and designations used in this report are not necessarily those of the organizations mentioned.

CONTENTS

LIST OF TABLES ix

LIST OF FIGURES xiv

PREFACE xv

SUMMARY 1

INTRODUCTION 12

   Background, 12

      Geography and Population Distribution, 12
      Political and Economic History, 15

   Recent Demographic Trends, 18

      Population Trends, 18
      National and Regional Trends in the Total
        Fertility Rate, 20
      Expectation of Life at Birth, 22
      Income Class Differences in Fertility and
        Mortality, 23

   Purpose and Structure of This Report, 25

PART I   FERTILITY DETERMINANTS AT THE NATIONAL LEVEL

1 THE PROXIMATE DETERMINANTS OF FERTILITY 29

   Marital Status and Mean Age at Marriage, 30

Marital Fertility, 35
Decomposition of Change in Birth Rates, 41
Role of the Proximate Variables, 42

> Contraceptive Use, 44
> Abortion, 49
> Breastfeeding/Postpartum Amenorrhea, 54
> A Speculative Overview of Trends in the Proximate Determinants of Total Fertility Rates, 1970-80, 56

Conclusions, 58

2 SOCIOECONOMIC DIFFERENTIALS IN FERTILITY   60

Education and Fertility Decline, 61
Family Income, 67
The Regional Dimension of Income Differences, 73
Conclusions, 77

3 DETERMINANTS OF BRAZIL'S RECENT FERTILITY DECLINE   79

Hypotheses Linking Socioeconomic Conditions to Fertility Decline, 80

> Increased Access to Fertility Control, 84
> Socioeconomic Factors, 90

Socioeconomic Factors and Fertility Decline Among Urban and Rural Women, 96

> Currently Married Urban Women, 97
> Currently Married Rural Women, 106

Conclusions, 113

4 ANALYSIS OF FERTILITY DETERMINANTS AT THE NATIONAL LEVEL   115

Urban Women, 116

> Analysis of Urban CEB Differentials in 1970 and 1976, 122
> Sources of Change in CEB from 1970 to 1976, 127

Rural Women, 133

Analysis of Rural CEB Differentials in 1970 and 1976, 136
Changes in Rural CED from 1970 to 1976, 142

Conclusions, 142

PART II FERTILITY DETERMINANTS AT THE LOCAL LEVEL

5 THE NIHR: PURPOSE AND METHODOLOGY — 145

6 THE TOTAL FERTILITY RATE: LEVELS AND TRENDS — 151

7 NUPTIALITY — 156

Type of Union, 156

   Distribution of Types of Union, 156
   The Role of Concensual Unions, 168
   Type of Union and Fertility, 172

Age at Marriage, 174

8 MARITAL FERTILITY — 178

9 THE PROXIMATE VARIABLES — 181

Contraceptive Use, 183

   Contraceptive Prevalence, 183
   Contraceptive Methods, 186
   Bongaarts' Index of Contraception, 189
   Postpartum Infecundability, 191

Abortion, 194

10 SOCIOECONOMIC FACTORS: FAMILY INCOME — 196

11 CONCLUSIONS — 202

Decomposition of General Fertility Rates, 202
Decomposition of Total Fertility, 204
Findings at the National/State and Local
   Levels, 205

NOTES — 208

APPENDIX: THE NIHR CONTEXTS — 209

REFERENCES — 235

LIST OF TABLES

1	Components of Population Growth, 1940-80	18
2	Total Fertility Rates, 1950-80	20
3	Expectation of Life at Birth, 1950-76	23
4	Income Class Differences in Total Fertility Rates and the Expectation of Life at Birth, 1970	24
5	Reported Percent Distribution of Women by Marital Status and Age, 1950-80	31
6	Percent of Single Women Who Report Having Had a Child, by Age, 1950-76	32
7	Singulate Mean Age at Marriage (SMAM), by Region, 1950-76	34
8	Age-Specific And Total Marital Fertility Rate Calculations, 1960, 1970, and 1976	36
9	Decomposition of Change in General Fertility Rate, 1960-76	41
10	Decomposition of Change in Crude Birth Rate, 1960-76	42
11	Contraceptive Prevalence, Summary of Survey Data	45
12	Components of Index of Contraception (C_c), 1970, 1976, and 1980	48
13	Reported Abortions, Summary of Survey Data	52
14	Reported Breastfeeding, Summary of Survey Data	55
15	Estimates of Proximate Determinants of Total Fertility Rate, 1970-80	56
16	Total Fertility Rates by Years of Schooling, 1970-76	63
17	Total Fertility Rates by Family Income Level (multiples of monthly minimum salary), 1970 and 1976	67
18	Total Fertility Rates by Family Income Deciles, 1970-76	70

19	Percent Distribution of All Women Aged 15-49 by Income Deciles, Years in School, and Rural-Urban Residence, 1970 and 1976	72
20	Unadjusted Total Fertility Rate by PNAD Region and Income Decile, 1970 and 1976	74
21	Percent Distribution of Women Aged 15-49 by PNAD Region and Income Deciles, 1970 and 1976	75
22	Percent Distribution of Married Women Aged 15-44, by Contraceptive Use Status and Household Income	88
23	Contraceptive Prevalence Survey Data on Percent of Currently Married Women Aged 15-44 Using Contraceptives, by Education	90
24	Source of Family Planning Supplies and Services, Currently Married Women Aged 15-44, CPS Data by State	91
25	Percent of Women Reported as Having No Schooling, by Age, 1960-80	93
26	Percent Distribution of All Women Aged 20-44 by Age and Years of Schooling, 1970 and 1976	94
27	Percent of Women Reported as Working, by Age and Years of Schooling, 1970 and 1976	95
28	Mean and Standard Error (S)[a] of Number of Children Ever Born, Currently Married Urban Women, by Age and Educational Attainment, 1970 and 1976	97
29	Percent Working and Percent Migrants Among Currently Married, Urban Women, 1970 and 1976	99
30	Distribution of Currently Married Women Aged 20-44 by Occupation, Work Status, and Educational Attainment, 1970 and 1976	101
31	Percent of Currently Married, Urban Women Living in Households Reporting Ownership of a Television, by Age and Education, 1970 and 1976	102
32	Average Number of Children Ever Born for Currently Married, Urban Women, by Age, Education, and Current Employment Status, 1970 and 1976	103
33	Average Number of Children Ever Born for Migrant and Nonmigrant Women, by Age and Educational Attainment, 1970 and 1976	104
34	Mean Number of Children Ever Born for Currently Married, Rural Women by Region, Educational Attainment, and Age, 1970 and 1976	108
35	Percent of Currently Married, Rural Women in Proletarian Households, Percent Working, and Percent Migrant, by Age and Region, 1970 and 1976	109

#	Title	Page
36	Mean Number of Children Ever Born for Currently Married, Rural Women Aged 20-44, by Region and Proletarian Status, 1970 and 1976	111
37	Mean Number of Children Ever Born for Currently Married, Rural Women Aged 20-44, by Region and Work Status, 1970 and 1976	112
38	Variable Labels and Definitions, Urban Women	118
39	Means (standard deviations) of Variables Used in Analysis of Differences in Average Parity for Urban Women, 1970 and 1976	121
40	Regression Analysis, Average Number of Children Ever Born (CEB), Married Urban Women, 1970	124
41	Regression Analysis, Average Number of Children Ever Born (CEB), Married Urban Women, 1976	125
42	Changes in Contribution of Independent Variables to Levels of CEB, 1970 and 1976	129
43	Regression Analysis and Test for Interactions, Merged 1970 and 1976 Data Files	130
44	Decomposition of Changes in Average Parity from 1970 to 1976 Using Regression Coefficient for Merged Data	131
45	Percent of Women with GAP Greater than One Standard Deviation from Mean, 1970 and 1976	133
46	Variable Labels and Definitions, Rural Women	137
47	Means (standard deviations) of Variables Used in Analysis of Differences in Average Parity for Rural Women, 1970 and 1976	138
48	Regression Analysis, Average Number of Children Ever Born (CEB), Married Rural Women, 1970	140
49	Regression Analysis, Average Number of Children Ever Born (CEB), Married Rural Women, 1976	141
50	Nine Contexts Defined in Terms of Modes of Production and Type of Involvement in the Development Process	148
51	Total Fertility Rates, Nine Contexts, 1965, 1970, and 1975	153
52	Mean Parity $1/2 \ (P_{25-29} + P_{30-34})$, 1965, 1970, and 1975	155
53	Percent Distribution of Ever-Married Women, by Type of Marital Union, Nine Contexts, 1960, 1970, and 1975	158
54	Percent Distribution of Ever-Married Women, by Type of Marital Union, 1960, 1970, and 1978	160
55	Distribution of Unions According to Order and Type	161

56	Distribution of Ever-Married Women by Type of First Union, for Three Marriage Cohorts: A (until 1960), B (1961-70), and C (1971-76), and for Nine Contexts	163
57	Distribution of Ever-Married Women by Type of First Union, for Three Marriage Cohorts: A (until 1960), B (1961-70), and C (1971-76), and for Five Urban and Four Rural Contexts	164
58	Distribution of Ever-Married Women According to Type of First Union, for Three Marriage Cohorts: A (until 1960), B (1961-70), and C (1971-76), Nine Contexts	166
59	Distribution of Consensual Unions by Different Types, Nine Contexts	170
60	Distribution of Consensual Unions, by Type for Three Marriage Cohorts, Recife	172
61	Mean Number of Children Ever Born Alive by Ever-Married Women, by Type of Marital Union, Nine Contexts, 1975	173
62	Mean Number of Children Ever Born, for Currently Married Women (first marriage), by Type of Union and Three Marriage Cohorts, Nine Contexts	174
63	Estimates for Nuptiality Parameters Using Coale's Method, Nine Contexts	175
64	Mean Age at Marriage (Hajnal method), Nine Contexts	176
65	Total Marital Fertility Rates, Nine Contexts, 1970 and 1975	179
66	Values for the Fertility Control Measure (m) Estimated by Coale's Method, 1970 and 1975	180
67	Currently Married Women Aged 15-49 Currently Using Contraception, by Types of Methods, Nine Contexts	182
68	Currently Married Women Aged 15-49 Currently Using Contraception, Nine Contexts	184
69	Age Distribution of Currently Married, Sterilized Women Aged 15-49, Nine Contexts	187
70	Estimates (in percent) for Use Efficiency of Contraceptives (e), for Currently Married Women, Nine Contexts	190
71	Index of Contraception, Nine Contexts	191
72	Percent of Breastfed Children at 4 Months of Age, by Various Studies	192
73	Values of "i" and C_i, Nine Contexts	194
74	Total Abortion Rates (TAR) and Bongaarts' Abortion Rate (C_a), Nine Contexts	195

75	Percent Distribution of Women Aged 15 and Over, by Per Capita Monthly Income (in fractions of one minimum wage), Five Urban Contexts, at Time of Survey	197
76	Average Number of Children Born to Ever-Married Women Aged 15 and Over, by Per Capita Monthly Income (in fractions of one minimum wage), Five Urban Contexts	199
77	Changes in General Fertility Rates Due to Age Structure, Marital Status, and Marital Fertility, Nine Contexts, 1970-75	203
78	Proximate Determinants of Total Fertility, Nine Contexts, 1975	206
A.1	Dynamics of the Population of Parnaiba (municipality), 1940-70	214
A.2	Dynamics of the Population of Cachoeiro do Itapemirim (municipality), 1940-70	217
A.3	Dynamics of the Population of Sao Jose dos Campos (municipality), 1940-70	221
A.4	Dynamics of the Population of Sertaozinho (municipality), 1940-70	228
A.5	Dynamics of the Population of Santa Cruz do Sul (municipality), 1940-70	231
A.6	Dynamics of the Population of Recife (municipality), 1940-70	234

LIST OF FIGURES

1	Total Fertility Rates by Urban-Rural Residence, 1950-80	2
2	Total Fertility Rates by Region, 1950-80	3
3	Changes in Selected Reproductive Measures Based on Bongaarts' Model, 1970-80	7
4	Percent of Married Women Aged 15-44, Currently Using Contraception, by Household Income for Specified Years	8
5	Age-Specific Fertility Rates, 1975	37
6	Age-Specific Marital Fertility Rates, ($ASMFR_{25-29} = 100$), Six Contexts	40
7	Total Fertility Rate by Years of Schooling, 1970 and 1976	65
8	Distribution of Women Aged 15-49 by Region and Income Group, 1976	76
9	National and Regional Trends in Commercial Distribution of Contraceptive Pills, 1965-81	86

PREFACE

Fertility and its determinants have been urgent topics for research in recent decades with the rapid expansion in world population. Attempts to control population growth have focused on reducing fertility, with some apparent effect. The peak rate of growth in the world's population has now been passed, but growth is still at a high level in almost all the developing countries. In absolute numbers, the increase in the world's population continues to rise; according to United Nations medium projections, more people will be added each year for the next 50 years than were added in 1980.

This report is one of a series of country studies of fertility determinants carried out by the Panel on Fertility Determinants of the Committee on Population and Demography. The Committee on Population and Demography was established in April 1977 by the National Research Council in response to a request by the Agency for International Development (AID) of the U.S. Department of State.

The causes of the reductions in fertility--whether they are the effect primarily of such general changes as lowered infant mortality, increasing education, urban rather than rural residence, and improving status of women, or of such particular changes as spreading knowledge of and access to efficient methods of contraception or abortion--are strongly debated. There are also divergent views of the appropriate national and international policies on population in the face of these changing trends. The differences in opinion extend to different beliefs and assertions about what the population trends really are in many of the less-developed countries. Because births and deaths are recorded very incompletely in much of Africa, Asia, and Latin America, levels and trends of fertility and mortality must be estimated, and disagreement has arisen in some instances about the most reliable estimates of those levels and trends.

It was to examine these questions that the committee was established within the Commission on Behavioral and Social Sciences and Education of the National Research Council. It was funded for a period of five and one-half years by AID under Contract No. AID/pha-C-1161 and Grant No. AID/DSPE-G-0061. Chaired by Ansley J. Coale, the committee has undertaken three major tasks:

1. To evaluate available evidence and prepare estimates of levels and trends of fertility and mortality in selected developing nations;
2. To improve the technologies for estimating fertility and mortality when only incomplete or inadequate data exist (including techniques of data collection);
3. To evaluate the factors determining the changes in birth rates in less-developed nations.

Given the magnitude of these tasks, the committee concentrated its initial efforts on the first two tasks. This work is detailed in a series of country and methodological reports from the National Academy Press, and the demographic estimation methodology developed for the country studies is laid out in a volume issued by the United Nations. Altogether, some 170 population specialists, including 94 from developing countries, have been involved in the work of the committee as members of panels or working groups. The committee, the commission, and the National Research Council are grateful for the unpaid time and effort these experts have been willing to give.

The committee initiated work on the third task in October 1979 when the separately funded Panel on Fertility Determinants was established. Research on the determinants of fertility change has been carried out by scholars from several disciplines, and there is no comprehensive accepted theory of fertility change to guide the evaluation. Because of this state of knowledge of the causes of reductions in fertility and the difficulty of the task, the Panel on Fertility Determinants includes scholars from anthropology, demography, economics, epidemiology, psychology, sociology, and statistics. Three committee members serve on the panel. The work program of the panel includes the preparation of a report that attempts to summarize and integrate scientific knowledge about the determinants of fertility (Academic Press, 1983) as well as a few illustrative cross-national analyses and studies of several developing countries (see inside back cover).

This report is the fourth panel country study. It has been prepared by Thomas W. Merrick, director, Center for Population Research, Georgetown University, and Elza Berquo, research scholar, Centro Brasileiro de Analise e Planejamento, Sao Paulo, Brazil, and a member of the panel. Although it is self-contained, the study is in part a companion to the report of the committee's Panel on Brazil, <u>Levels and Recent Trends in Fertility and Mortality in Brazil</u>, published earlier this year, which examines some of the demographic estimates that are incorporated in this report. Thomas Merrick served as a member of the Panel on Brazil.

The work on this study was carried out at Georgetown University and at the Centro Brasileiro de Analise e Planejamento. During its preparation, each author spent time at the other's institution and at the committee office. Both of the authors' institutions provided logistical support, and, more important, each institution essentially supported each author during the time they devoted to the preparation of this report. The panel and the committee are grateful to these institutions for all of this support.

Partial financial support for research assistance and computer use also was provided through an award from the Rockefeller and Ford Foundations' Research Program on Fertility, Mortality, and Development Interrelations. For Part I of this report, Mahesh Sharma provided capable programming and statistical assistance, and Pamela Nall made valuable contributions to the preparation of tables and in typing material for the report. For Part II, Marcelo Cesar Gouveia and Ivaldo Olimpio da Silva assisted in programming, Rebecca de Souza e Silva provided statistical assistance in preparing tables, and Oneida Maria Borges deserves credit for typing draft material for the report. Jose Alberto Magno de Carvalho, Hania Zlotnik, and Leo Morris provided comments and technical advice at various stages. Brazil's IPPF affiliate, BEMFAM, and the U.S. Centers for Disease Control were particularly helpful in providing information and advance copies of tables from the Contraceptive Prevalence Surveys cited in the report.

An early version of the draft report was discussed at a country studies workshop organized by the panel in

January 1982 with financial assistance from the Rockefeller Foundation. Finally, panel and committee reviewers provided advice and suggestions.

Several members of the panel and committee staff assisted in the preparation of this report. On the production side appreciation is expressed to Elaine McGarraugh of the panel staff for handling the production editing details, to Solveig Padilla and Irene Martinez for helping type the text and tables, and to Rona Briere for editing the report.

W. PARKER MAULDIN, Chair
Panel on Fertility Determinants

SUMMARY

Brazil experienced very rapid decline in fertility during the 1970s. Both the crude birth rate and more refined fertility measures such as the total fertility rate dropped by 25 to 30 percent during the decade; this represented a threefold acceleration in the pace of fertility decline over the previous decade. By 1980, Brazil's crude birth rate was close to 30 per 1,000, as compared to over 40 per 1,000 in the mid-1960s. Total fertility was close to 4.0, a decline of nearly two births per woman from the level of 5.8 births observed in the late 1960s. As shown in Figure 1, the decline was experienced in both rural and urban areas, as well as all of Brazil's major regions, including the Northeast, where fertility rates have traditionally been very high (see Figure 2). In Sao Paulo and other southern states, fertility had declined starting in the 1950s, but the pace accelerated after 1965.

The objective of this report is twofold: (1) to examine this accelerated fertility decline in light of changes in the proximate determinants of fertility; (2) to relate these latter changes in turn to socioeconomic changes that might account for the accelerated decline. The available data on which this report is based are limited in their geographic representation, their timeliness for measuring change, and their coverage of relevant demographic and socioeconomic variables, as well as their reliability in measuring the variables that are included. Despite these limitations, however, the available evidence provides strong support for the following hypotheses: (1) that declining marital fertility was the main demographic component of the accelerated decline; (2) that the principal proximate determinant of this decline consisted of increased fertility control within

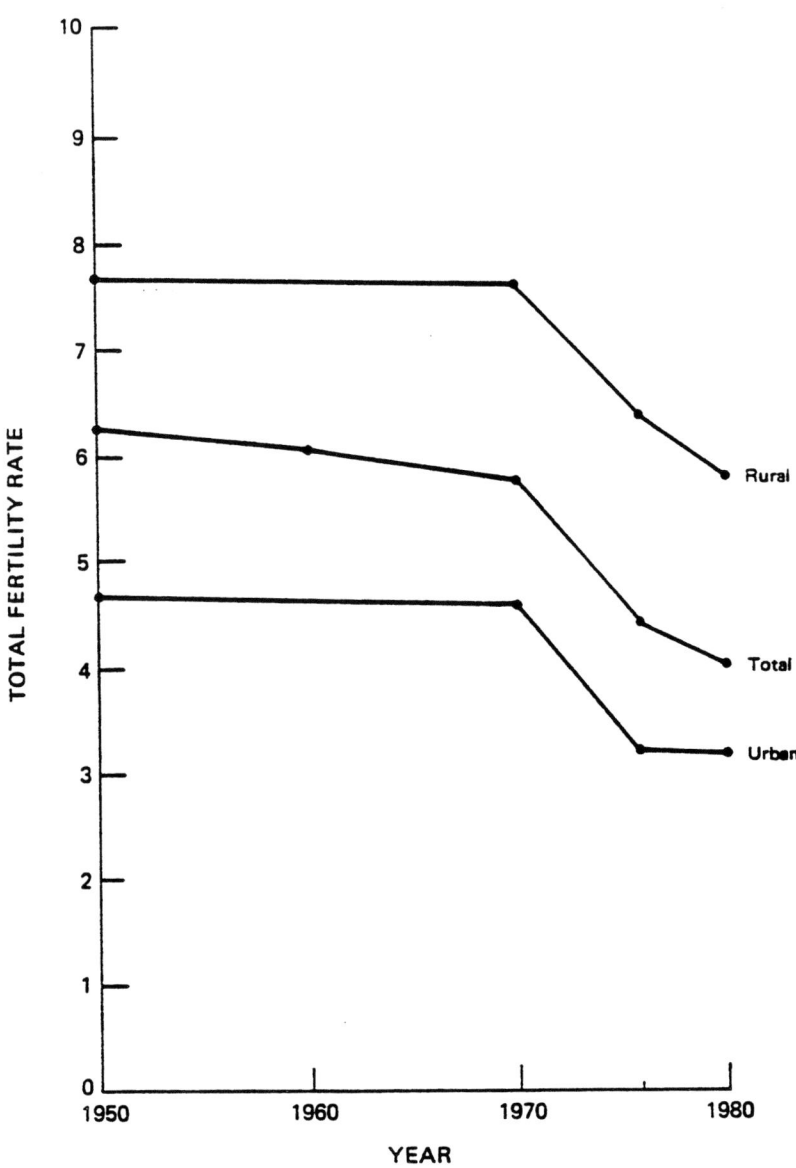

FIGURE 1 Total Fertility Rates by Urban-Rural Residence, 1950-80: Brazil

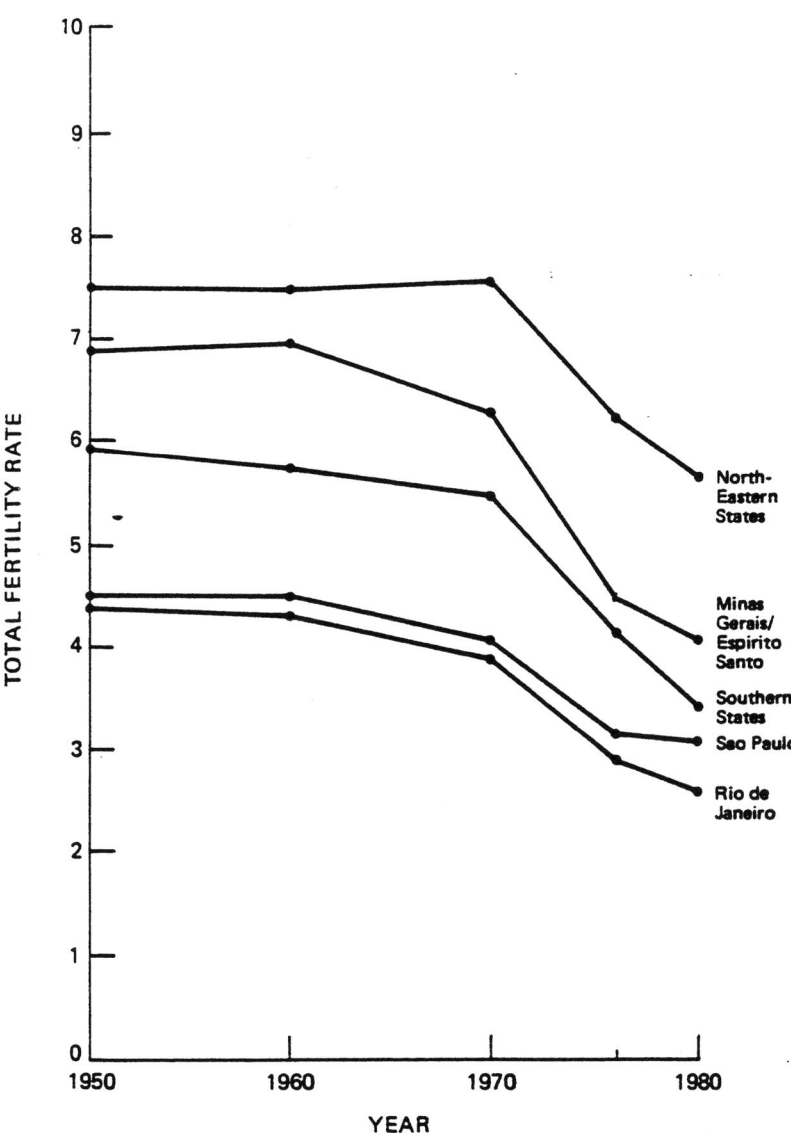

FIGURE 2 Total Fertility Rates by Region, 1950-80: Brazil

marriage (contraception, sterilization, and abortion), though it was not possible to specify precisely what the "mix" of these determinants was or how it may have changed; (3) that the decline in marital fertility can be attributed mainly to the spread of fertility control to lower-income regions and groups that had not participated in previous fertility declines; and (4) that these groups experienced socioeconomic changes (for example, increased educational attainment, increased ownership of such consumer durable goods as televisions, and increased female labor force participation) that were conducive to smaller family norms.

This report is based mainly on three sources of information. The first consists of national-level data collected by the Brazilian census bureau (Fundacao Instituto Brasileiro de Geografia e Estatistica--FIBGE), including the 1970 population census and a 1976 national sample survey (Pesquisa Nacional por Amostra de Domicilios--PNAD). Both included retrospective questions on fertility as well as on socioeconomic characteristics. The second source is the state-level Contraceptive Prevalence Surveys (CPS) conducted during the late 1970s by Brazil's International Planned Parenthood affiliate, BEMFAM (Sociedade Civil de Bem-Estar Familiar), with the assistance of the U.S. Center for Disease Control. Finally, a source at the local level is the CEBRAP National Investigation of Human Reproduction (NIHR), which consists of in-depth contextual studies of nine communities representing different types of socioeconomic structure in Brazil, as well as small sample surveys of the reproductive life histories of women in those settings. When possible, other sources are used to provide supplemental information.

The report is presented in two parts. The first uses the national- and state-level data to examine several hypotheses about how socioeconomic changes may have influenced the reproductive behavior of different groups in Brazil during the early 1970s. Tabular and multiple regression analyses of these data provide strong support for the argument that increased educational attainment of women contributed to the modernization of reproductive behavior, though the data do not provide enough information to specify precisely how this occurred. Nor do they permit as full a testing as one would desire of hypotheses about the way in which institutional forces and structural factors arising from class differences and economic pressures influenced reproductive patterns. The second part of the report consists of a detailed examination of the NIHR local-level data, providing a more focused perspective on Brazilian fertility patterns. These contextual data reveal a wide range of institutional forces that may have influenced fertility. However, the task of establishing the links between these factors and patterns of individual reproductive behavior reported in the sample survey component of the NIHR is still to be completed. The major conclusions of the report are summarized below.

THE PROXIMATE DETERMINANTS OF FERTILITY

The available evidence indicates that changes in the distribution of women by marital status, either through changes in the mean age at marriage or through increases in the proportion of women remaining single, was not a major factor in Brazil's accelerated fertility decline during the 1970s. This is a guarded conclusion because the data on marital status in Brazil are clouded by questions about their reliability, and about the effect of changes in reporting procedures. The most serious problem relates to consensual unions, particularly the extent to which true changes in the proportion of such unions and/or changes in their reporting affected measurement of the mean age at marriage. Because of doubts about mean age at marriage as an index of the effect of changes in marital status on fertility, an alternative measure—mean age at first birth—was also calculated. This measure indicated that changes in age at first birth (which is the main way that changes in age at marriage would affect fertility) did not contribute significantly to the accelerated fertility decline between 1970 and 1976. Thus the report concludes that declining marital fertility (with "marital" including both formal and informal unions) was the main contributor to Brazil's fertility decline. Among the major proximate determinants of marital fertility, the report draws the following conclusions.

Breastfeeding: Postpartum amenorrhea resulting from extended breastfeeding has contributed to fertility reduction in some populations; however, there is no evidence to suggest that changes in breastfeeding patterns played a major role in Brazil's accelerated fertility decline. Indeed, because the practice of breastfeeding is very limited in Brazil, it is difficult to fit models linking mean duration of breastfeeding and postpartum amenorrhea to Brazilian data.

Contraception: Increased control of marital fertility played a major role in Brazil's accelerated fertility decline (see Figure 3). Since there were no nationally representative "before" and "after" data by which to measure changes in contraceptive use, this conclusion is based on fragments of "circumstantial" evidence. This includes the state-level Contraceptive Prevalence Surveys, as well as information on the production and distribution of contraceptives through public- and private-sector institutions and commercial channels. The main unanswered question relates to the mix of fertility control means involved in this increase. The 1970s brought a dramatic increase in the production and distribution of pills in Brazil, and the surveys also report a high rate of surgical sterilization.

Abortion: The main unknown in the mix of fertility control in Brazil is abortion. While survey data reveal comparatively few abortions, the practice is reportedly widespread. Assuming that abortion and contraception were substitutes in the mix of fertility control measures actually used, the report uses a range estimate for the prevalence of abortion. The main flaw in this logic is that while most births in Brazil occurred among women in unions, a higher proportion of pregnancies may have been terminated by abortion among women who were not in unions.

DETERMINANTS OF FERTILITY DECLINE

Brazil's accelerated fertility decline coincided with a period during which lower- and middle-income urban households were raising their consumption expectations. They were also beginning to realize these expectations through increased purchases of housing and other consumer durables, including televisions and automobiles, with most purchases made on the installment plan. Because of unequal treatment of wages and credit obligations in Brazil's indexing system, it was more difficult for families to keep up with payments, and even to purchase basic necessities during periods of high inflation. A working hypothesis is that this pattern, combined with increased knowledge of and access to contraception, may have altered reproductive strategies and/or reduced

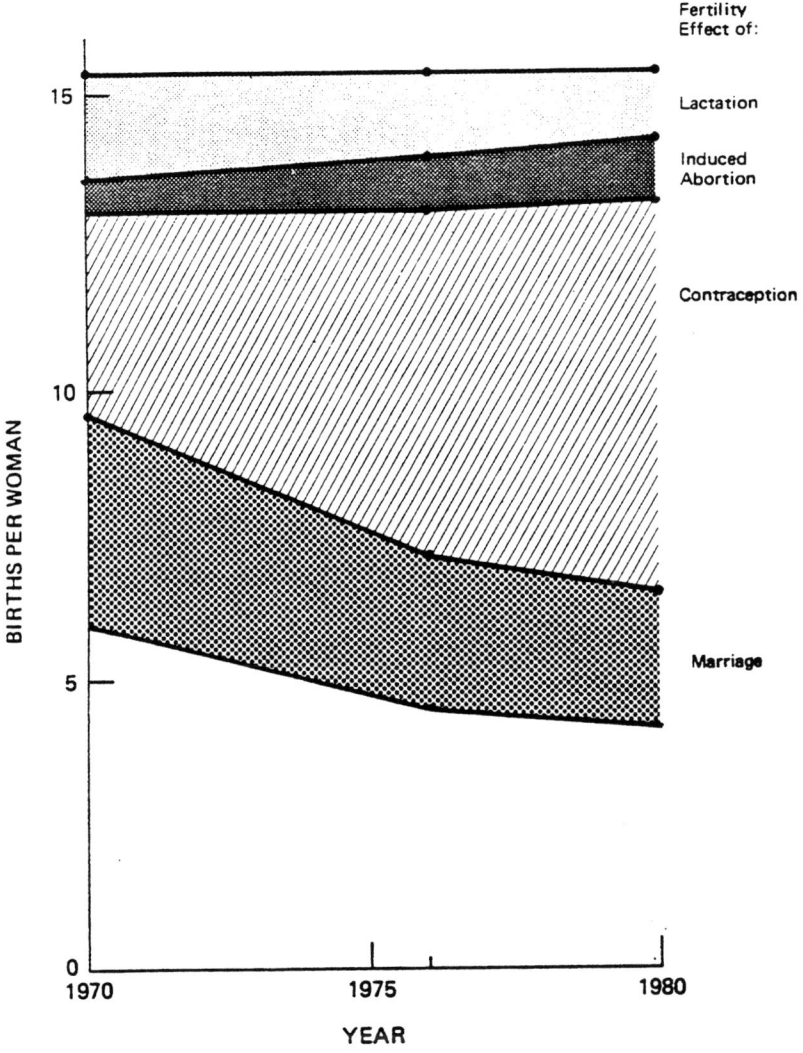

FIGURE 3 Changes in Selected Reproductive Measures Based on Bongaarts' Model, 1970-80: Brazil

family-size desires. While income was an important covariate of contraceptive use, survey evidence suggests that lower income women are also controlling fertility, particularly in the higher income southern region and in states that have established community-based family planning programs (see Figure 4). This explanation does

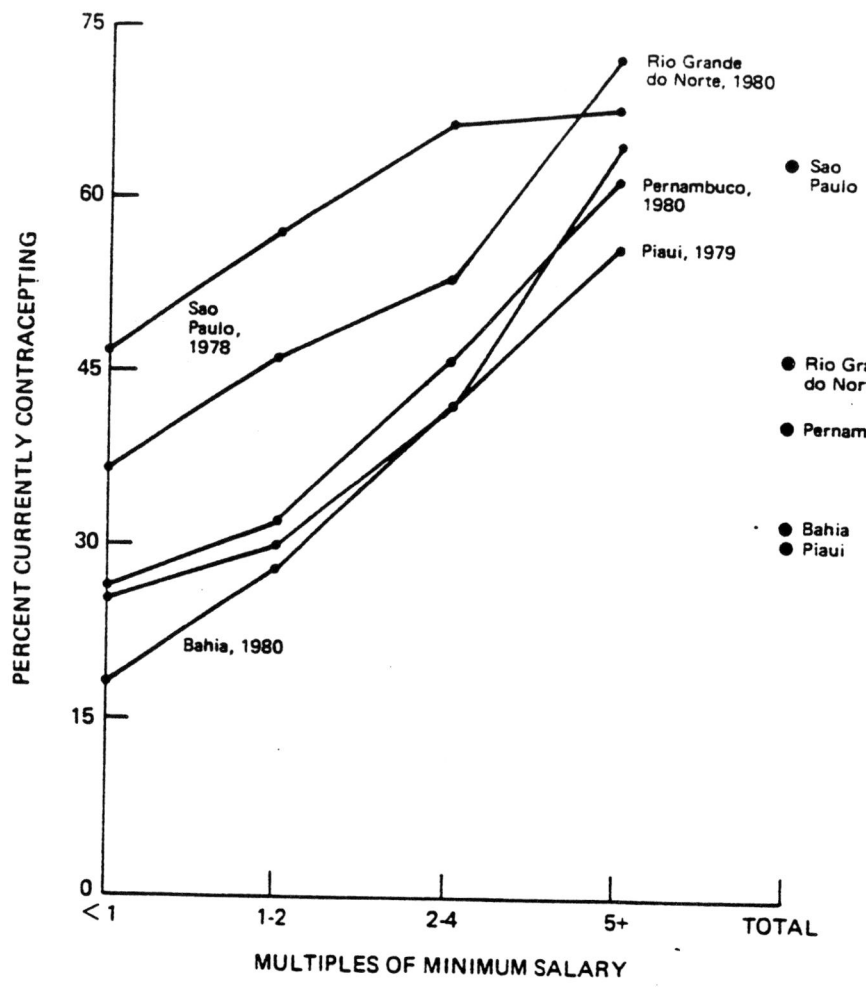

FIGURE 4 Percent of Married Women Aged 15-44, Currently Using Contraception, by Household Income for Specified Years: Brazil

not compete with more conventional explanations of fertility decline as part of the process of modernization, but is an extension incorporating other structural changes.

Part I of this report presents a three-step examination of these hypotheses. The first step consisted of calculating fertility rates based on reports of children ever born and children born in the year prior to census and survey interviews for women classified by income and education levels. These calculations revealed that fertility decline was greatest between 1970 and 1976 among urban lower- and middle-income women, and that increases in educational attainment among these women was a potentially important contributor to that decline. The calculations also raised questions about the interpretation of reports of recent births in the analysis of subgroup differentials, suggesting that the analysis be limited to data on children ever born.

The second step consisted of cross tabulations (controlling for differences in educational attainment) of 1970 and 1976 data on children ever born with questions relating to the hypotheses described above. Specific topics for the latter included female labor force participation, ownership of televisions, migration, and, for rural women, increases in the proletarianization of rural labor.

The third step consisted of multiple regression analysis of the data on children ever born. Among the research questions addressed in this analysis were the following: (1) What measures in the available data files could be used as appropriate indices of the modernizing forces and economic pressures discussed above? (2) How could the relation between these measures and average parity be specified? Were the relationships linear? Should interactions be taken into account? (3) Could the analysis be pushed beyond explanation of differentials in average parity in 1970 and 1976 to an assessment of the sources of changes in fertility during that interval? In other words, did declines in average parity reflect changes in the composition of the population of married women according to modernizing characteristics, or changes in the parameters reflecting the impact of these variables on parity? The latter are likely to reflect structural changes; one of the goals of the analysis was to incorporate variables in the specification for which such changes would be indicative of the specific structural forces hypothesized above, that is, increased economic pressures on household resources.

Most of the variation in average parity (CEB) that could be explained by multivariate regression analysis of data on individual married women from the Brazilian census and PNAD survey related to modernization variables, education, and average earnings. Most of the change that could be accounted for between 1970 and 1976 related to increases in educational attainment and earnings. An attempt to incorporate a variable measuring the relative economic position of urban households (GAP) indicated that there was a positive association between fertility and relative economic status; that is, CEB was higher on average for women whose husbands' current earnings exceeded the level that would be expected given their education and other characteristics. However, decomposition of changes in CEB from 1970 to 1976 did not show that change in GAP contributed to fertility decline.

These regression results do not suggest that increased modernization was the only reason for change. Changes in regression coefficients and in constant terms in the regression equations suggest that a variety of unmeasured factors could have contributed to unexplained variance. Measures that were available in the census and survey data file provide little insight into the nature of such changes--whether they were related to increased access to contraception through public or private channels, or to institutional changes associated with shifts in the Brazilian model of social and economic development.

The nine local studies of the NIHR examined in Part II cover a range of economic and social contexts, including Sao Jose dos Campos's (Sao Paulo State) concentrated industrial capitalistic mode of production, an area in Rio Grande do Sul where small owner-operated establishments predominate, and traditional latifundia-dominated production in the Northeast. Institutional variations were found to be reflected in reproductive behavior in a number of ways, including wide differences in both fertility levels and the proximate determinants of fertility. However, despite major differences in fertility patterns among the different contexts, all but one (Parnaiba-Rural in the Northeast) experienced a significant fertility decline during the early 1970s. CEBRAP's research has not progressed to the point of linking macrostructural differences and changes to recent fertility declines. However, the common experience of the different contexts suggests that societal--rather than local-level influences have contributed to the recent acceleration of fertility decline.

Consensual unions represent a higher and apparently increasing proportion of unions in Recife and other Northeastern contexts; this fact may have contributed to the lower age at marriage and higher fertility observed in those contexts. However, as in Part I, the major determinant of fertility decline is identified as declining marital fertility. Again as in Part I, the main proximate determinant of this decline in marital fertility was found to be increased use of contraception, particularly the more effective methods. This can in turn be related at the local level to shifts in family income: as in Part I, it is concluded that there is a positive association between higher family income and decreased family size.

INTRODUCTION

BACKGROUND

Brazil accounts for one-third of the population of Latin America, and nearly half that of South America. Its land area occupies 48 percent of the subcontinent, and is about equal in size to the United States, excluding Alaska. The population in 1980 was 120 million, more than double the 1950 total of 52 million. Starting in the late nineteenth century, Brazil experienced population growth rates in excess of 2 percent per annum, with a peak period of nearly 3 percent during the 1950s. Since then, the rate of growth has declined, and now stands at about 2.2 percent. Recent CELADE population projections, which incorporate new information on declining growth rates, indicate a population of about 185 million for Brazil in the year 2000; this means that about one-third of the increase in Latin America's population between now and the end of the century is expected to occur in Brazil.

Geography and Population Distribution

Brazil's geographic position, straddling the equator, has endowed it with both tropical and subtropical climates. Rainfall, latitude, and altitude contribute to the observed climatic conditions, ranging from very hot most of the year in the tropical rain forests of the Amazon region to chilly and damp during the Southern winters. A high plain (the planalto) encompassing much of the central Brazilian land mass is ridged by several low mountain chains running in a generally southwest to northeast direction. The first of these chains is the coastal escarpment that divides the relatively narrow coastal plain from the interior. Bordering the planalto are two large basins that spread out over the territory fed by Brazil's main river systems: the Amazon and its tributaries, which cut a wide path as they flow from west to east just below the equator, and the Parana system, which flows from north to south to become the Plata River dividing Argentina and Uruguay. A wide band of lands, starting at the northeast coast and jutting into the interior in a southwesterly direction, is known as the sertao, a semiarid high plain that has suffered many severe droughts.

Overall population density is low--14 persons per square kilometer. However, this figure is deceptive because of the high population density of the coastal regions and the very low density of the interior. This coastal concentration has decreased in recent decades because of internal migration both to rural areas and to cities on the agricultural frontier. Brazilian geographers have divided the country into five major regions for purposes of social and economic description (see map). The most populous of these regions is the Southeast, which accounts for 43 percent of the national total. Although it occupies only 11 percent of Brazil's land area, it includes the major urban-industrial centers, including Rio de Janeiro, Sao Paulo, and Belo Horizonte. This region dominates Brazil economically in all sectors, including agriculture; per capita income is half again as large as the national average. The second most populous region is the Northeast, with 29 percent of the total population and 18 percent of the land area. This is Brazil's poorest region, with a per capita income less than half the national average. Periodic droughts in its sertao region have contributed to its persistent rural poverty. A third region, the South, holds 16 percent of Brazil's population and is comparatively prosperous. It is endowed with good agricultural land, but has less industry than the Southeast. Droughts and frosts devastated large areas of the region during the 1970s, leading to substantial out-migration of rural families that had settled there during the 1950s and 1960s. The two remaining regions, which constitute Brazil's vast interior, have experienced substantial in-migration during the last two decades. The Central-West, with 22 percent of the land area, increased its share of total population from 3 to 6 percent from 1950 to 1980. The new national capital, Brasilia, is located there. The

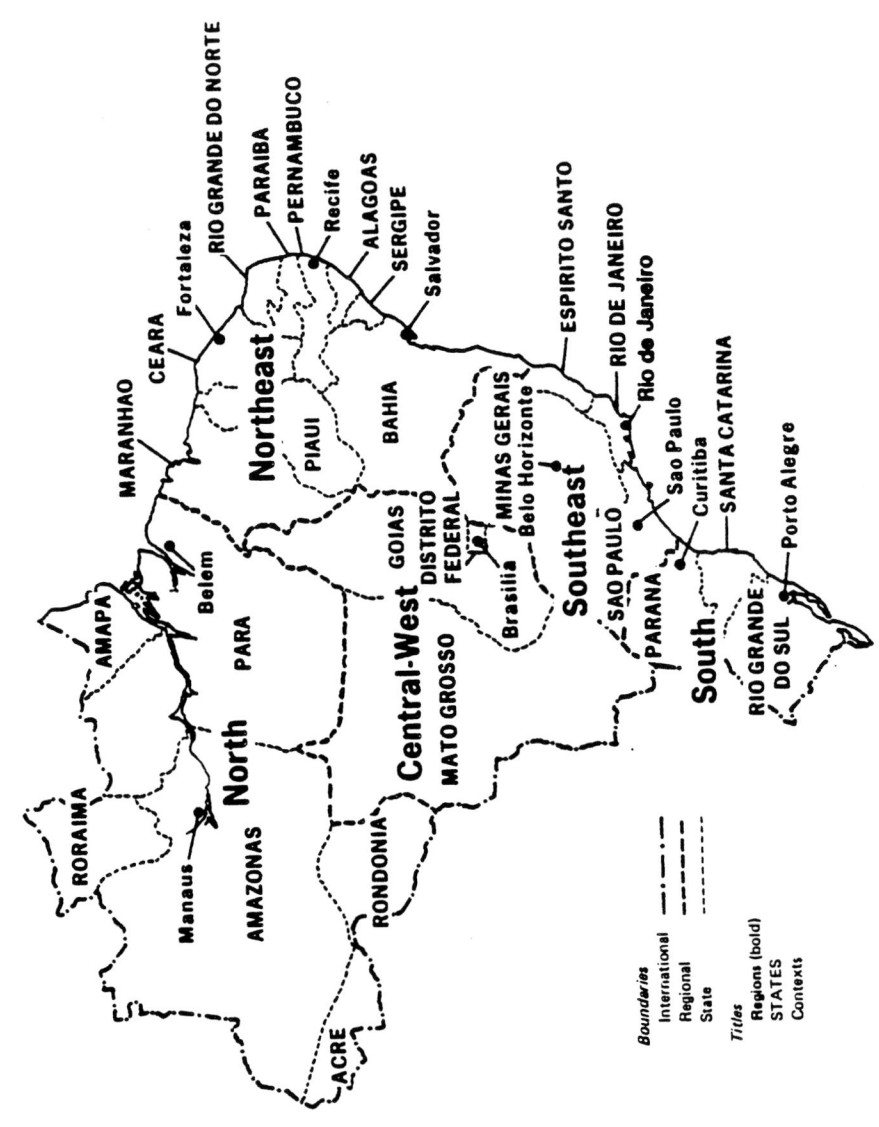

North, or Amazon, region occupies the largest part of Brazil's land area (42 percent) and is the least populated region (5 percent of the total). Although ambitious (and unrealistic) plans to resettle large numbers of poor farmers from the Northeast have been scaled down, hundreds of thousands of rural migrants from the South, Southeast, and Central-West regions flooded the territory (now a state) of Rondonia during the 1970s.

Political and Economic History

Brazil was first settled during the sixteenth century by the Portuguese who came in search of the gold that lured the Spanish conquistadores; however, they had to satisfy themselves with tropical agricultural production along the Northeastern coastal plain. A sequence of boom-bust export cycles punctuated the colonial period, beginning with brazilwood. Sugar production dominated the seventeenth century. The plantation system on which it was based required many unskilled laborers, and with no indigenous population to exploit, the Portuguese turned to the African slave markets. During the four centuries of the Atlantic slave trade, Brazil accounted for 36 percent of the total slave imports. The colonial heritage of the slave-based plantation system left a mark on the Northeast that even today is an important feature of its cultural diversity and economic backwardness.

During the eighteenth century, the Northeast drifted into economic stagnation; the center of gravity of the world sugar economy shifted to the Caribbean, while the Brazilian economy came to be dominated by gold and diamonds, which were discovered in Minas Gerais and Goias. Slaves were also employed in mining. Conflicts with Portugal over taxes on gold production, combined with the weakening of Portuguese power during the Napoleonic Wars, led to independence during the early nineteenth century.

During the nineteenth century, a new export cycle emerged, based on coffee and dominated by the state of Sao Paulo. Initial attempts to employ slave labor in coffee production proved unsatisfactory and slavery was eventually abolished. Paulista planters encouraged immigration, predominantly from Italy. These immigrants were able to secure better living conditions and a share of coffee profits; in fact, upwardly mobile immigrants and their offspring emerged as the urban industrial and entrepreneurial classes during Sao Paulo's industrialization in the twentieth century.

The two world wars and the Depression revealed the liabilities of dependence on exports for economic well being. As a consequence, Brazil adopted an import-substituting industrialization strategy during the 1950s. Brazil was more successful than many developing countries in establishing domestic manufacturing; it had achieved relative independence in nondurable goods even before World War II, and moved rapidly toward autonomy in durables and capital goods thereafter. However, the success of import substitution also brought problems: increased regional inequality because of the concentration of industrial activity in the Southeast; limited labor absorption because of the comparative capital intensity of imported manufacturing processes; increased dependence on foreign capital and petroleum (which Brazil has to import); and aggravated inequality in the distribution of income between those who benefited from the manufacturing boom and the growing masses of unskilled workers who migrated to the cities hoping to find greater opportunities.

Import substitution coincided with the period in which Brazil experienced its most rapid increase in population. Despite population growth rates of nearly 3 percent, per capita income grew at an average annual rate of around 5 percent, to stand at a level of about $1,600 by the late 1970s. This put Brazil near the top of so-called middle-income developing countries. However, as noted above, this national average masks major inequity in the distribution of income, among regions as well as among individuals and households. In 1972, the top 10 percent of households accounted for over 50 percent of household income, while the lowest 40 percent of households received only 7 percent. These differentials are echoed in other measures of welfare, such as infant mortality, access to public services, and housing conditions. While rapid population growth did not cause these problems, it surely aggravated them and does not make the task of overcoming them any easier.

The postwar period also brought rapid urbanization, as well as concentration of the urban population in large cities. The urban population increased from 36 percent of the total population in 1950 to 67 percent in 1980. The rural population declined in absolute terms between 1970 and 1980. The state of Sao Paulo (21 percent of Brazil's total population) is now 90 percent urban; the population of metropolitan Sao Paulo was 12.6 million in 1980, more than half of the state population.

Changes in Brazil's social and economic structure, combined with increased inflation and unemployment as the initial momentum of import substitution subsided, brought political turmoil and led to a military takeover in 1964. The military has traditionally played the role of arbiter in Brazilian politics, but their last intervention has been the most pervasive. Although there is currently a movement toward a return to civilian rule, the path is far from clear. Economic problems that have plagued Brazil since the mid-1970s and that dominate the current economic and political arena may play a key role. During the late 1960s, a combination of hard-handed military rule and civilian technical expertise restored stability to the Brazilian economy, with annual growth of industrial output exceeding 10 percent. One price for this stabilization program was deterioration of the earning power of lower-income groups; another was increased foreign debt. Then came the energy crisis, which inflated the cost of almost everything that Brazil imported, including the oil on which the economy was heavily dependent. Increased borrowing has put Brazil at the top of the list of indebted countries with a debt of over $60 billion; the cost of managing this debt adds further to balance-of-payments and inflationary pressures.

While social programs have not been a top priority of the military governments, they have not been neglected. During the past two decades, Brazil has invested in ambitious programs to increase access to public services and education, with a steady and sometimes impressive progress. Enrollment of the primary school population increased from 54 percent in 1955 to 85 percent in 1974, and secondary enrollment ratios rose from 3.7 percent in 1960 to 16.6 percent in 1976. The government has also sponsored a large-scale adult literacy program, as well as other types of adult education. Coverage of the urban population by social insurance (which includes basic health services) increased from 43 percent in 1960 to 79 percent in 1975. A National Housing Bank was established to finance low-income housing and urban services. Access to piped water in urban areas increased from 16 percent in 1950 to 68 percent in 1976, with much of the increase coming after 1970 under a national water and sanitation program. The cost of these programs has put further strain on the government budget; payroll taxes were recently increased to ease this budget pressure, exacerbating political tensions.

RECENT DEMOGRAPHIC TRENDS

Population Trends

At the beginning of the nineteenth century, the Brazilian population numbered about three and one-third million; two million were either slaves or former slaves who had been manumitted. By 1900, the population was nearly 18 million, with recent European immigrants representing an increasingly important group. Cultural and ethnic diversity, an important dimension of the Brazilian social structure, has proved difficult to measure in standard statistics. Complex patterns of interracial marriage and self-declaration of race in four categories (white, black, yellow, and mixed) in Brazilian censuses led to such skepticism about the validity of the data that the question was abandoned in 1970. Though the question was reintroduced in 1980, there is a major void in data on the ethnic aspects of Brazil's recent demographic history.

The demographic components of Brazil's population increase since 1940 are summarized in Table 1, which presents estimates of crude birth and death rates and the rate of population growth. The table indicates an increase in average annual growth rate from 2.39 percent in the 1940s to 2.99 percent in the 1950s. This resulted from the combination of a virtually constant birth rate and a 30 percent decline in the death rate, along with a limited amount of immigration. The growth rate declined slightly during the 1960s, and more rapidly during the 1970s; the reason for this accelerated decline during the 1970s was a more rapid decline in the birth rate of about 17 percent from 1960-70 to 1970-80.

TABLE 1 Components of Population Growth, 1940-80: Brazil

Period	Average Annual Rate of Population Increase	Crude Birth Rate	Crude Death Rate	Rate of Natural Increase
1940-50	2.39	44	20	24
1950-60	2.99	43	14	29
1960-70	2.89	41	13	28
1970-80	2.48	34	9	25

Sources: 1940-70 from Merrick and Graham (1979:Table III.5); 1970-80, see text.

As with other features of Brazilian economic and social history, these national-level data mask important regional differentials. The pace of change in both mortality and fertility has varied substantially between the more urbanized Southeast and the rest of Brazil, most strikingly in comparison with the Northeast. Both the level and timing of such regional differentials can be clarified by more refined measures of fertility and mortality, the total fertility rate, and the expectation of life at birth.

The main sources of national- and regional-level data on fertility and mortality rates in Brazil are the decennial censuses and the national sample survey program (Pesquisa Nacional por Amostra de Domicilios--PNAD). Though Brazil started to collect vital statistics at the national level in 1974, coverage is still not adequate to permit assessment of national levels and trends (Altmann and Ferreira, 1979). However, starting with the 1940 census, Brazil began reporting the number of children ever born and the number of children surviving by age of mother. A question on the number of births in the year prior to the interview was added in the 1970 census, and was continued in sample surveys taken in 1972 through 1975. In 1976, this question was modified to specify the date of the last live birth, a procedure that was also used in the 1980 census (see Leite, 1981:Table 1). Brazilian demographers, and more recently the Panel on Brazil of the Committee on Population and Demography, National Academy of Sciences, have derived estimates of fertility and mortality from these data using indirect estimating techniques. The panel based its estimates on the census data for 1940-70 and the PNAD survey data thereafter. As the present report was being written, preliminary tabulations of the 1980 census became available. These tabulations are based on an approximately one-percent sample of questionnaires processed in advance of the definitive tabulations, which are scheduled to appear on a state-by-state basis. Where possible, estimates based on these preliminary results are introduced. The Panel's fertility and mortality estimates for 1950-76 are reported in Tables 2 and 3, and detailed discussion of data sources and measurement techniques is presented in their report (National Academy of Sciences, 1979).

National and Regional Trends in the Total Fertility Rate

Table 2 presents data on national and regional trends in total fertility rates. The PNAD samples, which are the only source of regional data during the 1970-80 intercensal interval, are based on a somewhat different regional breakdown than the one described above because of sampling requirements. There are seven PNAD regions: the Amazon and Central-Western regions are combined in a region referred to as Frontier States (7), though only their urban population is included in the PNAD surveys; Brasilia is a separate region (6); Rio de Janeiro (1), Sao Paulo (2), and Minas Gerais/Espirito Santo (4) are broken out of the Southeastern group and reported as separate regions; and the Northeastern (5) and Southern (3) regions are maintained. For consistency, the report of the Panel on Brazil regrouped census data into PNAD regions, which are also shown in Tables 2 and 3.

At the national level, total fertility was nearly constant prior to 1960, and declined by about 6 percent during the 1960s. There was a marked acceleration in fertility decline during the 1970-76 interval, when total fertility fell by 24 percent, although the indirect measures make it difficult to determine when the acceleration actually started. The report of the Panel also

TABLE 2 Total Fertility Rates, 1950-80: Brazil and PNAD Regions

Region	1950	1960	1970	1976	1980
1. Rio de Janeiro	4.42	4.34	3.91	2.92	2.65
2. Sao Paulo	4.52	4.49	4.07	3.17	3.13
3. Southern States	5.96	5.75	5.48	4.20	3.47
4. Minas Gerais/ Espirito Santo	6.90	6.98	6.31	4.54	4.11
5. Northeastern States	7.52	7.50	7.58	6.30	5.71
6. Brasilia	--	--	5.52	3.83	3.63
7. Frontier States	7.14	7.32	7.08	--	5.07
Brazil: Total	6.32	6.18	5.83	4.44	4.10
Urban	4.68	--	4.61	3.48	3.47
Rural	7.70	--	7.71	6.36	5.83

Note: -- indicates that data were not available.

Sources: National Research Council (1983). Estimates for 1950 and 1960 are based on Carvalho's (1973) variant of the Brass method, which utilized the P/F ratio for women aged 20-29 as discussed in the text; estimates for 1970, 1976, and 1980 are based on National Academy of Sciences' variant of the Brass method, which employs the average of P/F ratios for women aged 20-24 and 25-29.

provides estimates of total fertility based on the own-children method which suggest that total fertility in 1969-70 was lower than 5.8. In all likelihood, the decline in the national total fertility rate accelerated in the late 1960s.

This national trend once again masks major regional differentials. The transition to lower fertility was already well underway in Rio de Janeiro and Sao Paulo during the 1950s, with total fertility nearly 2 children per woman lower than the national average by 1970. A more gradual decline was underway in the Southern states and in Minas Gerais/Espirito Santo. In contrast, fertility in the Northeast and in the Frontier states was high, possibly increasing, before 1970. Regional differentials increased during the 1950-70 period, but declines in the Southeast were not great enough to have a significant impact on the national trend. In the rural-urban breakdown, there was little change from 1950 to 1970 in either; this suggests that the limited national decline resulted in large part from the increased weight of the urban population in the total.

The 1970-76 period brought accelerated declines in all regions. In the Southern and Southeastern regions, rates fell by 22-28 percent, with the greatest decline occurring in region (4) (Minas Gerais/Espirito Santo). While the decline in the Northeast was less--17 percent--it signaled an important increase in the spread of accelerated fertility decline. At the same time, the Northeast-Southeast differential increased. Since rates of decline in the Southeastern states have reached comparatively low levels, continuation of the national trend will depend to a large extent on the pace at which Northeastern states catch up.

Estimates based on preliminary tabulations of the 1980 census indicate that the trend observed for the 1970-76 period continued during 1976-80, though at a slower pace. The 1980 total fertility rate for Brazil, 4.11, is 7.7 percent less than the 4.44 recorded in 1976 and 29.7 percent less than the 1970 rate of 5.83. Total fertility in the Southern region declined most (17.7 percent) during 1976-80, making this the region with the largest overall decline (36.7 percent) over the decade. Region (4) (Minas Gerais/Espirito Santo) ranked second in 1976-80, with 9.5 percent, and also second for the decade, with 34.9 percent. It is significant that the Northeast, which ranked last during the 1970-76 interval, was third in 1976-80 with a 9.4 percent decline, since this suggests that the spread of fertility decline to the

Northeast has continued and even accelerated. For the decade, this put the Northeast just ahead of Sao Paulo, which had a very small decline (1.3 percent) during 1976-80 and ranked last for the decade with 23.1 percent. Both Rio de Janeiro and the Frontier states were within a point or two of the national average, suggesting that omission of rural areas of the Frontier from the 1976 results probably did not bias the rate reported for Brazil at that date.

A surprising feature of the 1980 results is that they indicate that fertility decline during the 1976-80 period was limited to rural areas; total fertility for urban areas was practically unchanged over that interval. This raises a number of questions, to which the limited data published in the preliminary tabulations provide very few answers. One of these questions relates to the reliability of the sample frame on which the 1976 survey was based. It may be that the "Brazil" sampled in the 1976 survey underrepresented groups that experienced slower fertility decline, leading to an overstatement of the decline from 1970 to 1976 and an understatement of the decline from 1976 to 1980. If this was not the case, there is an even more interesting question of why urban fertility decline accelerated (to 24.5 percent) during the early 1970s and dropped to zero at the end of the decade. Was there a baby "boomlet" during the late 1970s? Clearly, we need a thoroughgoing assessment of the representativeness of the PNAD surveys, as well as a comparison of the advanced tabulations against the definitive 1980 census results. Although both of these tasks run well beyond the scope of this report, they have major implications for the present analysis of trends in the 1970s, which relies heavily on data from the 1976 survey.

Expectation of Life at Birth

Table 3 presents estimates of national and regional trends in the expectation of life at birth. In contrast with total fertility, there is a substantial increase (26 percent) in life expectancy at the national level. There are also important regional differentials, with the Northeast lagging behind the rest of the country by about 10 years of life expectancy; using the ratio of Sao Paulo to the Northeast as an index, the relative difference was about 27 percent. While all regions experienced increased

TABLE 3 Expectation of Life at Birth, 1950-76: Brazil and PNAD Regions

Region	1950	1960	1970	1976
1. Rio de Janeiro	48.7	60.3	60.3	68.5
2. Sao Paulo	49.2	60.3	61.6	67.1
3. Southern States	51.5	61.2	62.8	66.5
4. Minas Gerais/ Espirito Santo	46.9	55.2	58.4	65.0
5. Northeastern States	38.5	41.6	48.3	52.6
6. Brasilia	--	--	58.0	67.4
7. Frontier States	47.8	56.9	59.7	--
Brazil: Total	44.7	52.4	56.3	61.1
Urban	43.8	--	56.6	61.6
Rural	45.1	--	56.0	57.5

Note: -- indicates that data were not available.

Source: National Research Council (1983).

life expectancy during the 1950-70 interval, this pattern of regional differentials remained constant.

The pace of improvement in life expectancy increased during 1970-76. At the national level, it increased by 5 years in a 6-year period, compared to a 12-year increase over the previous 20 years. Percentage increases in Sao Paulo and the Northeast were about equal (9 percent), but Rio de Janeiro increased by nearly 14 percent. The pattern of rural-urban differentials shifted from a slight advantage for rural areas in 1950 to a slight advantage for urban areas in 1970, and a widening spread between urban and rural areas between 1970 and 1976.

Income Class Differences in Fertility and Mortality

Socioeconomic differences in fertility and mortality are another important dimension of recent Brazilian demographic trends, though there are fewer data with which to document them. Working with special tabulations of the 1970 census, Carvalho and Paiva (1976) reported a differential of over 4 children per woman in comparing total fertility rates for high- and low-income families. Their results are summarized in the top half of Table 4. For Brazil, total fertility in the 1-150 Cruziero per month

TABLE 4 Income Class Differences in Total Fertility Rates and the Expectation of Life at Birth, 1970: Brazil and Selected States

Region	Average Monthly Household Income (cruzeiros)			
	1–150	151–300	301–500	500+
Total Fertility Rates				
Central Northeast[a]	8.55	8.15	6.28	3.95
Minas Gerais/Espirito Santo	8.03	8.50	7.27	4.62
Rio de Janeiro	6.23	5.43	4.40	2.71
Sao Paulo	5.93	5.35	4.50	2.93
Santa Catarina/Rio Grande do Sul	6.08	5.79	4.97	3.25
Brazil	7.54	6.72	5.37	3.28
Urban	7.03	5.95	4.84	3.10
Rural	7.81	7.99	7.70	5.86
Expectation of Life at Birth				
Central Northeast[a]	43.8	46.1	50.3	54.4
Minas Gerais/Espirito Santo	53.8	55.4	58.6	62.3
Rio de Janeiro	54.1	54.8	57.6	62.1
Sao Paulo	54.7	56.1	58.7	63.9
Santa Catarina/Rio Grande do Sul	60.5	61.2	63.4	66.9
Brazil	49.9	54.5	57.6	62.0
Urban	46.0	53.7	57.6	62.2
Rural	51.4	55.9	57.6	60.0

[a]Ceara, Rio Grande do Norte, Parnaiba, Pernambuco (including Fernando de Noronha), and Alagoas.

Sources: Total fertility rates from Carvalho and Paiva (1976); expectation of life at birth from Carvalho and Wood (1978).

group was 7.54, compared to 3.28 for women in the 501 Cruziero and over group. Their data also reveal rural-urban and regional differentials within income classes: rural-urban differences increase with income, from less than one child to nearly three children; in contrast, regional differences narrow (using the Central Northeast and Sao Paulo as illustrative cases) from 2.6 to 1.1 children.

Equally dramatic mortality differentials were found. Using the same tabulations, Carvalho and Wood (1978) noted a striking 20-year differential between the life expectancy of low-income families in the Central Northeast and that of high-income families in Sao Paulo, and an even greater difference when the Northeast was compared to the Southern states of Santa Catarina and Rio Grande do Sul. Their results, summarized in the bottom half of Table 4, also suggest that for low-income households, life expectancy was higher in rural than in urban areas. However, caution is required in interpreting this difference since the income figures do not include income in kind, which was higher in rural areas; thus the true level of living among these groups may have been understated. In contrast to the fertility differentials, regional differentials in mortality were maintained at about 10 years as income increased, while rural-urban differences narrowed. Both sets of differentials highlight the importance of underlying socioeconomic variables in the regional differentials observed during the 1950-70 period; attention to changes in these variables will therefore be important in explaining the acceleration in Brazil's fertility decline after 1970.

PURPOSE AND STRUCTURE OF THIS REPORT

What changes could account for the accelerated fertility decline in Brazil since 1970? The evidence presented thus far suggests that a major factor was the spread of fertility decline after 1970 to new regions and socioeconomic groups, together with continued decline among those already affected. The objective of the present report is to examine this acceleration in greater detail. The discussion therefore focuses on some specific questions about what may have happened in the post-1970 period; it is not intended to be an exhaustive study of longer-term trends and differentials.

As noted above, the main sources of national-level data used here are the public use sample of the 1970 census of population and the 1976 PNAD national household survey. Both of these sources provide information on such socioeconomic characteristics as marital status, migration, rural-urban residence, income, and education; they also provide the data on births and surviving children needed to make indirect estimates of fertility and mortality. They do not include questions on contraception and other proximate variables, nor are other national-level survey data on these variables available. State-level data are found in reports of the Contraceptive Prevalence Surveys (CPS) conducted by Brazil's International Planned Parenthood Federation (IPPF) affiliate, Sociedade Civil Bem-Estar Familiar no Brasil (BEMFAM), with the cooperation of the U.S. Center for Disease Control; six such surveys were available when the report was prepared (Sao Paulo, Piaui, Rio Grande do Norte, Pernambuco, Paraiba, and Bahia). Local case study data on the proximate variables were assembled for the Centro Brasileiro de Analise e Planejament (CEBRAP) National Investigation on Human Reproduction (NIHR), which is examined in detail in Part II.

This study is organized as follows. Following the summary, Part I concentrates primarily on national-level data. Chapter 1 uses national census and survey data on fertility and nuptiality, together with CPS state-level data on contraception, abortion, and breastfeeding, to decompose recent fertility declines into the proximate determinants of fertility; this analysis is based on the standardization approach to decomposition of changes at the national level. In Chapter 2, national data are used to identify the level and amount of change in socioeconomic fertility differentials from 1970 to 1976. Chapter 3 examines hypotheses about links between changes in the proximate determinants and socioeconomic conditions in Brazil during the early 1970s, as well as national-level empirical evidence relating to these hypotheses. Chapter 4 uses multivariate regression analysis to clarify links between changing socioeconomic conditions and changes in average parity, with reference to the analytical questions raised in the previous chapter.

Although Part I makes some reference to relevant local-level NIHR findings, its primary focus, as noted above, is at the national level. Part II of this report focuses specifically on the NIHR to provide a more concentrated analysis of Brazilian fertility. Chapter 5 describes the purpose and methodology of the NIHR. Chapter 6 summarizes fertility levels and trends for the contexts studied, which are described in detail in the Appendix. Chapter 7 presents a discussion of local trends in nuptiality, including variations in union type and age at marriage. Chapter 8 examines data related to declining marital fertility, while Chapters 9 and 10 analyze the role of the proximate determinants and socioeconomic variables, specifically family income, respectively, in that decline. Finally, Chapter 11 presents some conclusions about Brazil's accelerated fertility decline based on the NIHR data. It is hoped that together, the broader and more focused perspectives offered in this report will provide a balanced understanding of Brazil's recent fertility trends.

PART I FERTILITY DETERMINANTS AT THE NATIONAL LEVEL

CHAPTER 1

THE PROXIMATE DETERMINANTS OF FERTILITY

The objective of this chapter is to analyze Brazil's accelerated fertility decline in demographic terms. Demographic theory indicates that two sets of variables are important: one is population composition, particularly age structure and marriage patterns, both of which mediate the relation between individual reproductive behavior and birth rates observed in a population; the other is comprised of the Davis-Blake (1956) "intermediate variables," such as frequency of intercourse, fertility control, breastfeeding, and abortion, which directly affect reproductive outcome. This chapter uses a standardization approach to identify compositional effects, and Bongaarts' (1980) method for decomposing natural fertility into its proximate determinants to identify intermediate variables.

This chapter is based on the available data for Brazil, which are fragmentary in both regional and time coverage. The approach is therefore essential detective work, piecing together clues from a variety of sources in an attempt to draw a picture at the national level. Changes in marriage patterns and age structure are always prime suspects in declining birth rates; therefore, the discussion begins by assessing changes in the distribution of women by marital status and in mean age at marriage, and then applies standardization techniques to check whether these changes and those in age structure played a major role in Brazil's fertility decline. The available evidence suggests that they did not. This suggests in turn that the primary factor in the decline was one of the intermediate variables affecting marital fertility. The Bongaarts framework is then used to explore this possibility. There are three potential factors responsible--breastfeeding, contraception, and abortion. Among these, the limited degree to which the first is practiced in Brazil is sufficient to eliminate it as a primary influence. The evidence implicating the second is stronger, though admittedly fragmentary. Finally, although the evidence is clearly circumstantial, it is strong enough to implicate abortion as an important, though necessarily indeterminate, influence on Brazil's fertility decline.

MARITAL STATUS AND MEAN AGE AT MARRIAGE

As noted above, the reporting of marital status in Brazilian data is problematic. The reported percentage distribution of Brazilian women aged 15-49 by marital status in the 1950, 1960, and 1970 censuses and in the 1976 PNAD survey are presented in Table 5; preliminary results of the 1980 census are also reported. Four marital status categories are shown--married, divorced and separated, widowed, and single. Each of these categories presents its own set of problems.

First, in the married category, there is a problem in the reporting of women in consensual unions. According to Henriques (1980), women in consensual unions account for an important share of Brazilian births, though Brazil has a lower proportion of such births than a number of other Latin American countries. However, although Brazilian data include women in consensual unions as a subcategory of married women, there is strong evidence that a number of those who report themselves as single may in fact be in consensual unions (Silva, 1979:14). This is suggested by data in Table 6, which shows the percent of women in the single category who reported having had a birth from age 15-19 to 40-49 in the censuses and PNAD survey.

Brazilian census authorities have attempted to improve on the reporting of consensual unions by broadening the number of categories of marital status to include the type of union. In 1950, when there was no subcategory for consensual unions, nearly four out of ten single women reported a birth by the end of their reproductive years, suggesting that most of these unions were grouped in the single category (Altmann and Wong, 1981a:356). This contrasts with 1960, when the consensual union category was introduced and the proportion of single women reporting a birth dropped to 11 percent. It should be recalled that tabulation of the 1960 census was delayed until the late 1970s because of administrative

TABLE 5 Reported Percent Distribution of Women by
Marital Status and Age, 1950-80: Brazil

Age	Married[a]	Divorced, Separated	Widowed	Single	Total[b]
1950					
15-19	14.8	0.0	0.1	85.1	100.0
20-24	51.9	0.0	0.7	47.4	100.0
25-29	70.4	0.1	1.8	27.7	100.0
30-39	76.3	0.2	5.1	18.4	100.0
40-49	71.2	0.3	14.1	14.4	100.0
1960					
15-19	14.0 (1.3)	0.7	0.1	85.2	100.0
20-24	53.3 (3.6)	2.6	0.4	43.7	100.0
25-29	74.0 (5.1)	3.4	1.1	21.5	100.0
30-39	80.9 (5.4)	3.9	3.1	12.1	100.0
40-49	76.2 (4.9)	4.8	10.1	8.9	100.0
1970					
15-19	12.0 (1.4)	0.5	0.1	87.4	100.0
20-24	46.9 (3.9)	2.0	0.3	50.8	100.0
25-29	71.3 (5.4)	3.0	0.9	24.8	100.0
30-39	80.2 (5.7)	4.1	2.8	12.9	100.0
40-49	76.2 (4.9)	5.6	8.9	9.3	100.0
1976					
15-19	11.2 (1.9)	0.6	0.1	88.1	100.0
20-24	46.2 (5.4)	2.0	0.2	51.6	100.0
25-29	69.8 (6.8)	3.0	0.8	26.4	100.0
30-39	79.5 (7.4)	4.9	2.6	13.0	100.0
40-49	77.7 (6.6)	5.9	8.4	8.0	100.0
1980					
15-19	16.3 (3.5)	0.5	0.0	83.2	100.0
20-24	53.2 (8.0)	2.0	0.3	44.5	100.0
25-29	72.6 (9.1)	3.2	0.7	23.5	100.0
30-39	79.9 (9.3)	4.5	2.3	13.3	100.0
40-49	77.0 (7.7)	6.3	7.7	9.0	100.0

[a]Figures in parentheses represents women in consensual unions as a percent of all women, when reported.
[b]The total excludes women who did not report marital status.

Sources: 1950-80 from population censuses; 1976 from PNAD survey.

breakdowns, and that procedures used in reconstructing it may have biased the results. The reported trend from 1960 to 1976 is puzzling, since it suggests that births to single women increased. It is possible that PNAD interviewers, who were more highly trained than census interviewers, were more careful in identifying single mothers.

TABLE 6 Percent of Single Women Who Report Having Had a Child, by Age, 1950-76: Brazil

Age Group	1950	1960	1970	1976
15-19	1.7	0.4	0.7	1.5
20-24	10.0	2.4	3.8	6.0
25-29	22.3	5.5	8.7	10.2
30-39	34.3	8.8	14.6	17.9
40-49	38.7	10.9	16.3	23.5

Source: Published tabulations of census and survey data.

The impact of misreporting of women in consensual unions appears to be greatest among younger women. For women aged 20-24, the proportion reported as married increases from 51.9 percent in 1950, when consensual unions were not included as a subcategory, to 53.3 percent in 1960, when the subcategory was introduced. To illustrate the possible influence of consensual unions on reporting, the percentage of women in the consensual union subcategory is indicated in parentheses in Table 5 next to the percent married after 1960 (the basis of this percentage is all women in the age category). The proportion of women aged 20-24 reported as married decreases from 1960 to 1976, then increases sharply to 53.2 percent (about equal to 1960) in the 1980 results. At the same time, the percent of women in consensual unions increases, particularly in 1980, when the figure is 8 percent of all women (15 percent of married women). Published tabulations of the preliminary 1980 results do not supply enough information to determine whether, in editing, single women with births may have been reclassified as being in consensual unions. The evidence suggests either that consensual unions have been increasing or that reporting of such unions has improved. In all likelihood, results for earlier periods understate the proportion of younger women reported as married. Such underreporting would bias the age-specific marital fertility rate for these women upward if that proportion were used in the calculation of the rate; it would also add a further bias to the extent that consensual unions were recognized when a woman gave birth to a child.

Although the impact of the underreporting of consensual unions is reduced by grouping all single women with births in the married category, it is not eliminated. One is still left with the problem of women in informal unions who have no children, but should be included in the denominator when fertility rates are calculated. This omission could bias calculation of rates for younger women, particularly when the beginning of an informal union is not clearly demarcated and the birth of a child leads to recognition (or admission) of the union. Including in the married category only those "single" women who had births will lead to overstatement of marital fertility rates. One way to compensate for this is to assume that the proportion of single women "at risk" is equal to that of married women; that is, if 50 percent of married women aged 20-24 report a birth, then assume that the single women aged 20-24 reporting a birth represent 50 percent of the single women at risk. This at-risk group can then be added to the married category. This procedure will be employed later in calculating the denominators for marital fertility rates. The issue of type of union and its relationship to fertility at the local level is explored in detail in Part II of this report.

A second problem of consistency in the Brazilian data on marital status relates to the reporting of separated and divorced women. Because Brazil legalized divorce only in 1977, its effects cannot be observed directly even in the 1976 survey. However, reporting of foreign divorces, legal separations, and a special Brazilian legal substitute for pre-1977 divorces (desquites) was increasing in the years prior to actual legalization. The contrast is sharpest between 1950, when practically no divorces and separations were reported, and the other data points. Because divorce was not legally recognized, it was fairly common practice for women who had entered a second union after separation to be declared as separated rather than married, leading to further underreporting of the proportion of women in unions.

Such problems with the reliability of marital status data suggest that considerable caution is required in the calculation and interpretation of measures incorporating those data. This applies not only to the proportion of women in unions, but also to measures of the average age at marriage and marital fertility rates. Table 7 summarizes the results of calculations of the singulate mean age at marriage (SMAM), which is based on the proportion

TABLE 7 Singulate Mean Age at Marriage (SMAM), by Region, 1950-76: Brazil

PNAD Region	1960	1970	1976
1. Rio de Janeiro	22.92	23.77	23.93
2. Sao Paulo	22.25	23.30	23.47
3. Southern States	21.66	22.17	22.80
4. Minas/Espirito Santo	22.36	23.36	23.66
5. Northeast States	22.18	22.90	23.13
6. Brasilia	20.45	23.38	23.73
7. Frontier States	21.21	22.04	--
Brazil			
Marriage	22.11	22.91	23.33[a]
First Birth	22.42	23.28	23.84[a]

[a]The Brazil figure for 1976 excludes rural areas of Region 7, which was not included in the PNAD survey.

Source: SMAMs calculated from census and survey distributions of women by marital status considering single women who reported having had children as married. First-birth measure based on same computation as SMAM, but substituting the proportion of women reported as childless.

of women reported as single at different ages. In order to reduce the impact of underreporting of consensual unions, single women reporting a birth were considered married. SMAMs were calculated for the PNAD regions and Brazil as a whole in 1960, 1970, and 1976. For Brazil as a whole, the data indicate a comparatively late average age at marriage and suggest that this average increased by more than one year between 1960 and 1976. Most of this increase came between 1960 and 1970, and resulted from a more than 6 percentage point rise in the proportion reported as single between the two dates. It was not possible to include single women with births in the calculation of the SMAM for 1980; nevertheless, with the decreased proportion reported as single in the preliminary results, the average age at marriage dropped back to the 1960 level of 22.1 years. It should also be noted that the preliminary 1980 results are not fully comparable to those for earlier dates since it was necessary to use 10-year age groups for women over age 30.

The breakdown of SMAMs by region indicates a fairly homogeneous pattern, with lower average ages in the Southern and Frontier states, and higher average ages in the Southeastern states (Regions 1, 2, and 4). The largest increase in average age at marriage is found in Region 6 (Brasilia); it may be observed that the composition of Brasilia's population changed significantly from the 1960s, when it was being constructed, to the 1970s, when it began to function fully as the national capital. For the remaining regions, increases range from .5 to 1.0 years in 1960-70 and .2 to .6 years in 1970-76.

Since there are questions about the reliability of the marital status data on which the SMAMs are based, another way of looking at the age at which exposure to the risk of childbearing starts is to consider the mean age at first birth. This can be derived from data on the proportion of women who remained childless at different ages using the same computational procedure employed in calculating SMAMs. The resulting index, calculated only for national-level data, is shown in the second row of results for Brazil in Table 7. For 1960 and 1970, the average age at first birth is .3 years higher than the age at marriage. This increases to .5 years in 1976. The 1980 average, not shown in the table, is 22.1 years, just equal to the average age at marriage.

MARITAL FERTILITY

How much did changes in the proportions married and age at marriage contribute to the acceleration of Brazil's fertility decline? Table 8 attempts to link total and age-specific fertility rates (ASFRs) to total marital fertility and age-specific marital fertility rates (ASMFRs) using the 1960, 1970, 1976, and 1980 data. The first column of the table shows ASFRs and total fertility rates calculated for the Brazil report of the Committee on Population and Demography, National Academy of Sciences. The total fertility rates are the same as those reported in Table 2, showing declines of about 6 percent from 1960 to 1970, 24 percent from 1970 to 1976,

TABLE 8 Age-Specific And Total Marital Fertility Rate Calculations, 1960, 1970, 1976, and 1980: Brazil

Age Group	ASFR[a]	Percent Married[b] (a)	Percent Married[b] (b)	ASMFR[c]	ASMFR[d]
1960					
15-19	.0799	14.0	15.3	.354[e]	
20-24	.2719	53.3	57.6	.472	
25-29	.3150	74.0	79.8	.395	
30-34	.2615	80.3	87.5	.299	
35-39	.1935	81.4	90.8	.213	
40-44	.0908	77.9	91.7	.099	
45-49	.0239	74.3	92.7	.026	
Total	6.18	58.9	65.7	9.29	
1970					
15-19	.0753	12.0	13.7	.373[e]	.352[e]
20-24	.2564	46.9	51.6	.497	.469
25-29	.2971	71.3	77.6	.383	.384
30-34	.2466	80.2	87.3	.282	.287
35-39	.1825	81.1	91.0	.200	.209
40-44	.0856	77.8	92.0	.093	.102
45-49	.0225	74.3	92.8	.024	.033
Total	5.83	55.5	62.8	9.27	9.18
1976					
15-19	.0733	11.3	14.1	.295[e]	.284[e]
20-24	.2062	46.3	52.3	.394	.379
25-29	.2240	69.8	76.5	.293	.292
30-34	.1874	78.8	87.4	.214	.222
35-39	.1292	80.3	91.6	.141	.147
40-44	.0588	79.4	93.7	.063	.071
45-49	.0108	75.7	94.2	.011	.015
Total	4.45	55.2	63.3	7.06	7.05
1980					
15-19	.0850	.163	.168	.278	
20-24	.2054	.532	.555	.370	
25-29	.2071	.726	.765	.271	
30-34	.1604	.799	.867	.185	
35-39	.1030	.799	.867	.119	
40-44	.0488	.770	.910	.054	
45-49	.0093	.770	.910	.010	
Total	4.10	58.5	64.8	6.44	

Sources:

[a]ASFR: Age-specific fertility rate: Panel on Brazil, Committee on Population and Demography, National Academy of Sciences.
[b]Percent married: in column (a) as reported in published tabulations; in column (b) adjusted to include all ever-married women; and, except for 1980 when data not available, single women "at risk" as explained in text.
[c]ASMFR: Age-specific marital fertility rate: computed using ASFR and percent married, variant (b).
[d]ASMFR: Age-specific marital fertility rate: computed from special tabulation of births in previous year for ever-married women, and and adjusted by P/F ratios for all women (1.32 in 1970 and 1.22 in 1976). Not available for 1960 and 1980.
[e]ASMFR for 15-19 computed as .75 ASMFR for women aged 20-24.

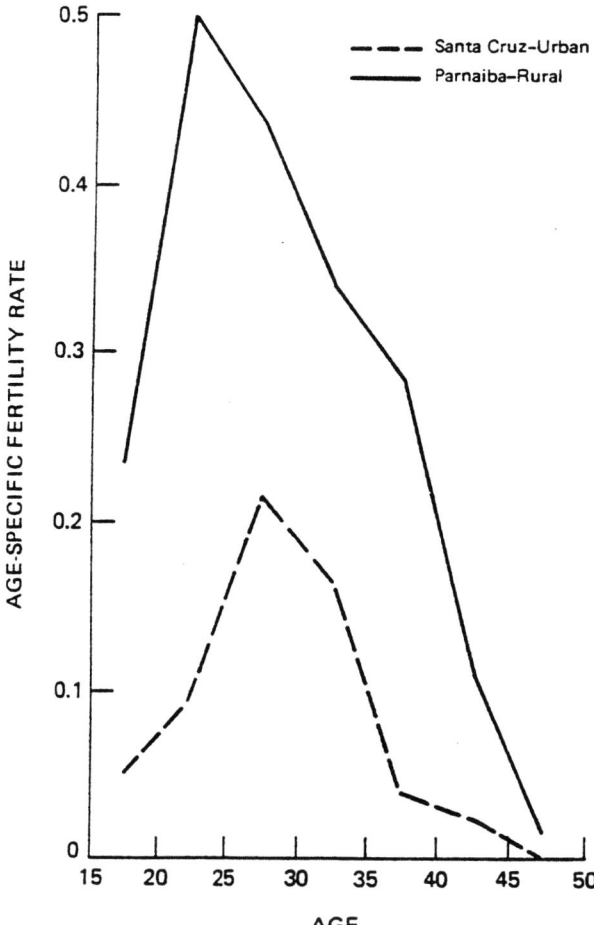

FIGURE 5 Age-Specific Fertility Rates, 1975: Brazil

and about 8 percent from 1976 to 1980. As can be seen in
Figure 5, the shape of the age-specific fertility rate
profile became somewhat flatter with the decline, which
was substantial for all age groups except the youngest.
The largest absolute decline occurred at ages 25-29, with
larger proportional declines among the older age
categories.

A first attempt was made to translate ASFRs into
age-specific marital fertility rates by using data on

marital status from published reports, as shown in column (a) under "percent married" in Table 8. Because of the underreporting of women in consensual unions, ASMFRs appear to be biased upward, particularly for women in their twenties. In 1970, for example, the ASMFR for the 20-24 group would be .547; this would mean that the fertility of Brazilian women exceeded that of the Hutterites, one of the populations on whose experience standard natural fertility schedules are based. To reduce this bias, the proportion "married" was adjusted to include all ever-married women, single women who reported a birth, and a prorated number of single women "at risk" based on the proportion of married women reporting a birth, as shown in column (b) under "percent married" in the table. This adjustment raised the percent married by about 7 percentage points for each observation; although this did not reduce the decline of about 5 percentage points in the proportion married among women 20-24 between 1960 and 1970, it did narrow the differences between 1970, 1976, and 1980. The increase in the proportion married among women in older age categories arises from the addition of widowed, separated, and divorced women.

Even with these adjustments, the ASMFRs and total marital fertility rates for 1960 and 1970 are quite high—nearly 9.3 for both dates. By 1976, total marital fertility falls to 7.06, a decline of 24 percent, with a further decline of 9 percent to 6.44 in 1980. While total marital fertility shows little change between 1960 and 1970, the rate for women aged 20-24 increases. This occurs because the decline in the ASFR for that group is less than the decline in the proportion married, even after adjustment. The rate for women aged 15-19 is similarly affected since it was calculated as .75 of the rate of those aged 20-24. Because these rates are so high, total marital fertility is very sensitive to such differences, which are as likely to be the result of differences in reporting (or editing, as suggested above) as they are to be real. Thus considerable caution is required in interpreting the 1960-70 period.

Access to public use sample files for the 1970 and 1976 data made it possible to tabulate the observed number of births by marital status in the year prior to interviews; this provided a check on the rates calculated from ASFRs. Observed births were adjusted by the P/F ratios used in adjusting ASFRs for that date. The resulting ASMFRs and total marital fertility rates are shown in the last column of Table 8. These rates are not exactly comparable to those calculated directly from ASFRs since the adjustment of observed births used in deriving ASFRs also included a factor to account for the one-half-year difference between women's reported age and their age when births actually occurred. Because it is inappropriate to apply this factor when the denominator is limited to ever-married women, the age profiles of ASMFRs differ with the two approaches. The main difference is that rates based on the tabulations are lower for women under 25 and higher for women over 30. Total marital fertility is slightly lower in 1970 and virtually the same in 1976 in the tabulated results. Comparison of the two sets of rates suggests that the decline in marital fertility probably was close to 24 percent over the 1970-76 period; however, there is a need to be cautious about both the level and age profile of marital fertility rates.

The age category most seriously affected is 20-24. Two factors could account for an overstatement of the age-specific marital fertility rate for this group. One is the underreporting of married women discussed above. The other is that the adjustment factors derived using the Brass technique may be too high for this group. Estimates of ASMFRs using model marital fertility schedules suggest that this may in fact be the case (see Berquo and Leite, 1979; Altmann and Wong, 1981a; Leite, 1981). One way to visualize the extent of possible bias is to compare observed ASMFRs to model schedules, as shown in Figure 6. Both of the 1970 ASMFR schedules from Table 8 are plotted against these model schedules. The models are based on a total marital fertility rate of 9.25, with the Coale-Trussel index of fertility control set at three levels: 0.0, the natural fertility level, and 0.3 and 0.5, indicating moderate fertility control. The model schedule with the index set at 0.5 provides a very close approximation to both of the observed 1970 ASMFR schedules for ages 25-29 to 40-44. The observed rates for age 20-24 exceed the model schedule, though the second schedule (estimated from births reported for "married" women, broadly defined) is closer than the rate calculated from dividing ASFRs by the proportion married. The comparison suggests that the 1970 base for calculating declines between 1970 and 1976 among the younger age groups may be too high, resulting in an exaggeration of declines for women in these age categories.

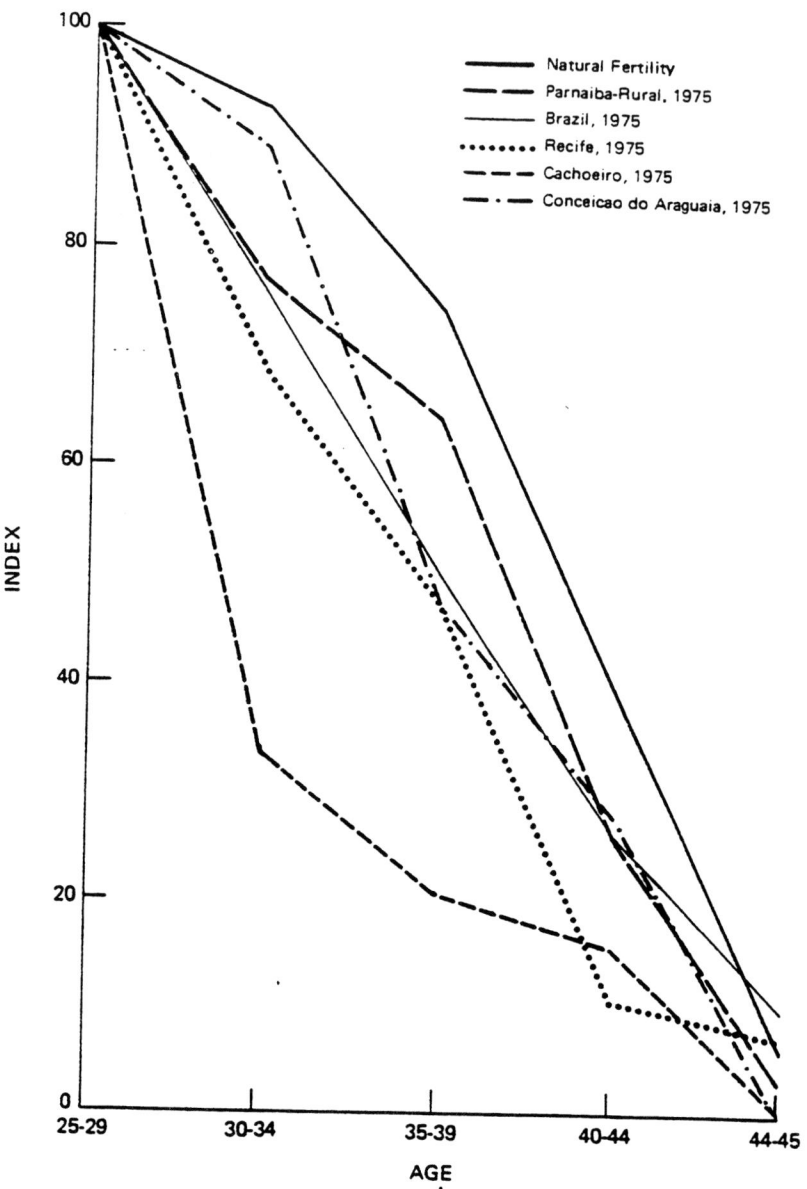

FIGURE 6 Age-Specific Marital Fertility Rates
($ASMFR_{25-29}$ = 100), Six Contexts: Brazil

DECOMPOSITION OF CHANGE IN BIRTH RATES

Standardization techniques to decompose the contributions of changes in marriage patterns and age structure and in marital fertility to declines in the general fertility rate (GFR) and crude birth rate (CBR) are described in United Nations Manual IX, The Methodology of Measuring the Impact of Family Planning Programs on Fertility (United Nations, 1979). The standardization method takes account of the contribution of shifts in age structure within the reproductive ages, as well as changes (for the CBR) in the proportion of women of reproductive age among the total population. All the measures required for these techniques are found in the Brazilian data for 1960, 1970, and 1976. However, considerable caution is required in interpreting results because of the poor reporting of marital status and possible overstatement of marital fertility rates discussed above.

For the GFR, the decomposition is as shown in Table 9. For the 1960-70 interval, there is a decline of 15 per 1,000 in the GFR. Of the three factors contributing to that decline, shifts in the marital status distribution account for the largest share (8 per 1,000). This reflects the reported decline in the percent married from 66 to 63 percent shown in Table 8; it should be viewed as skeptically as other measures depending on the marital status reporting of the 1960 census data. Marital fertility accounts for the smallest part of the decline in the GFR (2 per 1,000), while shifts in age structure within the reproductive ages make up the remaining 5 per

TABLE 9 Decomposition of Change in General Fertility Rate, 1960-76: Brazil

Component	1960-70	1970-76
GFR, base year	189.18	174.18
GFR, end year	174.18	136.42
Observed change (per 1,000)	-14.99	-37.76
Reproductive age structure	-4.89	0.78
Marital status distribution	-8.10	0.88
Marital fertility	-2.06	-40.49
Interaction	0.06	1.07

1,000. The composition of the much larger 1970-76 decline in the GFR (nearly 38 per 1,000) contrasts sharply with that of 1960-70. Marital fertility accounts for the entire decline; in fact, the decline would have been greater had not the marital status and age structure factors been slightly offsetting.

The standardization approach can also be used to decompose declines in the CBR with the addition of a factor to account for shifts in the proportion of women of reproductive age among the total population. For the two periods being studied, the breakdown is as shown in Table 10. The proportional contributions of the three components of the GFR to changes in the CBR remain the same, with marital status accounting for most of the change in 1960-70 and declining marital fertility being the only reason for the 1970-76 decline. The interesting addition in 1970-76 is the offsetting effect of the proportion of women of reproductive age among the total population. The larger cohorts born during the years of Brazil's peak birth rates entered the reproductive ages after 1970; their impact dampened the effect of the decline in marital fertility on the birth rate by about a fourth--2.3 out of 9.7 per 1,000.

ROLE OF PROXIMATE VARIABLES

Further insight into the nature of recent fertility trends in Brazil can be gained by examining the role of

TABLE 10 Decomposition of Change in Crude Birth Rate, 1960-76: Brazil

Component	1960-70	1970-76
CBR, base year	45.3	41.6
CBR, end year	41.6	34.4
Observed change (per 1,000)	-3.7	-7.2
Reproductive age women (total)	-0.12	2.28
Reproductive age structure	-1.17	0.19
Marital status distribution	-1.93	0.21
Marital fertility	-0.49	-9.72
Interaction	+0.01	+0.30

the proximate variables identified in the Davis-Blake (1956) framework, and more recently in Bongaarts' (1980) method for decomposing the difference between natural fertility and observed total fertility rates into four proximate determinants. Bongaarts' technique involves the computation of four indices: (1) C_m = the index of the proportion married, which equals one if all women of reproductive age are married, zero if none are; (2) C_c = the index of noncontraception, which equals one in the absence of contraception and zero if all women use 100 percent effective contraception; (3) C_a = the index of abortion, which equals one in the absence of induced abortion and zero if all pregnancies are aborted; and (4) C_i = the index of postpartum infecundability, which equals one in the absence of lactation and postpartum abstinence and zero if the duration of infecundability is infinite. Observed total fertility is linked to natural fertility (the number of births a women would have during her reproductive lifetime if none of the inhibiting factors were operative) by multiplying the number of births that would occur in a natural-fertility regime by each of the indices in succession: TFR = $15.3 \times C_m \times C_a \times C_c \times C_i$, where 15.3 represents an estimate of the total fecundity rate. It should be noted that the use of a single value to estimate the fecundability level of a population, set at 15.3 children per woman, has been questioned in light of the heterogeneity of populations in relation to a number of factors, such as state of health, duration of cohabitation, and so on. Thus, other values have been proposed for use in estimating this parameter for specific population subgroups (see Lesthaeghe et al., 1981 and Gaisie, 1981). In this report, however, 15.3 will be used.

Data requirements for calculating the four indices are geared to national-level fertility surveys, such as the World Fertility Survey, which include questions on breast-feeding and abortion as well as current contraceptive use. Census and survey data do provide enough information for calculation of the marriage index, which is the ratio of the total fertility rate to the total marital fertility rate, and which remained constant at a level of .63 from 1970 to 1976. In the absence of any nationally representative Brazilian data on the three remaining variables, the best that can be done is to piece together a national "guesstimate" from the fragments of subnational survey data that are available.

The two main sources of survey data for the 1970s are the local-level CEBRAP National Investigation on Human Reproduction (NIHR) and the state-level Contraceptive Prevalence Surveys (CPS), mentioned in Chapter 1. The NIHR interviews were conducted during 1975 in the states of Sao Paulo, Espirito Santo, Rio Grande do Sul, Pernambuco, Piaui, and Para (Berquo, 1976). The first CPS was conducted in Sao Paulo in 1978, followed by Piaui in 1979, and Pernambuco, Rio Grande do Norte, Paraiba, and Bahia in 1980 (Rodrigues et al., 1981a). Additional survey work was being conducted in Southern Brazil in 1981. Prior to these inquiries, the data were limited to a handful of surveys in specific localities: Rio de Janeiro was included in the comparative study of fertility and family planning in nine Latin American cities conducted by CELADE in 1963 (CELADE, 1972), and CEBRAP interviewed women in the municipality of Sao Paulo in 1965 (Berquo et al., 1977a); two other surveys include Martine's 1969 interviews of poor women who were using the services of a maternity clinic in Rio de Janeiro (Martine, 1975) and Etges' survey of women in Porto Alegre and two other localities in Rio Grande do Sul in 1973 (Etges, 1975). The subsections that follow assemble information on current contraceptive use, abortion, and breastfeeding from these surveys in a form that will permit calculation of the Bongaarts' indices.

Contraceptive Use

The index of noncontraception requires information on the percent of fecund married women of reproductive age currently using contraception, as well as a breakdown of methods by type to measure contraceptive effectiveness (Bongaarts, 1980). The available national-level Brazilian data are summarized in Table 11; as noted in Chapter 9, these data are paralleled by local-level NIHR data. The 1965 Sao Paulo survey is reported (Nakamura et al., 1979) to indicate that 66 percent of eligible women were using contraception, a higher proportion than was reported for Rio de Janeiro (38 percent) a year earlier. However, it is not apparent from reports on the Sao Paulo survey (Berquo et al., 1977a) whether the figure refers to current or ever use; if it is the latter, then 66 percent probably overstates current use. Both surveys indicate that methods other than the pill and sterilization were predominant. Martine's 1969 data on poor women in Rio

TABLE 11 Contraceptive Prevalence, Summary of Survey Data: Brazil

Site of Survey	Date	Users: Percent of Women	Method (percent)			Index	
			Pill	Sterilization	Other	E[a]	C[b]
Rio de Janeiro	1963	38.1	7.3	16.0	76.7	.763	.680
Rio de Janeiro	1969	31.3	45.0	n.a.	55.0	n.a.	n.a.
Rio Grande do Sul	1973	64.6	56.9	8.5	34.6	.839	.349
Sao Paulo, Sao Paulo	1978	63.4	47.3	21.9	30.8	.860	.345
Sao Paulo, Rest	1978	58.6	46.1	24.0	29.9	.864	.392
Piaui, Teresina	1979	44.9	26.1	62.8	11.1	.941	.493
Piaui, Rest	1979	28.8	33.9	46.7	19.4	.908	.686
Pernambuco, Metro Recife	1980	51.5	24.1	56.9	19.0	.919	.432
Pernambuco, Rest	1980	35.0	36.0	35.1	28.9	.877	.631
Rio Grande do Norte-Urban	1980	55.0	37.6	42.9	19.5	.904	.403
Rio Grande do Norte-Rural	1980	35.0	38.9	23.7	37.4	.849	.643
Bahia, Metro Salvador	1980	47.8	38.4	23.8	37.8	.848	.513
Bahia, Rest	1980	27.4	37.4	33.7	28.9	.876	.712
Paraiba	1980	43.2	36.3	33.1	30.6	.872	.548

[a] Index of effectiveness: sterilization = 1; Pills = .9; others = .7.
[b] Index of contraception: 1 - (proportion using x effectiveness index x 1.1 where 1.1 is sterilization factor.

Sources: 1963: CELADE (1972:178); 1969: Martine (1975:125); 1973: Etges (1975:95); 1978-80: Rodrigues et al. (1981b:Table 5); Paraiba 1980: Rodrigues et al. (1981a:Table 3).

indicate a sharp rise in pill use in the late 1960s; however, his survey is not comparable with the others since it did not include women who had been sterilized. The data on Rio Grande do Sul also show increased use of the pill, as well as a contraceptive use rate of nearly 65 percent.

The 1978 Sao Paulo CPS indicated that 63 percent of currently married women aged 15-44 were using contraceptives in the city of Sao Paulo, a figure slightly lower than that cited in the survey taken a decade earlier. Even if current use really was 66 percent in 1965, the 1978 survey indicates an important increase in effective contraception because of a shift to more effective methods, with the pill and sterilization accounting for nearly two-thirds of users in 1978 compared to less than one-fifth in 1965. The 1978 survey also indicated that contraceptive use was nearly as high in the rest of Sao Paulo, including rural areas, as it was in the capital city. The second CPS survey, conducted in 1979, shifted from Brazil's most developed to its least developed state, Piaui. Current users accounted for 45 percent of women in the capital city of Teresina and 29 percent in the rest of the state, which is predominantly rural. The most noteworthy feature of the Piaui data is the very major role played by sterilization, which represented 63 percent of all fertility control; the figure for the rest of the state was 47 percent. The 1980 Pernambuco and Rio Grande do Norte surveys tell a similar story: over 50 percent of women in Recife were currently using a method, with sterilization accounting for 57 percent of the total; in urban Rio Grande do Norte, sterilization and the pill were used in equal proportions. Finally, it should be noted that prevalence rates in general were higher in the rural areas of these states than in Piaui and Bahia, a reflection of the impact of community-based family planning programs organized by BEMFAM in cooperation with state governments (Rodrigues et al., 1981a).

The last two columns of figures in Table 11 provide estimates of the index of noncontraception (C_c) for each of the surveys for which the needed information was available. Computations were based on Bongaarts' formula: $C_c = 1 - (S \times E \times U)$, where "S" is a correction factor for sterility, "E" is a measure of average contraceptive effectiveness based on the share of each method in the total, and "U" is the proportion of married women currently using a method. The sterility correction factor was set at 1.1, Bongaarts' recommendation for less developed areas. Values of U were taken from the column showing the percent of current users. The value of E was determined from the three columns showing percent of total use for pills, sterilization, and other methods, with effectiveness ratings of 1.0, 0.9, and 0.7, respectively. Index values for the late 1970s range from about .35 for Sao Paulo to .70 for Bahia state, exclusive of Salvador.

The information in Table 11 falls far short of what is required to compute values of the index of noncontraception for Brazil during the 1970s. Most of the information relates to the later years of the decade, and only a fraction of the total population is represented. At best, these data are a rough guide to the extent of regional differentials, and serve as a basis for guesses at what the trends may have been. For illustrative purposes, they have been used to calculate national-level estimates of the index for three dates (1970, 1976, and 1980). The first step in making such calculations was to determine values for S, E, and U for the three dates, as shown in Table 12. National-level estimates of these measures were derived as follows. The sterilization index was assumed not to vary by region, and was set at 1.1 in 1970, then raised to 1.125 as the prevalence of sterilization increased. Values of U and E were assigned to each of six subdivisions of the Brazilian population, which was broken down by region (Northeast, South and Southeast, and North and Central-West) and by rural-urban residence. Those assignments were based on speculation about levels of these measures that would be consistent with the fragmentary trends suggested by the survey data.

For 1970, effectiveness was assumed to vary from .75 in the rural North and Northeastern regions to .85 in the urban Southeast. It was assumed that E converged on .90 for urban areas and on .85 for rural areas in 1980 as contraceptive use spread. The user rate was assumed to range from .05 for the rural North and Northeast to .55 in the urban Southeast in 1970, and was increased to .35 and .60 for the 1980 assumptions. It should be stressed again that these are merely illustrative figures; they are based on speculation about possible regional patterns of contraceptive use and effectiveness derived from the fragmentary evidence presented in Table 11. Actual numbers on which to base such an assessment simply do not exist. These illustrative figures will be incorporated below in the calculation of overall national-level estimates of the proximate determinants of fertility once similar speculative estimates of the prevalence of abortion and breastfeeding have been described.

TABLE 12 Components of Index of Contraception (C_c), 1970, 1976, and 1980: Brazil

Region	Weight	1970 Users	E	Weight	1976 Users	E	Weight	1980 Users	E
Northeast-Urban	.127	.10	.75	.138	.40	.85	.148	.50	.90
Northeast-Rural	.177	.05	.75	.160	.25	.80	.144	.35	.85
S. East/South-Urban	.389	.55	.85	.425	.60	.90	.460	.60	.90
S. East/South-Rural	.214	.35	.80	.174	.50	.85	.134	.55	.85
North/C. West-Urban	.044	.10	.75	.056	.40	.85	.069	.50	.90
North/C. West-Rural	.049	.05	.75	.047	.25	.80	.045	.35	.85
Brazil	1.00	.32	.80	1.00	.47	.86	1.00	.52	.88

Source: Derived from data presented in Table 11 using assumptions discussed in text.

Abortion

Abortion is illegal in Brazil, and the Brazilian penal code carries a sanction of several years of imprisonment at hard labor for both abortionists and women who practice it (Milanesi, 1970:12-13). However, the code is rarely invoked, except as a legal ploy in such efforts as the attempt to block the importation and use of the IUD as an "abortifacient." Abortion is believed to be widespread; rates of mortality and hospitalization resulting from abortion-related infections are high, though not well documented.

There are no reliable statistical data on abortions at the national level in Brazil, though there are reported estimates (based on some rather implausible extrapolations from the experience of hospitals in a few localities). According to these estimates, the annual number of abortions runs as high as three million per year, which would mean eight abortions for every ten live births (Rodrigues et al., 1975; Carvalho et al., 1981). The hard evidence that does exist suggests that poor, urban, and noncontracepting women are more likely to resort to induced abortion, and that only a fraction of these women identify themselves when the question is asked in survey interviews. Martine (1975) suggests that another reason for low observed abortion rates is the high mortality rate among women having abortions who, as a consequence, would not be accounted for. Questions on abortion have been asked in a number of fertility surveys conducted in Brazil since the early 1960s, including the NIHR and CPS; these provide a basis for calculation of the abortion index.

The way the incidence of abortion is reported varies by survey. For purposes of calculating Bongaarts' index of the effect of abortion on fertility, the ideal would be the total induced abortion rate; this is analogous to the total fertility rate and indicates the number of abortions a woman would have during her reproductive lifetime if current rates prevailed. Either annual age-specific abortion rates or the total number of abortions for women who have completed their reproductive life cycle could be used to calculate such a rate. However, samples are rarely large enough to give reliable estimates by the first method, and in only a few of the Brazilian studies are rates broken down by age. Variability in measures affects both the numerators and denominators of rates. In some cases, numerators refer to induced abortion, in others to all abortions (spontaneous and induced); some numerators indicate the number of abortions, others the number of women ever having had an abortion. Denominators include the number of women of reproductive age (usually restricted to women in unions) and/or the total number of pregnancies reported by these women.

Table 13 summarizes available statistical information on abortion in Brazil. Hutchinson's data on Rio de Janeiro in 1963 indicate that 9 percent of married women of reproductive age had experienced an abortion, while a 1965 CEBRAP study of Sao Paulo reveals that 18 percent of pregnancies ended in abortions, about one-third of which were induced. Martine's data on poor women in Rio de Janeiro in 1969 suggest a substantially higher incidence of abortion among low-income groups. Etges' study of three municipalities in Rio Grande do Sul in 1973 shows a higher rate of induced abortions as a percent of all pregnancies in Porto Alegre than in two smaller municipalities that he sampled. Questions on abortion have been included in all six of the CPSs for which tabulations are available. Women were asked how many abortions (spontaneous and induced) they had experienced, and whether their last abortion was spontaneous or induced. The proportion of induced abortions in the 1978 Sao Paulo survey was much lower (closer to one-ninth) than the one-third figure of the 1965 Sao Paulo survey; this suggests (1) that induced abortion is underreported in the CPS data, and/or (2) that a higher level of contraceptive use in 1978 may have resulted in a substitution of contraception for abortion (Nakamura et al., 1979:17). The proportion of women reporting having had an induced abortion was higher in urban areas of Sao Paulo. In other CPSs, the proportion of __women__ reporting that they had ever had an abortion was higher in rural areas, but the proportion of __pregnancies__ ending in abortion was higher in urban areas. CPS abortion data have been tabulated by women's age; this permitted a rough approximation of the total abortion rate, which was calculated as the proportion of the difference between the total pregnancy rate and the total fertility rate that could be attributed to induced abortion. This difference averaged .57 per woman in the Northeast, where the total fertility rate was 6.3 per woman. If the reported 10-15 percent share of induced abortion were accepted, the total abortion rate would be a very low .06 to .08 per woman; if all reported terminations of pregnancy were attributed to induced abortion, then the total induced abortion rate would be .57 per woman.

Berquo (1980) has calculated total abortion rates for the nine localities included in the NIHR survey. These range from .068 abortions per woman in Santa Cruz-Urban in the state of Rio Grande do Sul to .735 in Parnaiba-Rural in the state of Piaui. There is no consistent rural-urban pattern, though there is a suggestion that abortion rates are higher in larger cities and in poorer regions. It is also possible to speculate on total abortion rates using CPS data on the proportion of pregnancies ending in abortion. In Salvador, Bahia, for example, assuming that one-third of reported abortions are induced and the total fertility rate is about 4, the total induced abortion rate would be about .2 per woman; for Bahia-Rural, with a total fertility rate of 7, the total abortion rate is about the same. For Recife, calculation based on a total fertility rate of 4 yields an abortion rate of .25 per woman, about half of the rate indicated in the NIHR data; this is again consistent with the interpretation that (1) the CPSs underreport abortion more than does the NIHR survey, and/or (2) increased contraceptive use is being substituted for abortion.

The Bongaarts index for measuring the effect of abortion on the fertility rate is defined by the expression

$$C_a = \frac{TFR}{TFR + 0.4(1+u)TAR},$$

where "u" is the parameter already estimated when calculating the contraception rate. C_a becomes zero if all pregnancies are aborted, and is equal to 1 if all are successful. In applying this index to recent Brazilian fertility trends, one can at best speculate on orders of magnitude suggested by these survey results for the total induced abortion rate. There are several qualifications to be noted here. First, it is very likely that the survey data presented above greatly understate the abortion rate. Second, in addition to showing the prevalence of abortion, variation in Bongaarts' abortion index also reflects the level of fertility and of contraceptive use (to the extent that both, in turn, are related to the potential number of pregnancies to be aborted). Thus abortion, contraception, and fertility must be balanced in any calculations. Finally, uncertainty about the level of the abortion rate also relates to the impact of

TABLE 13 Reported Abortions, Summary of Survey Data: Brazil

Site of Survey	Date	Rate	Abortion Measure/Base Population	Source
Rio de Janeiro	1963	9.2	Induced Abort./Married Women 20-50	Hutchinson (1964:23)
Sao Paulo	1965	6.2	Induced Abort./Pregnancies	Berquo et al. (1977a:389)
Sao Paulo	1965	18.0	All Abort./Pregnancies	Berquo et al. (1977a:389)
Rio de Janeiro	1969	22.5	Induced Abort./Low Income Women	Martine (1975:38)
Porto Alegre-RGS	1973	13.2	Induced Abort./Pregnancies	Etges (1975:44)
Sao Leopoldo-RGS	1973	4.6	Induced Abort./Pregnancies	Etges (1975:44)
Caxias do Sul-RGS	1973	5.2	Induced Abort./Pregnancies	Etges (1975:44)
Sao Paulo-Capital	1978	14.8	All Abort./Women 15-44	Nakamura et al. (1979:Table 19)
Sao Paulo-Other Urban	1978	14.1	All Abort./Women 15-44	Nakamura et al. (1979:Table 19)
Sao Paulo-Rural	1978	16.8	All Abort./Women 15-44	Nakamura et al. (1979:Table 19)
Piaui-Teresina	1979	13.1	All Abort./Women 15-44	Rodrigues et al. (1981c:65)
Piaui-Rest	1979	19.3	All Abort./Women 15-44	Rodrigues et al. (1981c:65)
Piaui-Teresina	1979	9.4	All Abort./Pregnancies	Rodrigues et al. (1981c:65)
Piaui-Rest	1979	8.4	All Abort./Pregnancies	Rodrigues et al. (1981c:65)
Rio Grande do Norte-Urban	1980	15.2	All Abort./Women 15-44	Rodrigues et al. (1981b:Table 11)
Rio Grande do Norte-Rural	1980	18.0	All Abort./Women 15-44	Rodrigues et al. (1981b:Table 11)
Rio Grande do Norte-Urban	1980	9.5	All Abort./Pregnancies	Rodrigues et al. (1981b:Table 11)
Rio Grande do Norte-Rural	1980	8.4	All Abort./Pregnancies	Rodrigues et al. (1981b:Table 11)

Location	Year	Rate	Measure	Source
Pernambuco-Recife	1980	20.2	All Abort./Women 15-44	Rodrigues et al. (1981b:Table 11)
Pernambuco-Other Urban	1980	20.1	All Abort./Women 15-44	Rodrigues et al. (1981b:Table 11)
Pernambuco-Rural	1980	21.8	All Abort./Women 15-44	Rodrigues et al. (1981b:Table 11)
Pernambuco-Recife	1980	16.3	All Abort./Pregnancies	Rodrigues et al. (1981b:Table 11)
Pernambuco-Other Urban	1980	13.3	All Abort./Pregnancies	Rodrigues et al. (1981b:Table 11)
Pernambuco-Rural	1980	9.3	All Abort./Pregnancies	Rodrigues et al. (1981b:Table 11)
Bahia-Salvador	1980	18.2	All Abort./Women 15-44	Rodrigues et al. (1981b:Table 11)
Bahia-Other Urban	1980	20.8	All Abort./Women 15-44	Rodrigues et al. (1981b:Table 11)
Bahia-Rural	1980	21.8	All Abort./Women 15-44	Rodrigues et al. (1981b:Table 11)
Bahia-Salvador	1980	14.2	All Abort./Pregnancies	Rodrigues et al. (1981b:Table 11)
Bahia-Other Urban	1980	10.2	All Abort./Pregnancies	Rodrigues et al. (1981b:Table 11)
Bahia-Rural	1980	8.2	All Abort./Pregnancies	Rodrigues et al. (1981b:Table 11)
Cachoeira-Urban (RS)	1975	.179	Total Induced Abortion Rate	Berquo (1981:Table 11)
Santa Cruz-Urban (RGS)	1975	.068	Total Induced Abortion Rate	Berquo (1981:Table 11)
Santa Cruz-Rural (RGS)	1975	.104	Total Induced Abortion Rate	Berquo (1981:Table 11)
Sao Jose-Urban (SP)	1975	.462	Total Induced Abortion Rate	Berquo (1981:Table 11)
Sertaozinho-Rural (SP)	1975	.454	Total Induced Abortion Rate	Berquo (1981:Table 11)
Recife-Urban (PB)	1975	.478	Total Induced Abortion Rate	Berquo (1981:Table 11)
Conceicao Araguaia-Rural (PA)	1975	.263	Total Induced Abortion Rate	Berquo (1981:Table 11)
Parnaiba-Urban (PI)	1975	.617	Total Induced Abortion Rate	Berquo (1981:Table 11)
Parnaiba-Rural (PI)	1975	.735	Total Induced Abortion Rate	Berquo (1981:Table 11)

nonmarriage. It is one thing to assume that most births accrue to women in unions; it is quite another to assume that all pregnancies, particularly those that are aborted, are within unions. In all likelihood, a significant fraction of abortions may be experienced by women who are not in unions. To the extent that these abortions are understated, the estimate of nonmarriage may be overstated.

For illustrative purposes, a range for the total abortion rate of 0.5 to 1.5 per women may be assumed. With an estimated 1976 total fertility rate of 4.4, yielding about 3.75 million births in Brazil, a range estimate of between 500,000 and 1,250,000 annual induced abortions is implied. While these figures fall well below the 3 million annual abortions derived by extrapolation from newspaper and other reports, they seem more plausible than the very low abortion rates yielded by survey data.

Breastfeeding/Postpartum Amenorrhea

Statistical data on breastfeeding and postpartum amenorrhea in Brazil are also quite deficient. Questions on breastfeeding were included only in more recent inquiries--the NIHR and CPS. However, the data are more consistent for the purpose of calculating Bongaarts' index of the effect of postpartum infecundibility on fertility than was the case with abortion. Mean or median months of breastfeeding are provided in reports on the NIHR and CPS by Anderson et al. (1981) and Berquo (1980), as shown in Table 14. Calculation of the Bongaarts index requires a transformation of mean or median months of breastfeeding to months of postpartum amenorrhea, which is the "i" in the formula for the index: $C_a = 20/18.5 + i$. Anderson calculated i for Bahia, Pernambuco, Rio Grande do Norte, and Paraiba using the Lesthaege-Page model schedules, and a formula based on this schedule was used to transform the remaining observations.

While not representative of the entire Brazilian population, the data in Table 14 do span a broad enough spectrum of experience, from poorer Northeastern areas to the industrialized Southeast and the more developed rural areas of the South, to permit speculation about a plausible national-level index. The index values in the table, as well as the breastfeeding data on which they are based, show that the practice of breastfeeding is

TABLE 14 Reported Breastfeeding, Summary of Survey Data: Brazil

Site of Survey	Date	Months of Breastfeeding Mean	Months of Breastfeeding Median	Months of Amenorrhea Median	Index c_i
Sao Paulo-Urban	1978		<1	2.0	.97
Sao Paulo-Rural	1978		7.4	4.4	.87
Piaui, Teresina	1979		3.3	2.7	.94
Piaui-Rest	1979		9.1	5.3	.84
Bahia, Salvador	1980	4.8	<1	2.9	.93
Bahia-Rest	1980	9.4	3.8	4.0	.89
Paraiba-Urban	1980	4.7	<1	2.4	.96
Paraiba-Rural	1980	5.5	1.8	3.2	.92
Pernambuco, Recife	1980	3.7	<1	2.2	.97
Pernambuco-Rest	1980	4.4	<1	2.1	.97
Rio Grande do Norte-Urban	1980	4.2	<1	2.5	.95
Rio Grande do Norte-Rural	1980	5.0	<1	2.8	.94
Cachoeira-Urban (ES)	1975	8.5		5.0	.85
Santa Cruz-Urban (RGS)	1975	4.2		3.0	.93
Santa Cruz-Rural (RGS)	1975	5.5		3.6	.90
Sao Jose-Urban (SP)	1975	6.0		3.8	.90
Sertaozinho-Rural (SP)	1975	7.3		4.4	.87
Recife-Urban (PE)	1975	3.3		2.7	.94
Conceicao A.-Rural (PA)	1975	8.5		5.0	.85
Parnaiba-Urban (PI)	1975	4.8		3.3	.92
Parnaiba-Rural (PI)	1975	6.3		3.9	.89

Sources: 1975 data from Berquo (1980:Table II); all other data from Anderson et al. (1981:Table 5).

very limited. Indeed, Brazil falls at the very low end of the spectrum of countries for which breastfeeding data are available, including Latin American countries, which have low rates compared to other regions of the world (Kent, 1981). The index values range from .84 to .97, with lower values (higher breastfeeding) in rural areas and higher values in the cities. Values are also higher in areas in which contraceptive use is higher, suggesting that the practice of breastfeeding decreases as contraceptive use increases. These values are much more comparable to those of other industrialized countries than to those of developing countries; they are high even in comparison with other Latin American countries that also have higher values in comparison with other developing regions.

For purposes of computing an index of postpartum infecundability at the national level, an initial 1970 level of 4 months was assumed. Since there is evidence to suggest that increased contraceptive use leads to a decrease in breastfeeding, the assumption was reduced to 3.5 months in 1976 and 3 months in 1980 in the national-level estimates of proximate determinants that follow.

A Speculative Overview of Trends in the Proximate Determinants of Total Fertility Rates, 1970-80

Table 15 links estimates of the total fertility rate to the total fecundity rate (assumed to be 15.3 births per woman), using the evidence on contraception, abortion, and postpartum amenorrhea presented in the previous three sections on Bongaarts' indices for each of these proximate determinants. It also incorporates the information on marriage rates discussed earlier in this chapter. Two variants are presented for each of the three observation points: one assumes the lower value in the range of estimates of the total abortion rate, with higher levels of contraceptive use (lower levels of the index of non-contraception); the other assumes lower contraceptive

TABLE 15 Estimates of Proximate Determinants of Total Fertility Rate, 1970-80: Brazil

Measure and Variant	1970		1976		1980	
	A	B	A	B	A	B
Assumptions						
Percent users (U)	0.32	0.25	0.47	0.41	0.52	0.46
Effectiveness (E)	0.80	0.80	0.86	0.86	0.88	0.88
Sterilization factor	1.10	1.10	1.125	1.125	1.125	1.125
Months of infecundity	4.0	4.0	3.5	3.5	3.0	3.0
Total abortion rate	0.5	1.5	0.5	1.5	0.5	1.5
Results[a]						
Total fecundity rate	15.3	15.3	15.3	15.3	15.3	15.3
Infecundity index	0.89	0.89	0.91	0.91	0.93	0.93
Natural marital fertility	13.6	13.6	13.9	13.9	14.2	14.2
Abortion index	0.96	0.88	0.94	0.84	0.93	0.82
Contraception fertility	0.72	0.78	0.54	0.60	0.49	0.55
Total marital fertility	9.34	9.39	7.04	7.03	6.42	6.42
Nonmarriage index	0.63	0.63	0.63	0.63	0.64	0.64
Total Fertility Rate	5.89	5.92	4.43	4.43	4.11	4.11

[a]Data in second panel have been rounded; total fertility rate based on data before rounding.

use, and the higher estimate of the total abortion rate. This is only one of several tradeoffs that a range of values in the abortion rate implies. Higher abortion rates could also imply less effective contraception, as well as a lower impact of nonmarriage to the extent that abortions are used to terminate the pregnancies of women outside of unions.

The underlying assumptions are summarized in the first panel of the table. The contraceptive use and effectiveness rates in variant "A" are based on Table 12. The reduction in the contraceptive use rate in variant "B" is proportional to the increase in the abortion index implied by the higher total abortion rate. Both variants assume that there is a decline in postpartum infecundity of about 0.5 months from 1970 to 1976 that relates to increased contraceptive use, with a similar decline for 1976 to 1980. No change is assumed between 1970 and 1976 in the index of nonmarriage, which is consistent with the observed trend for that period, while a small increase is shown for 1980.

In variant "A", the main factor accounting for the decline in the total fertility rate from its level of around 5.9 in 1970 to 4.4 in 1976 is the decrease in C_c; this reflects increased contraceptive use, as well as increased effectiveness deriving from a higher proportion of more effective methods (the pill and sterilization) among those used. To the extent that variant "A" understates the abortion rate, this conclusion should be modified by assuming a smaller increase in contraceptive use, less improvement in contraceptive effectiveness, or a lower level of nonmarriage. Variant "B" illustrates the first of these possibilities.

Extrapolating to 1980, the table suggests that the pace of the decline in total fertility could be slower in the last half of the decade. This is partly a result of using levels of C_c in 1976 large enough to account for the 1970-76 decline, combined with C_c values for 1980 that are consistent with the survey results reported in Table 11. Variant "B" suggests an even slower decline in C_c, assuming that abortions played a greater role in the decline in total fertility than is implied in variant "A." It is worth noting that special tabulations of the 1977 and 1978 PNAD survey data in fact suggest a slowing of the pace of the decline of total fertility (Leite, 1981). An alternative hypothesis is that flaws in the design of the 1976 survey produced an overstatement of the decline, a point that will prove difficult to test until data for making alternative estimates of fertility during the decade become available (i.e., 1980 census data, for which the own-children method could be applied).

CONCLUSIONS

The 1970s brought a significant acceleration in the decline of fertility in Brazil: the crude birth rate fell from 41 per 1,000 in the late 1960s to 34 per 1,000 in the late 1970s; the total fertility rate, a more refined measure of fertility, declined from around 5.8 births per 1,000 women around 1970 to around 4.4 births by 1976. Of the three demographic factors that could account for a decline in the birth rate (proportions married, age structure, and marital fertility), declining marital fertility was clearly responsible for the change.

Assessment of the effect of nuptiality on fertility is complicated by the questionable reliability of reported marital status in the available census and survey data. A number of factors suggest that the proportion of younger women (up to age 25) reported as married has been understated. Doubts about the proportions married remain even after adjustments to include single women reporting births and separated women who might have entered into a second union and did not report it because divorce was not legally recognized. The whole question of pregnancies to women not in unions and the termination of such pregnancies remains a major area of doubt in examining the proximate determinants of Brazil's fertility decline. Calculations of the singulate mean age at marriage (SMAM) from census and survey data indicate a rise of about 0.8 years in the mean age at marriage between 1960 and 1970, and about half that from 1970 to 1976. An alternative measure of the age at which women begin being exposed to the risk of childbearing, the singulate mean age at first birth, reveals a similar trend. Even after adjustment of the marital status data to account for possible underreporting of the proportions married among women in their early twenties, there is little evidence of change between 1970 and 1976; this suggests that changes in marital status had only a limited effect on fertility decline during that interval. Because of the demographic echo of increased births in the 1950s and 1960s, the age structure of the Brazilian population had a slightly positive impact on birth rates.

Thus, on the basis of an admittedly speculative reconstruction of "what could have happened" when Brazil's accelerated fertility decline is decomposed into demographic components and into the proximate determinants of fertility, it can be concluded that a decline in marital fertility was the primary factor responsible. This decline in marital fertility can in turn be traced to an increased use of effective contraception, combined with an indeterminate abortion component both within and outside of marriage. Though national-level data on the proximate variables are lacking, survey data can be used to construct a national-level index of noncontraception, which declined from .72-.78 in 1970 to .54-.60 in 1976 and .49-.55 in 1980, suggesting that increased contraception played a major role in the decline. Survey data also indicate a very low prevalence of breastfeeding, and suggest a moderate attenuation of the fertility-reducing effect of postpartum amenorrhea as contraception increased. The major unknown variable is abortion. The more one accepts the fragments of evidence that abortion is widespread in Brazil, particularly among low-income groups, the more one must adjust the importance attached to increased contraception and no change in marriage rates.

Finally, it should be emphasized that doubts remain about the reliability of data on marital status, particularly since a significant number of pregnancies among women not in unions may be terminated by abortion, and informal unions may be formalized only after a live birth. Census and survey data on the proportion of women in unions may therefore reflect after-the-fact social adjustment processes more than the exact demographic accounting needed to decompose the proximate determinants of fertility.

CHAPTER 2

SOCIOECONOMIC DIFFERENTIALS IN FERTILITY

The evidence presented in Chapter 1 indicated that fertility had already declined prior to 1970 in more developed regions such as the Southeast, particularly among higher-income groups, but not among lower-income groups and regions. It also suggested that the overall accelerated decline after 1970 probably resulted from the spread of lower fertility to those latter groups. The objective of the present chapter is to identify these groups more precisely. This should make it possible to focus an explanation of the post-1970 accelerated decline more sharply on particular groups, and on specific socioeconomic changes that may have affected their reproductive behavior.

Evidence presented in this chapter is based on data from the public use sample of the 1970 census and the 1976 PNAD national sample survey, both of which include questions on average parity and on births in the year prior to the interview. Responses were tabulated by household income, education of women, rural-urban residence, and region. Indirect estimating techniques were used to derive total fertility rates for women in different education and income categories. Considerable caution is required in interpreting the results since most of the assumptions on which the techniques are based are violated in such an exercise. This problem is complicated by the fact that the severity of these violations can vary between categories of income and education into which the population has been grouped. For example, the assumption of constant fertility would be violated to a greater extent among higher income and education groups if they had been experiencing more rapid fertility decline than lower income and education groups--the situation in Brazil in 1970. Moreover, once the population has been divided into education and income classes, these cannot be considered "closed" populations, another requirement for valid application of the techniques. Sampling error is a further problem when such divisions are made, particularly for reported births in the year prior to the interview. These biases can be reduced but not eliminated by using fewer categories of each variable to increase sample size. In the study of fertility differences by income category cited in Chapter 1, Carvalho and Paiva (1976) reported that such a procedure reduced the impact of interclass mobility on their estimates. This problem may be less serious for breakdowns of the population by education than by income since most women, except the small proportion with university education, would have completed their education by the time they reached their late teens.

EDUCATION AND FERTILITY DECLINE

To examine the relation between fertility and education, women were divided into three broad education categories, with education defined according to years of schooling completed: women with no schooling, those with 1-4 years of schooling, and those with 5 or more years. This breakdown sacrifices some specificity among higher educational groups for a reduction in sampling error and in the mobility bias mentioned above. In preliminary tabulations, the effect of education on fertility varied by rural-urban residence, suggesting that rural and urban women should be separated in the discussion of educational differences. To reduce the sampling error that resulted from having so few rural women with more than 4 years of schooling, only two rural education classes were created: "none" and "any education."

Computations of total fertility rates for women in different education groups are based on the adapted Brass methodology described in Indirect Techniques for Demographic Estimation (United Nations, 1983); in this method, reference period error in the reporting of births during the year prior to the census or survey is corrected using a factor derived from comparisons between reported parity at different ages and the parity that would accrue if current fertility were cumulated (P/F ratios). Although reference period error would be expected in the 1970 data, which are based on a question about births in the last year, that error should have been minimal in the

1976 survey, which recorded the date of the last birth. Estimates prepared for the Panel on Brazil indicated an average P/F of 1.32 for Brazil in 1970 and 1.22 in 1976; this falls to 1.07 in estimates of total fertility based on advanced tabulations of the 1980 census. The 1976 P/F ratios suggest that reference period error was still present; one reason for this is that the survey was conducted over several weeks, and the year interval identified in the tabulations may have excluded recent births. The Panel on Brazil elected to employ the P/F ratio adjustment in 1976, as discussed further in its report.

These problems, as well as the others mentioned above (interclass mobility, interclass differentials in recent fertility decline, and sampling error), have undoubtedly affected the results reported in Table 16, which presents estimates of total fertility for women grouped according to educational attainment and rural-urban residence. The results are arranged in separate panels for 1970 and 1976. The first row in each panel shows unadjusted rates based on reported births in the previous year; the second row gives the average P/F ratio for women aged 20-24 and 25-29. The unadjusted data suggest a strong negative correlation between years of schooling and total fertility. The question arises of whether reference period error was higher among less-educated women. In 1970, the P/F ratio was 1.37 for urban women with no education and about .10 lower for urban women with some education. It is doubtful that enough women in their twenties shifted from the "none" class to the 1-4 group for interclass shifts to have accounted for this. On the other hand, it is possible that the P/F ratio for the 5+ group may be exaggerated since these women had been experiencing more rapid fertility decline prior to 1970.

Although the 1976 results suggest that fertility decline has indeed spread to lower education groups, problems arising from P/F ratios make it very difficult to determine how much. Interclass shifting of women may have had a greater effect since P/F ratios dropped from 1.27 in the "none" group to 1.07 in the 5+ group at the same time that the percent of women in the "none" group declined from 13.6 in 1970 to 9.5 in 1976; the 5+ category increased from 22.1 to 30.7 percent. The 1976 results could also reflect higher reference period error among less-educated women. That survey's enumerators were better trained and supervised than those of the census, a point which suggests that reference period error, if present in 1976, could be related to the

TABLE 16 Total Fertility Rates by Years of Schooling, 1970-76: Brazil

Year and Measure	Total	Urban			Rural	
		None	1-4	5+	None	Some
1970						
Unadjusted TFR	4.37	5.02	3.77	2.28	6.31	5.27
P/F Ratio[a]	1.33	1.37	1.26	1.27	1.32	1.32
Adjusted TFR	5.81	6.90	4.74	2.91	8.31	6.94
Percent Distribution	100.0	13.6	27.6	22.1	20.8	15.9
1976						
Unadjusted TFR	3.64	4.51	3.26	2.22	5.99	4.63
P/F Ratio[a]	1.22	1.27	1.24	1.07	1.31	1.12
Adjusted TFR	4.42	5.70	4.06	2.37	7.84	5.18
Percent Distribution	100.0	9.5	28.2	30.7	12.9	18.7
Percent Decrease						
Unadjusted TFR	16.7	10.2	13.5	2.6	5.1	12.1
Adjusted TFR	23.9	17.3	14.5	18.6	5.7	25.4
Mean Age[b] at First Birth						
1970	23.28	21.86	22.75	25.04	21.95	23.48
1976	23.84	21.91	22.30	26.08	22.08	23.70

[a] Adjustments based on average of P/F ratios for women aged 20-24 and 25-29.
[b] Based on reported percent of women with zero parity, after El Badry correction of nonreporting women (see United Nations, 1983).

Sources: Derived from 1970 census and 1976 PNAD sample files.

ability to recall the date of the last birth. If so, education, rather than the quality of interviewing, would account for differentials in reference period error. However, if fertility actually did decline more rapidly between 1970 and 1976 among less-educated women, this, too, could have inflated their P/F ratio.

Educational differentials in fertility with and without the P/F adjustment can be summarized according to differences between rates for women reporting a given level of education and women with no education. In 1970, unadjusted total fertility for urban women with 1-4 years of school was 1.25 children lower than for women with no schooling, and 2.74 lower for women with 5 or more years of schooling. These differentials increased to 2.15 and

3.99 children, respectively, when rates were adjusted using observed P/F ratios. The differential between rural women with no education and some education was one child when unadjusted data were used, and 1.37 children with the adjustment; though rural P/F ratios are equal, the adjustment process increases the differential between the two groups because of the larger base rate for women with no education. In 1976, the differential between unadjusted fertility rates for urban women with no education and those with 1-4 years of schooling was again 1.25 children, but decreased to 2.29 children for the 5+ group. With the adjustment, the differentials were 1.64 children and 3.33 children, respectively. Either way, educational differentials in fertility appear to narrow among urban women (when these differentials are expressed in numbers of children). For rural women, the opposite is true, since the 1976 differential was 1.36 with unadjusted data and 2.66 after the adjustment (see Figure 7).

The pattern of differentials in fertility decline between 1970 and 1976 is highly sensitive to P/F adjustments. For urban women, the category that appears least affected is the 1-4 group, whose decline was about 14 percent; however, its P/F ratios could have been biased upward both by fertility decline and by population shifts. For women with no education, the decline increases from 10 percent in the unadjusted rates to 17 percent after adjustment. For women with 5+ years of schooling, the decline increases from 3 percent to nearly 19 percent; the P/F ratio drops from 1.27 in 1970 to 1.07 in 1976 for that group. Although the results for rural women with no education are not affected by the adjustment, it causes the decline for rural women with some education to double.

It is difficult to draw firm conclusions about educational differentials in fertility decline from these results. For urban women, unadjusted data suggest that declines were greatest for women with 1-4 years of school. Adjusted results suggest that declines were greater among women with 5 or more years of schooling. Since there is reason to suspect that the 1970 P/F ratio for women in the 5+ group was biased upward by declining fertility, the 1970-76 decrease indicated by the adjusted data is probably exaggerated. A conclusion, tentative at best, is that urban fertility decline was probably more rapid among women with less education, leading to a narrowing of educational differentials among urban women; for rural women, those with no education experienced the least decline, leading to a widening in these differentials.

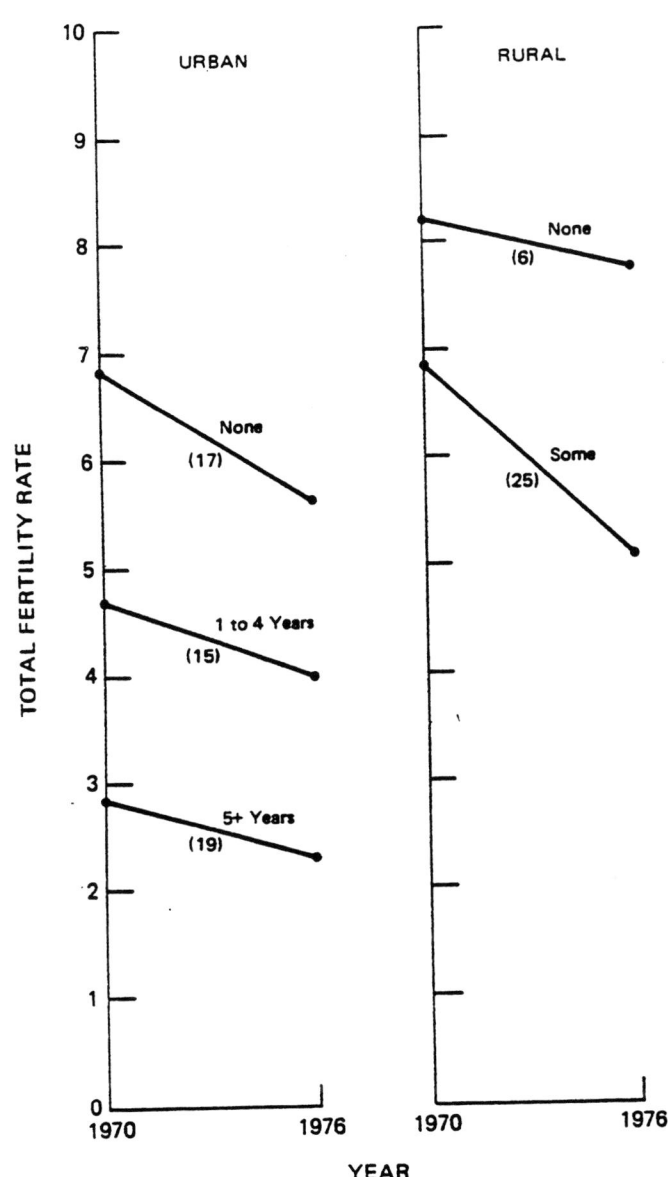

FIGURE 7 Total Fertility Rate by Years of Schooling, 1970 and 1976: Brazil

Note: Percent decreases shown in parentheses.

It is also important to observe that the total percentage fertility decline between 1970 and 1976 exceeded the decline in all but one education/residence category (the adjusted rates for rural women with some education). This is because the percentage distribution of women among education/residence categories changed between 1970 and 1976. The percentage of women in the urban "none" class declined from 13.6 percent to 9.5 percent, while the rural "none" dropped from 20.8 percent to 12.9 percent. The shares of the urban 5+ class increased from 22.1 percent to 30.7 percent, while the rural "some" group rose from 15.9 to 18.7 percent. The urban 1-4 group was more stable in percentage terms, though it is important to recognize that this stability masks considerable shifting into and out of the group as a consequence of changes in the shares of adjacent groups. Because of these changes in composition, the average decline for all classes combined exceeds percentage declines within classes.

Insights into the relationship between education and fertility that can be extracted from tabulations of questions on children ever born and children born in the last year are not limited to computation of total fertility rates. Tabulations of first births from these data make it possible to measure educational differences in the singulate mean age at first birth using the technique described earlier. These averages are shown in the last panel of Table 16. In 1970, there is a difference of less than one year between urban women in the "none" category and those with 1-4 years of schooling. A much larger difference, 2.3 years, separates the 1-4 and 5+ groups. There is a differential of about 1.5 years between rural women with no schooling and those with some schooling.

The main change in 1976 is that the average age at first birth for urban women in the 5+ group increases to 26.1 years, while the average for women in the 1-4 group drops slightly, increasing the difference between these groups to nearly 4 years. Since the reliability of these measurements could have been affected by the shifting of women from one education group to the next, by declining fertility, and by sampling error, caution is required in interpreting them. However, it is probably safe to say that these differences in age at first birth are one of the main features of educational differentials in Brazilian fertility. This could be the result of later marriage, labor force participation, and other aspects of the changing roles associated with increased education. Educational differences in the singulate mean age at marriage measure were not computed because of previously mentioned doubts about the reliability of the reporting of marital status.

FAMILY INCOME

Published results of the 1976 PNAD survey included tabulations of fertility questions according to household income categories (in multiples of the monthly salary at the time of the survey). Berquo (1980) has compared estimates of total fertility based on these tabulations to estimates of fertility by minimum salary groups in 1970 census data, with results as shown in Table 17. These estimates suggest that the greatest decline in total fertility between 1970 and 1976 occurred among the lowest-income groups. This suggests important changes in the pattern of income-related fertility differentials in Brazil because declines prior to 1970 clearly had been concentrated in higher-income groups. These changes have stirred considerable interest in the question of why rapid fertility decline spread to low-income women. Before this question is explored in detail in subsequent chapters, the remainder of the present chapter describes more precisely

TABLE 17 Total Fertility Rates by Family Income Level (multiples of monthly minimum salary), 1970 and 1976: Brazil

Monthly Income: Multiples of the Minimum Salary	Total Fertility Rate		Percent Decline
	1970	1976	
≤ 1	7.66	6.11	20.2
<1 to ≤ 2	6.20	5.94	4.2
<2 to ≤ 5	4.35	4.07	6.4
>5	2.60	2.54	2.3

Source: Berquo (1980), using 1970 census and 1976 PNAD survey data.

changes in the relationship between income and fertility in Brazil.

There are several ways in which the rates reported in Table 17 are ambiguous or might have been distorted. One relates to the effect of changes in the composition of women by income class. Again, in no group, including the lowest-income, does the decline exceed the 24 percent average for all groups combined, suggesting that changing composition has been at work. The effects of changing composition by income class are more complicated than the changes in education described above. There is an added problem of definition: the meaning of minimum salary categories as indices of poverty or wealth changed over the period from 1970 to 1976 because of deterioration in the purchasing power of the minimum salary; thus fertility changes observed for a particular minimum salary class could reflect the movement of women into or out of the class, or changes in the way that the class reflects income distribution. In 1970, 39 percent of families reported income levels of one minimum salary or less, and 21 percent had two or more. By 1976, the share of families with less than one minimum salary had fallen to 21 percent, while those with two or more had increased to 54 percent. The extent to which these shifts represent interclass mobility rather than changes in the meaning of minimum salary classes is ambiguous. Either could explain why the largest fertility declines seem limited to the lowest minimum salary group. Nearly half of the women in the one-two class in 1976 belonged to the less than one class in 1970, which means that they could well have experienced a decline from 7.66 to 5.94 (22 percent), a figure that is closer to the national average.

Another ambiguity relates to the extent to which these changes in composition, as well as interclass differentials in prior fertility decline and sampling error, may have distorted P/F ratios used to adjust total fertility rates reported in Table 17. If the tabulations by educational level are a valid indication, there could be major problems.

A third ambiguity, also suggested by the education results, arises from the possible masking of quite different rural and urban patterns in income group averages that combine rural and urban women.

Access to the raw data files for both the 1970 census sample and the 1976 PNAD survey make it possible to experiment with alternative tabulations by income class aimed at reducing, or at least clarifying, these distortions. To avoid the definitional problem arising from categorizing income groups according to minimum salary, families were regrouped into family income deciles (with families in multifamily households considered as separate units). In doing this, a choice had to be made between total family income and family income per capita. Neither measure was entirely satisfactory: for a given level of income, grouping by total income understated the relative prosperity of smaller households, whereas grouping by income per capita led to a clustering of higher-fertility women in the lower-income category. When total fertility rates for women categorized as low-income by both definitions were compared to results for women with no education, the rate for the low per capita category was higher, enough so that the grouping by total family income was selected.

In tabulating questions on fertility for different family income deciles, decile categories were grouped to reduce sampling error and the impact of interclass mobility. The following groups were adopted: in urban areas, deciles 1-3 were labeled "low," deciles 4-6 "middle," and deciles 7-10 "high"; in rural areas, the top two groups were combined because of sampling error arising from the limited number of cases in the 7-10 category. Interclass mobility is reduced but not eliminated by this grouping since the deciles refer to the distribution of all families, and the composition of groups could change as a result of changes in the distribution of women by place of residence or income.

Total fertility rates calculated from responses to fertility questions tabulated for groups of family income deciles are presented in Table 18. The format of the table is similar to that of Table 16, which described fertility differences by educational level: unadjusted rates in the first row, followed by observed P/F ratios, adjusted rates, and the percentage distribution of women in 1970 and 1976. The table also shows percentage decreases in rates from 1970 to 1976 and singulate mean ages at first birth for both dates.

In the unadjusted rates for 1970, total fertility for the urban low group was actually .4 children less than for the middle group. The reason that this did not show up in Table 16 is that in 1970, the majority of low-income women resided in rural areas, which weighs heavily in the overall low-income average. Unadjusted total fertility for urban women in the high-income class was over 2 children lower than for those in the middle class, and in

TABLE 18 Total Fertility Rates by Family Income Deciles, 1970-76: Brazil

Year and Measure	Total	Urban			Rural	
		Low	Middle	High	Low	High
1970						
Unadjusted TFR	4.37	4.36	4.75	2.69	6.71	4.99
P/F Ratio[a]	1.33	1.38	1.22	1.44	1.19	1.53
Adjusted TFR	5.81	5.99	5.82	3.88	8.00	7.66
Percent Distribution	100.0	10.8	16.5	35.8	17.8	19.1
1976						
Adjusted TFR	3.64	3.98	3.95	2.08	6.50	4.11
P/F Ratio[a]	1.22	1.10	1.14	1.45	1.03	1.45
Adjusted TFR	4.42	4.37	4.52	3.02	6.70	5.86
Percent Distribution	100.0	12.2	18.6	37.7	13.4	18.1
Percent Decrease						
Unadjusted TFR	16.7	8.7	16.8	22.7	3.1	17.6
Adjusted TFR	23.9	27.0	22.3	22.2	16.3	22.2
Mean Age[b] at First Birth						
1970	23.28	22.03	21.46	25.16	20.51	24.28
1976	23.84	21.32	21.52	26.30	20.48	24.70

[a] Adjustments based on average of P/F ratios for women aged 20-24 and 25-29.
[b] Based on reported percent of women with zero parity, after El Badry correction of nonreporting women (see United Nations, 1983).

Sources: Derived from 1970 census and 1976 PNAD sample files.

rural areas about 1.7 children lower for middle and high deciles combined. Unadjusted total fertility declined by about 17 percent overall from 1970 to 1976. Rates for the urban low and middle groups were about the same, and the pattern of differences among other groups was similar to that of 1970. The rural low group declined least; however, the weight of this group decreased, while that of low urban women increased. The unadjusted rates suggest that fertility decline was greater among the middle- and high-income groups.

The picture changes considerably when rates are adjusted using the observed P/F ratios: income differentials narrow for both urban and rural women because of the high P/F ratios of high-income women. This is surely a distortion that reflects the declining fertility of women in this group. Because 1976 P/F ratios were lower for all women except those in the urban high-income group, the adjusted rates suggest more rapid declines than do the unadjusted rates. The pattern of fertility decline by income class also changes, with the adjusted rates indicating that decline to have been greatest among low-income urban women and least among low-income rural women. Though the P/F ratio of high-income women is probably distorted, there is little change in it from 1970 to 1976; thus the percentage decline for the group is unaffected.

The insights provided by these results about income class differentials in the level and percentage decline of fertility between 1970 and 1976 are thus clouded by distortions in the P/F ratios. However, they do suggest a need to modify the conclusion reported earlier that fertility decline was concentrated in the lowest-income group and that little or no decline occurred at higher levels. Moreover, the results indicate that if fertility decline was greater among low-income women, it was among low-income urban women; in fact, they suggest that the rate of decline was lowest among low-income rural women. Otherwise, the evidence reported here indicates that fertility decline was more evenly spread across income classes. If this is so, education may have played a more important role than income in differentials in the rate of decline between 1970 and 1976. There may also be an interaction between education and income; that is, fertility change may be related to a woman's level of education, but the nature of this relation may vary by income class.

The last bit of information about income class differentials in fertility relates to the measure of mean age at first birth. The patterns here are similar to those observed in the educational breakdowns, with a differential of about 3 years separating high-income women from other groups in 1970 and an increase in this differential to about 4 years for urban women in 1976. This again raises the question of what socioeconomic forces led to increases in age at first birth for these women and not for women in lower income and education groups; it also raises the question of how differences by income and education relate to each other.

A partial answer to the last question is provided by an examination of joint percentage distributions of women by educational attainment and family income level, as shown in Table 19. The base for the percentages is the total number of women aged 15-49; thus each cell in the

TABLE 19 Percent Distribution of All Women Aged 15-49 by Income Deciles, Years in School, and Rural-Urban Residence, 1970 and 1976: Brazil

Year and Income Decile	Years of Schooling				
	Urban			Rural	
	None	1-4	5+	None	Some
1970					
Urban Low	4.78	4.46	1.52	--	--
Urban Middle	4.93	8.27	3.26	--	--
Urban High	3.83	14.83	17.29	--	--
Rural Low	--	--	--	12.20	5.54
Rural High	--	--	--	8.73	10.36
1976					
Urban Low	3.74	5.79	2.62	--	--
Urban Middle	3.46	9.34	5.79	--	--
Urban High	2.32	13.10	22.27	--	--
Rural Low	--	--	--	7.21	6.20
Rural High	--	--	--	5.69	12.44

Sources: Tabulations of 1970 census and 1976 survey data files.

table shows the percent of women in a particular income/education group, with the sum of all cells rather than either rows or columns adding to 100 percent. The distributions show that there is a loose correspondence in the data, but hardly an exact fit, between income level and educational attainment. This correspondence, measured by comparing percentages in each cell, is closer when one examines the distributions of educational attainment within income groups (reading across rows); the picture is less clear in the distribution of women by income level within education categories (reading down columns). There is a closer correspondence in rural areas and at higher levels of income and education in the urban population: for example, the majority of women with higher educational attainment are found in higher-income deciles. This is not true of urban women with lower educational attainment, who appear to have a better chance of attaining the middle- or upper-income deciles. This indicates a need to take account of the role of education and other features of the urban environment (particularly labor force participation) in examining differentials in fertility by income class, and vice versa.

THE REGIONAL DIMENSION OF INCOME DIFFERENCES

The regional dimension of declines in total fertility by income level is examined in Table 20.[1] Rates were calculated for three groups of PNAD regions, which were combined to preserve an adequate sample size in the tabulation by income deciles. Regions 1 and 2 (Rio de Janeiro and Sao Paulo), which represent the highest levels of income and socioeconomic development in Brazil, were combined and are labeled as "RJ-SP". A second combination consists of PNAD regions 3 and 4 (Parana/Santa Catarina/Rio Grande do Sul and Minas Gerais/Espirito Santo), which represent intermediate levels of income and other development indicators and are labeled as "Other." Region 5 consists of Brazil's poorest region, the Northeastern states, so labeled. PNAD regions 6 and 7 are not shown because only their urban population was available in the 1976 sample. Family income groups were also consolidated to reduce sampling error: in urban areas, the lowest six and highest four deciles were combined, and all rural women were combined. The discussion is limited to unadjusted total fertility rates.

In 1970, previously observed (Chapter 1) patterns of interregional differentials in fertility were maintained within each broad category of family income. Fertility was lowest in the high-income region and highest in the low-income region. Interregional differentials were greatest among low-income urban women. Within regions, the differential between low- and high-income urban women was greatest in the Northeast and least in Rio and Sao Paulo. However, the differential between low-income urban women and rural women generally (most of whom are lower-income) is greatest in the middle group.

In 1976, the pattern changed. Most importantly, rates for women in middle-income regions moved closer to those for women in Rio and Sao Paulo. In fact, the rates for urban low-income women were lower in the "other" region, so that the within-region differential for urban women

TABLE 20 Unadjusted Total Fertility Rate by PNAD Region and Income Decile, 1970 and 1976: Brazil

	PNAD Region		
Year and Decile	RJ-SP (1-2)	Other (3-4)	Northeast (5)
1970			
Urban/Low-Middle	3.85	4.27	5.41
Urban/Middle	2.47	2.67	3.37
Rural/All	4.82	5.62	6.39
1976			
Urban/Low-Middle	3.51	3.32	4.85
Urban/High	2.01	2.04	4.43
Rural/All	4.42	4.43	6.06
Percent Decrease			
Urban/Low-Middle	8.8	22.2	10.4
Urban/High	18.6	23.6	29.1
Rural/All	8.3	21.2	5.2

Source: Unadjusted total fertility rates derived from special tabulations of census and survey files.

was less for this region than for RJ-SP. The reason for this is that fertility rates for all classes of women declined more rapidly in the former. Declines were least rapid in Rio and Sao Paulo since their rates were lower to begin with in 1970. The greatest percentage decline occurred among high-income urban women in the Northeast, while the lowest percentage decline was among rural women in that region.

In assessing these patterns, it is also important to take account of the relative size of each region's income classes, since both the percentage decline and weight of each group in the total number of women account for their contributions to the overall fertility decline. Table 21

TABLE 21 Percent Distribution of Women Aged 15-49 by PNAD Region and Income Deciles, 1970 and 1976: Brazil

Year and Decile	PNAD Region				
	RJ-SP (1-2)	Other (3-4)	Northeast (5)	(6-7)	Total
1970					
Urban/Low-Middle	7.8	7.8	9.2	2.5	27.3
Urban/High	19.9	9.0	4.7	2.2	35.8
Rural/All	4.6	15.5	16.8	a	36.9
Total	32.3	32.3	30.7	4.7	100.0
1976					
Urban/Low-Middle	9.7	8.7	9.7	3.1	31.2
Urban/High	19.7	10.7	4.7	2.3	37.4
Rural/All	3.7	13.2	14.5	a	31.4
Total	33.1	32.6	28.9	5.4	100.0

aRegions 6-7 included for comparison, but rural population of these regions not included in total.

Source: Special tabulations of census and survey data files.

shows the percentage distributions of women aged 15-49 by region and income class for 1970 and 1976. The total number of women at each date is the base of the percentages. The group with the largest share (nearly 20 percent) of women--the higher-income deciles in Rio and Sao Paulo--had an 18.6 percent fertility decline. Although this was below the national average since this group already had comparatively low fertility in 1970, it was important because of the weight of this group in the total. The group with the greatest percentage decline in fertility--the higher-income women in the Northeast--accounted for a relatively small share (less than 5 percent) of women (see Figure 8).

The important groups in terms of larger weight in the total and higher percentage declines were women in the middle-income "other" region. They accounted for a little less than one-third of all women, and experienced

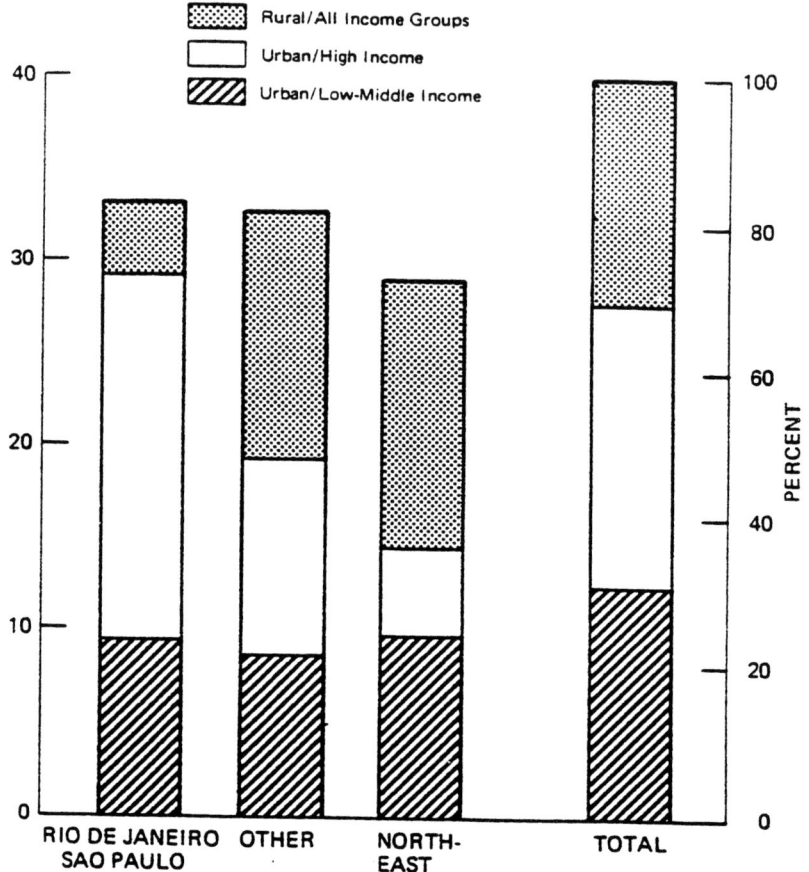

FIGURE 8 Distribution of Women Aged 15-49, by Region and Income Group, 1976: Brazil

fertility declines of 21-24 percent. Rural fertility decline in this region was about 22 percent, and these rural women accounted for about 14 percent of the total. This contrasts with rural women in the Northeast, whose decline was only 5 percent, and who accounted for a roughly similar percentage share of all women.

These comparisons add further weight to the conclusion stated earlier: that the spread of fertility decline to new regions and income groups, combined with its continuation among women experiencing pre-1970 declines, accounted for the accelerated fertility declines of the 1970s.

These comparisons also suggest that in the future, fertility decline at the national level will depend to an even greater extent on declines among low-income groups in both urban and rural areas. Fertility decline among urban middle- and upper-middle deciles, which contributed substantially to the declines of the 1970s, will be more limited since the fertility of these groups has reached comparatively low levels.

CONCLUSIONS

The objective of this chapter was to identify differences in fertility among Brazilian women according to levels of educational attainment and family income in 1970 and 1976, as well as differential rates of fertility decline between these two sets of data by education and income. A further objective was to determine the possible effects of changes in the distribution of women by education and income on the overall rate of decline and to pinpoint which groups contributed most to the decline because they had greater percentage declines, greater weight in the total number of women aged 15-19, or both.

The main finding of the chapter is a confirmation of the hypothesis stated in Chapter 1 about the reason for Brazil's accelerated fertility decline in the 1970s: during the 1970s, there was continued, though slowing, fertility decline among middle- and upper-income women in Rio de Janeiro and Sao Paulo (women who had experienced declines prior to 1970), combined with the spread of fertility decline to women in lower- and middle-income regions that had experienced only limited decline before 1970. The chapter also suggests a number of lines of analysis that might indicate why the 1970s brought the particular combination of fertility declines that it did. These data, while basically descriptive, suggest that interactions between income level, educational attainment, age, and other aspects of the socioeconomic environment should be studied in greater detail. An examination of links between female labor force participation, migration, and household consumption patterns is warranted, with account taken of regional and rural-urban dimensions of these changes. These factors will be included in the analyses presented in the next two chapters.

The present chapter has also raised a number of methodological questions, particularly about the reliability of data on births in the year prior to the interview as tabulated for subpopulations like the income and education groups identified here. The distortions in P/F ratios associated with the shifting of women between groups, differential fertility between groups, and sampling error are so severe that adjustments based on these ratios are questionable if not misleading. Though it would be desirable to use data on current rather than cumulative fertility in analyzing recent changes, the questionable reliability of current fertility measures as applied to subpopulations suggests that data on parity by age and other characteristics are more likely to yield unbiased results. Imaginative use of these data, such as a focus on childlessness and on cohort changes (for example, the difference between the average parity of women in a particular education/income class who were 20-24 in 1970 and the parity of the same group at age 26-30 in 1976) may be a way to compensate for some of the information on recent fertility that is lost by not using the data on births in the last year.

CHAPTER 3

DETERMINANTS OF BRAZIL'S RECENT FERTILITY DECLINE

During the 1970s, marital fertility in Brazil declined by about 30 percent. Previously, it had been stable or decreased only slightly, though there were declines among women in higher-income classes. What accounts for this major shift in Brazilian reproductive patterns? A working hypothesis is that the change was triggered by the convergence of two sets of forces. One of these was the increased availability of effective means of contraception, particularly for lower-income groups and regions of the country that had not participated in the earlier fertility decline. The other was the emergence of socioeconomic conditions conducive to smaller family norms, which motivated couples to use available contraception to reduce, delay, or end childbearing.

The decomposition of the Brazilian fertility decline during the 1970-76 period presented in Chapter 2 of this report identified increased use of effective contraception as the key proximate variable determining that decline. The questions raised by this finding relate to the way access to fertility control increased in a country providing no official support for fertility control at the national level, as well as what factors motivated people to make use of available contraception when previously they had not.

Rapid fertility decline began during a period (1967-73) when the Brazilian economy was experiencing a very rapid rate of growth in aggregate income per capita, and accelerated when the boom faltered as a result of rising energy costs after 1973. In this period, Brazil also made major strides in achieving increased educational attainment for women (and men); moreover, important changes in social structure were occurring, including very rapid urbanization, increased female labor force participation, and increased exposure to mass communications. At the same time, declining fertility took place in a society characterized by a very unequal distribution of the benefits of growth, and among groups that profited least from the boom and whose relative economic position may actually have deteriorated during this period. This raises the question of how modernizing forces, combined with changes in the capability to realize childbearing and other economic and social expectations, have influenced reproductive norms and behavioral patterns among the groups that contributed to fertility decline.

Brazil's diversity of regions and social classes, together with associated differences in the level and pace of change in demographic variables, would suggest that multiple changes in socioeconomic and demographic variables led to the accelerated fertility decline of the 1970s. This chapter examines hypotheses and supporting evidence used to explain recent shifts in Brazilian reproductive behavior, focusing on the spread of contraceptive use to women in lower and middle socioeconomic classes who accounted for much of the accelerated decline, and on socioeconomic changes that might explain this change in contraceptive use.

First, it explores hypotheses linking socioeconomic conditions to fertility decline. Next, it examines the available data on changes in Brazil's contraceptive patterns, and on socioeconomic factors associated with those changes. Finally, because of the essential institutional differences between urban and rural women, the hypotheses and data linking socioeconomic factors to fertility decline are applied separately to these two groups.

HYPOTHESES LINKING SOCIOECONOMIC CONDITIONS TO FERTILITY DECLINE

A number of hypotheses about the effects of changing socioeconomic conditions on Brazil's fertility decline can be formulated. One of these, coming under the general heading of "modernization," refers to the influence on reproductive behavior of rising income, changes in the costs of children relative to other goods, and shifts in social norms and aspirations. This hypothesis emphasizes the role of income and costs of children and other goods, focusing on tradeoffs between the number of children and other goods (including child quality). These tradeoffs are influenced by increases in the value of women's time as they achieve higher levels of education, by related changes in the opportunity and direct costs of children (who are time-intensive compared to other goods), and by changes in overall household consumption patterns as a result of increased income and changing tastes. The logic of this hypothesis can be used to show that such changes lead to reduced demand for children and increased motivation to use family planning, particularly when the subjective and monetary costs of fertility control have fallen below those of an unplanned additional pregnancy.

A limitation of this framework is that there is no easy way to assess the influence of institutional forces at both the family and societal levels on reproductive norms and aspirations. This limitation is particularly important when fertility change is occurring in a context of rapid socioeconomic change. When only a few measures reflecting such changes are available, it may be difficult to identify the causal relationships between such variables and fertility. Female educational attainment and labor force participation are good examples. Education is strongly associated with fertility differentials, and is used in economic models as a measure of the value of time. However, education may also embody attitudes about women's roles, the value of children, and the practice of contraception. Increases in female labor force participation may indeed be responding to changes in female education and household income, but institutional forces that influence the labor markets in which jobs for women are available may also play an important role.

An institutional factor of particular concern in the Brazilian case is the distribution of income. It is true that during the period in which the decline of fertility accelerated, the rate of growth of per capita income was around 7 percent per annum; however, it should also be remembered that the distribution of the benefits of this growth was highly skewed. It is estimated that two-thirds of household income in Brazil accrued to the top 20 percent of households in 1972, with only 7 percent going to the lowest 40 percent (World Bank, 1981:Table 25). The 20 million people (20 percent of the Brazilian population in the early 1970s) with incomes growing more rapidly than Brazil's already impressive national average represent a substantial force in the direction of modernization, whose impact on fertility was clearly evident in the data presented in Chapter 2.

Nevertheless, lower-income groups experienced the most rapid fertility declines after 1970. To use the term "modernization" to characterize the social and economic changes that accompanied these declines seems incongruous with the living conditions implied by their position in Brazil's income distribution. While there is still considerable debate about the interpretation of Brazilian income distribution data, particularly with reference to nonmonetary items and the impact of inflation on the welfare of the poor, there is general agreement on points that are relevant to the question of fertility decline. One is that there are substantial numbers of people and families who are poor in the absolute sense of living with substandard levels of health, housing, nutrition, and other basic needs. Lluch (1981) estimates that the lowest three deciles of families classed by family income per capita in 1970 fell into this category, and that they were located in both rural and urban areas. A second point is that inflation has had an adverse impact on the buying power of lower-income groups. This is a result of the way in which the Brazilian system of wage and price indexing operated during the late 1960s and early 1970s, with the indices that controlled prices and credit obligations being allowed to increase more rapidly than the wage index. Lower-income groups suffered the most from this, and particularly hard-hit were urban working class families (the lower-middle income deciles), whose incomes were more closely linked to the wage index by virtue of employment in sectors governed by minimum salary arrangements.

The fact that fertility declines in the early 1970s were concentrated among the absolute poor and the lower-middle income families has suggested alternative hypotheses about the link between deterioration in buying power and reproductive behavior. Berquo (1980) has argued that the living conditions of the poor deteriorated so much during this period that their psychological and physiological capacity to reproduce was affected--a sort of "immiseration" hypothesis. She suggests that poor nutrition, fatigue associated with the need to work long hours to earn enough income to buy food, and poor nutrition may have caused a loss of the will to reproduce, a reduction in coital frequency, and a possible reduction in fecundity. However, assessment of such effects would require much more in-depth interviews than those available from the Contraceptive Prevalence Surveys (CPS). Certainly, the threshold at which amenorrhea and anovulation are caused by malnutrition and psychological stress is high enough that such effects would be observed only in extreme circumstances. Still, it is possible that the fecundity of very low-income Brazilian women could have been affected by poor nutrition. A national nutrition and household consumption survey taken in 1974-75 provides nutritional indices for children under age 18. That survey indicated that 37 percent of Brazilian children were affected by first degree malnutrition (average body weight 76 to 90 percent of FAO/WHO norms), 20 percent by second degree malnutrition (61 to 75 percent of the norm), and 1 percent by third degree malnutrition (less than 60 percent of the norm) (World Bank, 1979). While data on mothers were not provided, such indices suggest that subfecundity may have affected a portion of low-income women. The possibility that physiological and psychological factors were involved in the fertility decline among Brazil's low-income groups should therefore not be ignored; however, it appears unlikely that they would account for a significant share of that decline.

Another hypothesis draws on elements of the modernization framework outlined above, but stresses increased economic pressures on the buying power of low-income households as a key determinant of changes in reproductive behavior. Carvalho et al. (1981) have argued that pressures to preserve living standards in the face of adverse economic conditions have forced poor families to adapt by delaying or curtailing their reproductive aspirations. In such circumstances, couples recognize that they cannot afford another child because of its direct impact on their limited income, as well as its opportunity cost in the time of mothers who must work to supplement family income. With increased accessibility, knowledge, and acceptability of contraception, fertility control is one of the few options available as a survival strategy; the decline of fertility among lower-income families is seen as an indication that they are choosing this option.

Extending this argument, it has been suggested that lower- and middle-income families, particularly in urban areas, raised their consumption expectations during early stages of Brazil's economic boom and were beginning to realize those expectations through increased purchases of housing, consumer durables, and even automobiles. Most of these purchases were made with small down-payments and required extended installment payments that were subject to Brazil's indexing system. Unequal treatment of credit obligations and wages in the indexing process forced these families to allocate an increasing share of their monthly income to those installment payments. In these circumstances, avoiding the expense of an additional child, again given increased accessibility, knowledge, and acceptability of contraception, was an option. The rapid decline of fertility among these groups suggests that this may indeed have been their response.

The hypotheses summarized in the preceding paragraphs suggest a number of mechanisms through which changes in socioeconomic conditions in Brazil during the 1970s could have contributed to the acceleration of fertility decline. These hypotheses suggest differing views of the process in that the "modernization" hypothesis focuses on changes in couples' reproductive aspirations and their ability to realize them, while hypotheses focusing on economic pressures and structural change place greater emphasis on institutional forces. However, the various hypotheses are not necessarily competitive. In fact, given the range of changes in fertility observed at both the regional and socioeconomic class levels, it is likely that recent experience reflects a combination of reinforcing factors rather than any single mechanism.

Data with which to test any of these hypotheses are very limited. Most of the evidence provided by the 1970 census and 1976 survey data consists of broad measures having a bearing on several of the hypotheses; none of these measures offers the precision needed to specify causal models in support of one hypothesis to the exclusion of the others. At the same time, the data suggest that socioeconomic changes consistent with such explanations were in fact occurring. The next two subsections examine the data available on the primary aspects of the hypotheses presented above: increased accessibility, knowledge, and acceptability of contraception, and socioeconomic factors related to changing patterns of contraceptive use.

Increased Access to Fertility Control

While Brazil is one of the few developing countries without a national policy in support of fertility control, Brazilian women are not necessarily denied access to fertility control. In fact, the private sector has played a major role in increasing the availability of contraceptives in Brazil, both through commercial channels and through private agencies, the most important being Brazil's International Planned Parenthood Federation (IPPF) affiliate Sociedade Civil Ben-Estar Familiar no Brasil (BEMFAM).

Commercial distribution networks were an important factor in the fertility decline among Brazilian middle- and upper-income classes prior to 1970, with pills, condoms, and surgical sterilization being the most common means adopted. Pills are manufactured in Brazil, with an increase in annual production from 1.7 million cycles in 1964 to 61.2 million in 1980. The largest percentage growth occurred during 1964-70, when there was an eightfold increase to 13.5 million cycles. The following six years, 1970-76, brought a larger absolute increase to over 49 million cycles, nearly four times the 1970 level. This trend is shown graphically in Figure 9. Regionally, the market for pills has been concentrated in the Southern and Southeastern states. Regional shares of the total market are also shown in the figure, with separate panels for Sao Paulo, Rio de Janeiro, Minas Gerais, the three Southern states (Rio Grande do Sul, Santa Catarina, and Parana), and the remaining states in the Northeastern, Northern, and Central-West regions. Sao Paulo alone accounts for over 30 percent of the market; when its share is combined with that of Minas Gerais and Rio de Janeiro, the figure is close to 60 percent. The contribution of traditional methods such as withdrawal and periodic abstinence is also significant, even though these are less effective means.

BEMFAM has played an important role in extending access to modern methods, particularly the pill, to lower-income groups and regions. According to industry sources, 9 percent of pills produced in Brazil in 1976 were distributed to BEMFAM. Several state governments, including five in the Northeast, have entered into cooperative agreements with BEMFAM for the provision of community-based family planning services. While the number of women served by such programs is not large enough to account for all of the increase in contraceptive use that has been observed, BEMFAM's impact is clear from a comparison of data for states in which it is active with those in which it is not.

Another important factor in increased access is what appears to be a significant but not highly publicized shift in the attitude of the Brazilian public health care system toward the provision of family planning services and surgical sterilization. Though the Brazilian govern-

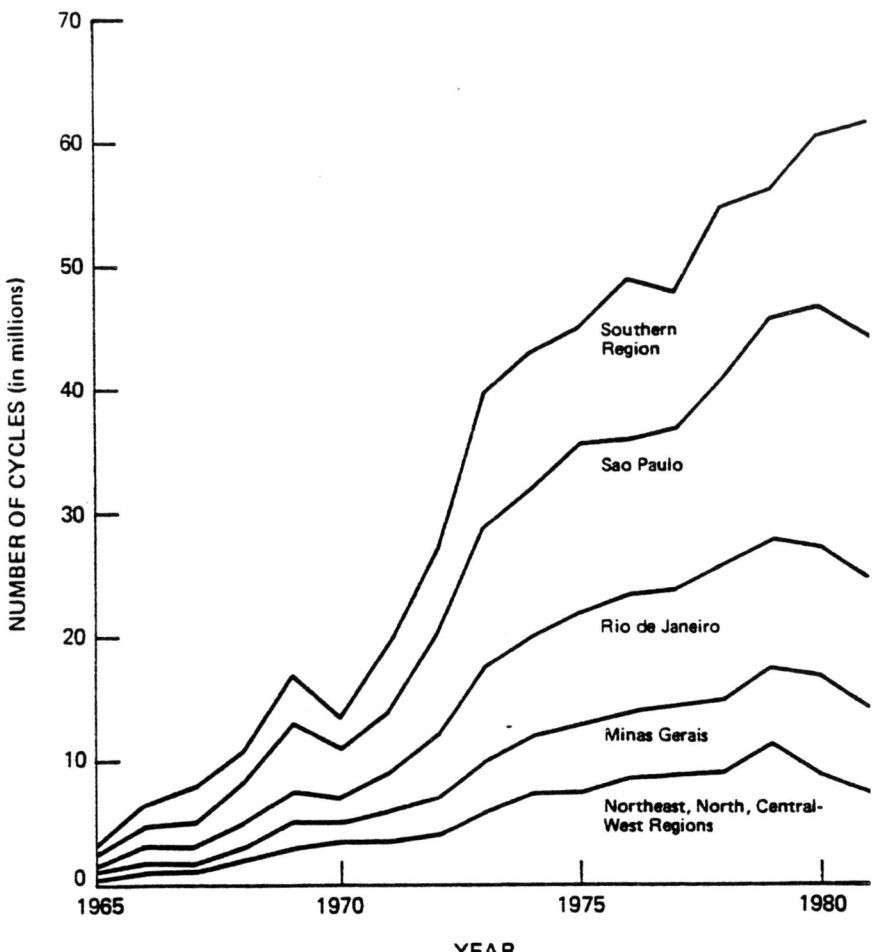

FIGURE 9 National and Regional Trends in Commercial Distribution of Contraceptive Pills, 1965-81: Brazil

ment has not yet adopted a national health plan that would eventually include family planning among its services, the health care system appears to have adopted a more liberal approach than it had before, at least in allowing private physicians working within the system to prescribe oral contraceptives and perform sterilizations.

The main sources of statistical data on contraceptive use in Brazil are the state-level Contraceptive Prevalence Surveys (CPS) and the local-level CEBRAP National Investigation on Human Reproduction (NIHR). Since the latter is discussed in detail in Part II, the present chapter focuses on the CPS results. It should be noted that because none of these surveys was conducted prior to 1976, they provide an ex post view of the impact of increased access to family planning on fertility decline. Table 22 presents the percentage distributions in five of these surveys of married women aged 15-44 by household income level and contraceptive use status. The first row of figures for each survey shows that the percentage of women currently using contraception increased with household income, which is broken down in multiples of the average monthly minimum salary. The contraceptive use differential between women in upper- and lower-income groups was least in Sao Paulo, Brazil's most urbanized and industrialized state, and greatest in Bahia, located in the lower Northeast. The remaining states shown in the table are also located in the Northeast. Through cooperative arrangements with state governments, BEMFAM has operated community-based family planning programs (CBPs) in Rio Grande do Norte since 1973, followed by programs in Pernambuco and two other Northeastern states in 1976, and in Piaui in 1979.

Survey results for Rio Grande do Norte, the state in which the CBPs had been operating longest, indicate that the differential between higher- and lower-income women was less than that in Piaui and Bahia, states in which such programs did not exist prior to the survey. As for contraceptive methods, a higher proportion of women in upper-income groups had been sterilized, particularly in the Northeast; pills were more important relative to other methods among lower-income women. This is especially evident in Rio Grande do Norte, where pill users accounted for 43 percent of women currently contracepting in the low-income group, and 25 percent of high-income contraceptors. Sterilization, in contrast, accounted for 22 percent of low-income current users and 47 percent of high-income users. Other methods, mainly rhythm and withdrawal, were also important among low-income current users; these methods, along with condoms, were important as well among low-income women in the state of Sao Paulo.

When educational attainment is substituted for income as the measure of socioeconomic differences in contraceptive use, the results are virtually identical, at least for the four states with available tabulations on which to base a comparison. Table 23 shows the percentage of currently married women aged 15-44 using contraception for four education categories, ranging from none to some

TABLE 22 Percent Distribution of Married Women Aged 15-44, by Contraceptive Use Status and Household Income: Brazil

State and Date	Multiples of Minimum Salary				
	<1	1-2	2-4	5+	Total
Sao Paulo (1978)[a]					
Currently Using	47.4	57.4	67.4	68.5	63.9
Orals	6.4	28.9	34.0	22.0	27.8
Sterilization	5.4	11.0	15.2	22.0	16.1
Other	35.6	27.5	18.2	24.5	20.0
Not Using	53.6	42.6	32.6	31.5	36.1
Total	100.0	100.0	100.0	100.0	100.0
Rio Grande do Norte (1980)					
Currently Using	37.0	46.6	53.4	72.9	47.0
Orals	15.9	18.2	20.9	22.9	17.9
Sterilization	8.4	17.3	23.1	34.4	17.4
Other	12.7	11.1	9.4	15.6	11.7
Not Using	63.0	53.4	46.6	27.1	53.0
Total	100.0	100.0	100.0	100.0	100.0
Piaui (1979)					
Currently Using	25.1	30.5	42.6	57.0	30.9
Orals	9.3	10.5	12.7	17.1	10.0
Sterilization	9.9	14.9	25.5	34.1	15.4
Other	5.9	5.1	2.4	5.8	5.5
Not Using	74.9	69.5	57.4	43.0	69.1
Total	100.0	100.0	100.0	100.0	100.0
Pernambuco (1980)					
Currently Using	26.2	32.4	46.5	62.9	41.4
Orals	8.0	10.6	13.0	16.4	12.5
Sterilization	9.1	12.9	22.9	40.2	18.9
Other	9.1	8.9	10.6	6.3	10.0
Not Using	73.8	67.6	53.5	37.1	58.6
Total	100.0	100.0	100.0	100.0	100.0

TABLE 22 (continued)

	Multiples of Minimum Salary				
State and Date	<1	1-2	2-4	5+	Total
Bahia (1980)					
Currently Using	18.7	28.4	42.8	65.9	31.1
Orals	6.9	13.5	15.3	15.7	11.7
Sterilization	7.1	7.4	13.2	26.3	9.6
Other	5.7	7.5	14.3	23.8	9.8
Not Using	81.3	71.6	57.2	34.1	68.9
Total	100.0	100.0	100.0	100.0	100.0

[a]Source breaks Sao Paulo data by more detailed income classes. Weighted averages were used to collapse income categories for Sao Paulo into classes that were comparable to those reported for other states. Since cell weights were not available, figures may differ from those derived from direct tabulation using collapsed income classes.

Source: Rodrigues et al. (1981a:Table 7).

secondary or more, in Piaui, Pernambuco, Rio Grande do Norte, and Bahia. Percentages for the "none" group are quite similar to those for the lowest-income groups in the respective states, with those for the "secondary and over" category falling somewhat below what was observed for the 5+ minimum salary group.

The CPS data presented in Table 22 support the view that access to family planning has spread to women of lower socioeconomic classes in the industrialized Southeast and to a lesser extent in the Northeast. Differences in contraceptive use in the Northeast appear to be related, at least in part, to whether organized family planning programs were operative. These programs appear to have filled the gap in access between lower- and higher-income women, with the latter being able to rely more heavily on private physicians, clinics, and pharmacies.

Further partial information on access is provided by tabulations of CPS survey data on sources of services for two of the main methods, surgical sterilization and oral contraceptives. Table 24 shows that for Sao Paulo, where

TABLE 23 Contraceptive Prevalence Survey Data on Percent of Currently Married Women Aged 15-44 Using Contraceptives, by Education: Brazil

State	Education			
	None	Primary, Incomplete	Primary, Complete	Secondary or More
Piaui	22.3	29.3	44.6	47.0
Pernambuco	27.8	36.6	50.2	60.0
Rio Grande do Norte	37.0	45.2	45.1	61.1
Bahia	16.0	32.9	40.7	59.9

Source: Rodrigues et al. (1981a:Table 6).

organized programs are more limited, 97.5 percent of pill users relied on private physicians; this is also true of Bahia. In Rio Grande do Norte, Pernambuco, and Paraiba, where CBPs had been operative, the BEMFAM-State/Municipal Hospital system provided around 60 percent of services. Table 24 also shows a similar, though less differentiated, pattern for surgical sterilization: again the contribution of private hospitals and clinics is highest in Sao Paulo and Bahia, whereas public-sector sources play a greater role in Rio Grande do Norte, Paraiba, and Pernambuco. One reason that the pattern for sterilization is not as sharply differentiated as that for pills is that sterilization in state/municipal hospitals is not provided through the CBP program. This may be a factor in the lower share of sterilizations among low-income women reported in Table 22. (Sample-size limitations prevented tabulation of the data in Table 24 by source and income level.)

Socioeconomic Factors

Increased use of contraceptives in Brazil during the 1970s was accompanied by a variety of socioeconomic changes, particularly among the regions and income groups responsible for the acceleration in fertility decline. This raises the question of how these two sets of forces may have interacted to bring about that accelerated decline. Important socioeconomic shifts include the

TABLE 24 Source of Family Planning Supplies and Services, Currently Married Women Aged 15-44, CPS Data by State: Brazil

	Sao Paulo 1978	Piaui 1979	Rio Grande do Norte 1980	Paraiba 1980	Pernambuco 1980	Bahia 1980
Oral Contraceptives						
State and municipal hospitals	0.3	35.9	63.2	50.5	59.8	7.6
BEMFAM	0.6					
INPS	1.3	2.4	1.6	0.5	2.6	9.6
Private physician/ clinic/pharmacy	97.5	58.9	33.6	48.0	34.0	81.7
Other	0.3	2.8	1.6	1.0	3.7	1.1
Total	100.0	100.0	100.0	100.0	100.0	100.0
Surgical Sterilization						
State and municipal hospitals	23.4	68.1	62.5	49.4	32.9	23.1
INPS	36.0	24.8	23.1	27.2	44.6	42.0
Private hospital/ clinic	34.8	6.2	12.7	22.9	20.5	33.2
Other (incl. not stated)	5.8	0.9	1.6	0.5	1.9	1.7
Total	100.0	100.0	100.0	100.0	100.0	100.0

Source: Rodrigues et al. (1981a).

changing status of women, as reflected in their educational attainment and labor force participation, as well as changes in household income and consumption patterns, such as the diffusion of consumer durables like television receivers, refrigerators, and gas stoves among lower-income groups. These changes could have reduced the desire to have more children and increased motivation to use the means of fertility control that were becoming more available.

Data presented in Chapter 2 on differences in the level and percentage of fertility decline by years of schooling revealed significant increases in the educational attainment of women during the 1970s. The data also revealed a close, though not exact, correspondence between the distribution of women by educational attainment and household income deciles (Table 19). In examining socioeconomic changes, the present chapter does not repeat that breakdown by income deciles. Moreover, such a breakdown is not used in the present discussion of the relationship between education and labor force participation. To do so would introduce a circularity arising from the contribution of women's earnings to the income of their households: it would create the misleading impression that the proportion of women who work is higher among households in higher-income deciles, when in fact one of the reasons that such households fall into those higher deciles is because these women work. The relevant income variable is household income without these women's contributions. At this point, the discussion focuses on changes in educational attainment and their relationship to differences in labor force participation.

Table 25 suggests that increases in female educational attainment were greater in the 1970s than in the 1960s. The table shows the proportion reporting no schooling among women aged 20-49 by five-year age groups, in 1960, 1970, 1976, and 1980. For women in their twenties, the proportion with no schooling was around 40 percent in 1960, declining to about 33 percent in 1970, and to below 20 percent by 1976. Increased female school enrollment during the 1960s accounts for part of this increased decline in the proportion with no schooling. Another factor is various types of adult education programs, including adult literacy classes and special courses leading to certification of equivalency at various grade levels. Many employers in the formal sector require such certification, even for semiskilled labor, and these

TABLE 25 Percent of Women Reported as Having No Schooling, by Age, 1960-80: Brazil

Age Group	1960	1970	1976	1980
20-24	39.1	30.6	15.8	16.9
25-29	42.7	35.4	21.7	19.6
30-34	44.4	38.1	24.8	}26.9
35-39	52.2	42.5	30.8	
40-44	54.5	45.5	35.4	}36.7
45-49	57.0	49.8	39.3	

Source: Population census 1960 and 1980.

courses have helped women to move from informal-sector jobs such as domestic service to formal-sector employment. Data from preliminary tabulations of the 1980 census are also shown. While they confirm the changes that occurred during the 1970s, they also suggest that the 1976 survey may overstate improvements, either through underrepresentation of less-educated women or inconsistency between the survey and census reporting of educational attainment.

Table 26 uses tabulations from the 1970 census and 1976 survey data files to present further detail on the changes that occurred during that interval. For each five-year age group, the percentage of women in each of four educational attainment categories (none, 1-4, 5-9, and 10+ years of schooling) is shown. Again there is a reduction in the percentage of women in the "none" category and increases in other groups. Only a part of this decline represents a "cohort" effect, where succeeding higher-attainment groups replace those with lower attainment. A contributing factor in increases for the 10+ category among women aged 25-29 in 1976 is the fact that some of them were still in school in 1970. Adult education could also account for the changes observed among older women. However, the caution suggested above about the representativeness of the 1976 data and the consistency of reporting in the survey and census sources should be applied to the amount of increase in educational attainment indicated by the table.

TABLE 26 Percent Distribution of All Women Aged 20-44 by Age and Years of Schooling, 1970 and 1976: Brazil

Age Group	Education							
	None		1-4		5-9		10+	
	1970	1976	1970	1976	1970	1976	1970	1976
20-24	30.4	15.6	41.8	39.9	17.3	27.1	10.5	17.5
25-29	35.2	21.2	42.3	42.3	13.9	19.6	8.6	16.9
30-34	38.3	24.2	42.4	47.9	12.9	16.4	6.4	11.5
35-39	42.2	30.1	41.1	47.0	11.9	14.0	4.8	8.9
40-44	45.2	34.4	38.5	45.2	11.9	13.2	4.4	7.2

Note: Each row adds to 100 percent for each year.

Source: Tabulations of census and survey sample data files.

The 1970s also brought increases in female labor force participation. Table 27 presents tabulations of the percentage of women reported as working by age and educational attainment. The education categories are the same as those in Table 26. Rates are shown for all women and for currently married women. In comparing data on labor force participation from the census and survey, it is important to recognize that the two sources define participation differently: in the census, a person was considered active if market work was his or her principal activity during the year prior to the interview; in the survey, a person who worked during the week prior to the interview was considered active. The census definition tends to understate economic activity for those employed part-time or on an intermittent basis, generally younger and older people and women more than middle-aged males (for further discussion of this point see Merrick and Graham, 1979:167). This could lead in turn to an overstatement of increases in labor force participation for such groups when the census and survey data are compared.

Data for all women in Table 27 indicate that in 1970, women with higher educational attainment (10+ years of schooling) were three to four times as likely to be working as women with no education. Increases in labor force participation among women in lower educational attainment categories narrowed this differential to a

TABLE 27 Percent of Women Reported as Working, by Age and Years of Schooling, 1970 and 1976: Brazil

	Education							
	None		1-4		5-9		10+	
Age Group	1970	1976	1970	1976	1970	1976	1970	1976
All Women								
20-24	18.0	29.2	26.4	35.5	35.1	40.5	52.9	55.5
25-29	14.8	24.8	19.4	28.9	30.7	36.9	66.3	63.3
30-34	14.6	28.1	17.7	28.3	29.7	34.9	66.0	65.4
35-39	15.3	28.9	18.7	29.5	30.0	37.2	66.8	67.8
40-44	16.4	28.5	18.3	27.6	28.6	33.9	66.5	64.8
Currently Married Women								
20-24	5.7	12.2	6.3	13.0	13.4	16.6	39.9	38.5
25-29	6.2	15.0	8.0	17.2	15.5	21.9	54.1	47.5
30-34	6.9	20.5	9.7	20.2	18.0	24.0	56.4	55.0
35-39	8.2	21.6	11.3	22.7	21.0	29.3	58.9	59.5
40-44	7.8	20.9	11.0	21.5	19.5	26.2	56.1	56.4

Source: Tabulations of census and survey data files.

little more than two times in 1976. Percentage point increases in both the "none" and 1-4 education categories were greater for women over age 30. For women in the 10+ educational attainment category, the percent reported as active declined in three of the five age groups.

These increases in labor force participation among less-educated women, particularly those over age 30, show up even more strongly in rates for currently married women, as shown in the second panel of Table 27. In 1970, only 7-8 percent of married women over age 30 in the "none" education group were working; in 1976, this proportion increased to over 20 percent. Similar increases can be observed in the 1-4 year education group, though there was less change for women over 30 because they started from a slightly higher base in 1970. In the 10+ education group, rates declined for the first three age groups and increased only slightly for the other two. As a consequence, the magnitude of differentials in participation rates between women with no education and those with 10+ years of schooling decreased from 7 or 8 to 1-2 or 3-1.

Increased educational attainment, higher labor force participation among more-educated women, and the narrowing of differentials in participation between more- and less-educated women between 1970 and 1976 combined to double the proportion (from 15 percent to 30 percent) of women who were working during the six-year period under study. Although caution is required because of possible upward bias in the 1976 data resulting from definitional differences mentioned above, the data suggest that important changes in women's roles were occurring. Increases in labor force participation, associated with increases in the proportion of women with higher levels of education, suggest an improvement in these women's status; on the other hand, these trends among women in the lower education classes may mean that more women were working out of economic necessity.

SOCIOECONOMIC FACTORS AND FERTILITY DECLINE AMONG URBAN AND RURAL WOMEN

While the hypotheses about relationships between socioeconomic factors (modernization, increased economic pressures on families) and fertility decline in Brazil outlined above are broadly applicable to both urban and rural women, differences in institutional factors suggest that these groups be examined separately. For example, increased ownership of televisions, while not exclusively an urban phenomenon, is much more pronounced in urban areas. Likewise, the influence of land availability and increased proletarianization of farm labor is probably more direct in rural areas. While indirect effects could reach urban areas via migration, they are much more difficult to capture with the census and PNAD survey data files. Based on separate samples for urban and rural women extracted from these files, the next two subsections present a more detailed examination of the characteristics of currently married urban and rural women, and how these characteristics relate to differentials in average parity. The focus in both subsections is restricted to currently married women because the analysis of proximate determinants of fertility presented in Chapter 1 identified declining marital fertility as the main component of the recent decline in Brazilian birth rates.

Currently Married Urban Women

Data presented in Chapter 2 on levels and changes in fertility rates by socioeconoic class revealed that major differentials were associated with female educational attainment. To see how these differentials are reflected in the average parity of currently married urban women, and to permit further comparisons by other characteristics of these women, subsamples of about 17,000 women each were extracted from the census and survey data files. (Cost considerations dictated the decision to use subsamples.) Table 28 presents tabulations of the mean number of children ever born to currently married urban women in 1970 and 1976 by age and educational attainment. Standard errors of means for the age/education breakdowns of the two subsamples are also shown. While most cells

TABLE 28 Mean and Standard Error (S)[a] of Number of Children Ever Born, Currently Married Urban Women, by Age and Educational Attainment, 1970 and 1976: Brazil

Age Group	Education							
	None		1-4		5-9		10+	
	Mean	(s)	Mean	(s)	Mean	(s)	Mean	(s)
1970								
20-24	2.51	(.08)	1.79	(.04)	1.43	(.05)	0.70	(.06)
25-29	3.91	(.09)	3.07	(.05)	2.39	(.06)	1.50	(.06)
30-34	5.04	(.10)	4.08	(.06)	3.20	(.08)	2.30	(.07)
35-39	6.16	(.12)	4.75	(.08)	3.82	(.10)	3.12	(.11)
40-44	6.64	(.15)	5.11	(.10)	3.75	(.12)	3.20	(.16)
N (unweighted)	4,059		8,081		3,252		1,396	
Percent (weighted)	24.2		48.1		19.4		8.3	
1976								
20-24	2.07	(.08)	1.72	(.04)	1.23	(.03)	0.69	(.04)
25-29	3.65	(.10)	2.69	(.04)	1.99	(.04)	1.30	(.04)
30-34	4.86	(.12)	3.70	(.05)	2.99	(.07)	2.03	(.05)
35-39	6.26	(.14)	4.57	(.07)	3.44	(.08)	2.68	(.08)
40-44	6.47	(.16)	5.00	(.08)	3.58	(.11)	2.78	(.10)
N (unweighted)	2,632		8,019		4,205		2,828	
Percent (weighted)	16.0		47.9		22.1		14.0	

[a](s) is standard error of sample means.

Source: Tabulations of subsamples of census and survey data files.

are large enough at this level to minimize sampling error, further breakdowns could be affected, particularly when a small percentage of women fall into a given category. Further tests of the significance of educational and other differences in the number of children ever born are presented in the next chapter using multiple regression.

The basic pattern of educational differences in the mean number of children ever born is similar in 1970 and 1976: comparing women in the age 40-44 category, the mean number of children ever born in 1970 drops from 6.6 children for women with no education to 3.2 children for those with 10+ years of schooling; in 1976, the figures are 6.5 children for women with no education and 2.8 for those with 10+ years of schooling. The earlier average age at marriage of women with no education is a major factor in differences among younger women, who had 2.5 births in 1970 compared to 0.7 for the 10+ group, and 2.1 compared to the 10+ group's 0.7 in 1976. The values for older women with 10+ years of school are a problem in that the average of 2.8 for women aged 40-44 in 1976 is <u>lower</u> than the 3.1 reported for those aged 35-39 in 1970. Sampling error is the most likely culprit, since the .95 confidence intervals of the standard errors of the two means intersect. Shifts of women from the 5-9 class in 1970 to the 10+ class in 1976 could not account for this since they would bias the 1976 figure upward rather than downward.

How do other characteristics such as work status and migrant status affect fertility differentials? The generalizations in the previous section about increases in educational attainment and labor force participation hold for currently married urban women. From 1970 to 1976, the proportion of urban women reporting no education declined from 24.2 percent to 16.0 percent, while that of women with 10+ years of schooling increased from 8.3 to 14.0 percent. Patterns of labor force participation by level of educational attainment are similar to those shown in Table 27, though the differences between education categories are less. The top panel of Table 29 presents participation rates for urban women. Part of the large differential between more- and less-educated women in Table 27 resulted from the lower educational attainment and labor force participation of rural women. For urban women, the order of magnitude of differences between the top and bottom education categories was four to five, narrowing to a range of three to four in 1976. Larger proportional increases among less-educated women over age

TABLE 29 Percent Working and Percent Migrant Among Currently Married, Urban Women, 1970 and 1976: Brazil

Age Group	Education							
	None		1-4		5-9		10+	
	1970	1976	1970	1976	1970	1976	1970	1976
Percent Working								
20-24	6.8	8.1	6.1	11.0	12.1	13.1	32.6	37.8
25-29	6.8	12.1	9.2	15.0	15.8	20.6	50.7	46.8
30-34	7.5	15.6	10.2	19.4	17.8	22.7	54.9	54.5
35-39	10.9	19.8	13.5	22.1	21.3	26.5	54.7	57.2
40-44	8.3	16.7	12.5	19.0	19.4	24.0	56.6	55.6
Percent Migrant								
20-24	31.3	31.9	28.0	28.7	31.0	24.1	34.4	30.4
25-29	26.0	24.0	22.1	21.7	17.5	20.5	28.3	25.7
30-34	20.6	17.2	17.0	15.9	15.7	12.8	21.9	16.7
35-39	14.6	10.7	12.1	11.7	11.0	10.7	12.0	13.7
40-44	13.3	12.6	10.5	9.7	8.0	7.1	7.0	12.8

Source: Tabulations of census and survey data files.

30 are observed, but they are not as great as in Table 27. This suggests that definitional differences affecting 1970-76 comparisons may have introduced greater bias in the reporting of work status for rural women.

Another potential source of variation in fertility among urban women is migration, particularly if work status were related to fertility differences and if migrants were more likely to be working than nonmigrants. To assess the possible impact of migration, women were classified by migration status, with those who had resided in their municipality of current residence for less than 6 years being considered migrants. The second panel of Table 29 shows the percentage of currently married urban women who qualified as migrants according to this definition for each of the age and education categories previously identified. The percentages of migrants are greatest for the 20-24 age category and for the lowest and highest education groups. The variation by age is much greater than that across education categories. The limited amount of variation by education raises questions about the link, mentioned above, between migrant status, work status, and fertility. Tabulations (not shown) of the percentage of currently married women reported as working by age and migration status revealed no differences between migrants and nonmigrants. This suggests that motives for migration other than work--most probably marriage--account for the variation in the proportion of migrants shown in the table.

Returning to the question of increases in female labor force participation and educational attainment, the question of whether these increases indicate changes in women's socioeconomic status can be further clarified by examining the kinds of jobs involved in the increased proportions reporting employment. For this purpose, the occupations of employed women were grouped into four broad status categories: (1) high-status service occupations, including managerial, technical, and professional positions, as well as higher-status jobs in the commercial and financial sectors; (2) low-status service occupations, including domestic and personal services, as well as low-status commercial jobs, counter attendants, waitresses, and clerks; (3) occupations in manufacturing; and (4) others, consisting of nonmanagerial public-sector jobs, any primary-sector jobs held by urban women, and poorly defined occupations.

Table 30 presents the percentage distributions of currently married urban women according to these status categories and their educational attainment. The status distributions also include the proportion of women not working (columns sum to 100 percent), indicating which status categories absorbed employment increases in each educational group between 1970 and 1976. Education can be seen to determine the kinds of jobs women hold: of the 8.2 percent of women in the "none" education category who were working in 1970, 6.8 percentage points (83 percent of workers) were in the low-status service and other categories; of the 50.8 percent working among women in the 10+ education category, 49.3 percentage points (97 percent of workers) were in the high-status service categories. Increases in labor force participation among less-educated women consisted mainly of more jobs in the same category as their 1970 employment. The participation rate of women with no education increased by 6.8 percentage points between 1970 and 1976, with low-status service and other occupations accounting for 90 percent of jobs held by this group. Lower status-jobs also accounted for most of the increases in employment in the middle two education classes, though manufacturing also contributed

TABLE 30 Distribution of Currently Married Women Aged 20-44 by Occupation, Work Status, and Educational Attainment, 1970 and 1976: Brazil

Occupation and Work Status	Education				
	None	1-4	5-9	10+	All
1970					
High Status	0.3	2.0	9.9	49.3	7.1
Manufacturing	1.1	2.8	2.2	0.3	2.1
Low Status	5.1	3.8	3.2	0.3	3.7
Other	1.7	1.8	1.9	0.9	1.7
Not Working	91.8	89.6	82.8	49.2	85.4
Total	100.0	100.0	100.0	100.0	100.0
1976					
High Status	0.8	2.5	10.3	49.4	10.5
Manufacturing	2.3	5.7	5.3	1.0	4.4
Low Status	8.5	7.2	4.8	1.6	6.1
Other	4.4	3.7	2.3	1.1	3.1
Not Working	84.0	80.9	77.3	46.9	75.9
Total	100.0	100.0	100.0	100.0	100.0

Source: Tabulations of census and survey data files.

a small amount. These data suggest that if improvements in women's status occurred through employment, they did so because of increased participation among women in higher educational attainment categories rather than the opening of higher-status jobs to women with lower educational attainment. The fact that increased employment among women with lower or no education consisted mainly of low-status jobs suggests that increased employment for these groups may indicate not so much a return on investment in education, but a desire to maintain or increase household income.

The census and survey data files on which this chapter is based permit only the broadest sort of speculation about changes in household consumption and earning patterns that may be behind these increases in the employment of married women. It was suggested earlier that increased purchases of consumer durables on credit, combined with an inflationary squeeze on household income-generating capacity, may have contributed to increased employment among married women in lower socioeconomic groups. The data files provide information on ownership of a few consumer durables (televisions, gas and electric stoves, refrigerators, and automobiles), but no information on whether the purchase was with cash or credit; however, given the widespread use of credit and the high cost of most of these items relative to the average monthly earnings of lower-class households, it is likely that most of these purchases were made on credit.

Data on television ownership illustrate the diffusion of consumer durables among lower socioeconomic groups during the early 1970s. Table 31 shows the percentage of currently married urban women residing in households with a television, again broken down by age and educational attainment. Although increases are observed among all of the education groups, the larger proportional increases are concentrated in the two lower groups. Among women aged 25-29, the percent with TVs increased from 12.2 in 1970 to 29.5 in 1976 for the "none" education group, and from 36.0 to 62.7 for the 1-4 group. Similar, though less dramatic, increases were found in the ownership of gas and electric stoves and of refrigerators, though tabulations for those items are not shown. While impressionistic, such evidence supports the view that diffusion of consumer durables among lower-income groups and the resultant increased demands on family budgets may have contributed to the increases in labor force participation observed among women in lower socioeconomic groups.

Did such increases in labor force participation have any influence on fertility? Data on average parity suggest that differences between working and nonworking women were greater in 1970 than in 1976. Table 32

TABLE 31 Percent of Currently Married, Urban Women Living in Households Reporting Ownership of a Television, by Age and Education, 1970 and 1976: Brazil

	Education							
	None		1-4		5-9		10+	
Age Group	1970	1976	1970	1976	1970	1976	1970	1976
20-24	11.8	24.7	29.0	47.6	48.2	67.6	77.1	87.6
25-29	12.2	29.5	36.0	62.7	60.1	80.0	82.9	94.4
30-34	15.8	27.4	41.3	68.6	66.6	84.5	88.7	97.0
35-39	17.2	37.8	45.7	70.5	72.0	86.0	89.9	96.5
40-44	21.3	37.3	51.4	73.7	73.6	91.2	93.3	98.3

Source: Tabulations of census and survey data files.

TABLE 32 Average Number of Children Ever Born for
Currently Married, Urban Women, by Age, Education, and
Current Employment Status, 1970 and 1976: Brazil

	Education									
	None		1-4		5-9		10+		All	
	Currently Employed									
Age Group	No	Yes	No	Yes	No	Yes	No	Yes	No	Yes
1970										
20-24	2.5	2.5	1.8	1.3	1.5	1.1	0.8	0.6	1.8	1.3
25-29	3.9	4.0	3.1	2.6	2.4	2.1	1.7	1.3	3.1	2.2
30-34	5.1	4.0	4.2	3.4	3.3	2.8	2.4	2.2	4.2	3.0
35-39	6.3	5.4	4.8	4.5	3.9	3.6	3.3	3.0	5.0	4.1
40-44	6.7	5.5	5.2	4.2	3.8	3.4	3.6	2.9	5.4	3.9
1976										
20-24	2.0	2.7	1.8	1.4	1.3	0.9	0.8	0.6	1.5	1.0
25-29	3.7	3.5	2.7	2.4	2.1	1.6	1.5	1.1	2.6	1.8
30-34	4.9	4.8	3.8	3.5	3.0	3.1	2.1	2.0	3.6	3.1
35-39	6.3	6.3	4.5	4.2	3.5	3.4	2.7	2.7	4.6	4.0
40-44	6.5	6.3	5.0	5.0	3.6	3.5	3.0	2.6	5.0	4.4

Source: Tabulations of census and survey data files.

presents averages of the number of children ever born for
working and nonworking currently married women by their
age and educational attainment. In 1970, the average number of children was generally lower for working women.
For all education groups combined, the number of children
ranges from 1.8 for ages 20-24 to 5.4 for ages 40-44 among
nonworking women, compared to 1.3 to 3.9 for working
women. The effect of work status varies according to the
level of educational attainment and age. For women with
no education, average parity is lower for working women
after age 30. For women who reported some schooling, the
averages are lower for all age categories, with the
largest absolute differences (.5 to 1.0 children) occurring in the 1-4 class. In 1976, there is an overall
narrowing of differentials between working and nonworking
women: there is no difference for women with no education, and the differences for women in the 1-4 group are
reduced to less than .4 children per woman; for women
with 5-9 and 10+ years of schooling, differences are also
reduced. This overall narrowing of differentials raises

the question of whether the relationship between work status and average parity changed between 1970 and 1976, or whether the narrowing reflects changing composition by educational attainment that occurred during this interval. This question is addressed using multivariate regression analysis in the next chapter.

Differences in average parity by migration status, again controlling for age and educational attainment, are shown in Table 33. Age and education influence the direction of differences by migrant status. Overall, there are no differences between migrant and nonmigrant women under age 35, but higher averages for migrant women in the 35-39 and 40-44 age groups. When the data are broken down by education, younger nonmigrant women have higher average parity in the "none" education and 1-4 years of schooling categories. A shift to higher averages for migrant women in the two upper age groups also occurs in these categories. There are no differences between migrants and nonmigrants in the 5-9 education group, but higher averages show up again for three of the four cells

TABLE 33 Average Number of Children Ever Born for Migrant and Nonmigrant Women, by Age and Educational Attainment, 1970 and 1976: Brazil

	Education									
	None		1-4		5-9		10+		All	
	Migrant									
Age Group	No	Yes	No	Yes	No	Yes	No	Yes	No	Yes
1970										
20-24	2.7	2.2	1.8	1.7	1.4	1.4	0.7	0.7	1.8	1.7
25-29	4.0	3.6	3.1	3.1	2.4	2.4	1.5	1.4	3.0	2.9
30-34	5.1	4.9	4.0	4.3	3.2	3.2	2.3	2.1	4.0	4.1
35-39	6.2	6.1	4.7	5.3	3.8	3.7	3.1	3.4	4.8	5.2
40-44	6.6	6.9	5.0	5.8	3.8	3.6	3.2	3.8	5.1	5.8
1976										
20-24	2.1	1.9	1.8	1.6	1.2	1.2	0.7	0.6	1.5	1.4
25-29	3.6	3.7	2.7	2.6	2.1	1.6	1.3	1.2	2.4	2.2
30-34	4.9	4.7	3.7	3.5	3.0	2.9	2.1	1.7	3.5	3.3
35-39	6.2	7.3	4.4	4.6	3.5	3.3	2.6	3.1	4.4	4.6
40-44	6.3	7.7	4.9	6.5	3.6	3.8	2.8	2.8	4.7	6.1

Source: Tabulations of census and survey data files.

containing older migrant women in the 10+ education category. The higher average parity among older migrant women probably reflects the fact that these women made recent moves as members of a family unit, whereas a large share of the moves of recent younger migrants may have been associated with or occurred before marriage; this could explain why nonmigrants with lower educational attainment had higher average parity.

The data on links between selected measures of the socioeconomic status of currently married urban women and differentials in their average parity raise several issues for further analysis. After controlling for age, the greatest differentials in average parity are those associated with educational attainment, with significantly lower levels of average parity being observed among women with higher levels of education. Since there were important shifts of women to higher education categories between 1970 and 1976, increased education stands out as a key factor among the socioeconomic variables associated with fertility declines during that interval. However, the question remains of whether the impact of education was mainly a change in the distribution of women by educational attainment, or whether and how education may have interacted with other variables, perhaps with changes in its relationship to fertility differentials resulting from changes in those variables. For example, average parity was lower among working than nonworking women, but the nature of this relationship was conditioned by education. Work status itself was closely associated with educational attainment, with a greater proportion of working women among those with higher education. However, increases in the percentage of women working between 1970 and 1976 were greatest for those in lower educational categories. One effect of this was a narrowing of the differential in average parity between working and nonworking women between 1970 and 1976. This suggests that something beyond changes in educational composition may have been at work, perhaps along the lines of the argument suggested earlier about increased work to maintain household income or to finance increased consumption of consumer durables. Though the census and survey files provide little supporting evidence for this idea, the data on increased ownership of televisions among less-educated women support such a view. Although the links between migrant status and differences in average parity are less clear, those that do appear were conditioned by education and age.

Currently Married Rural Women

For currently married rural women, differences in average parity may reflect not only variation in individual and household characteristics, but also institutional factors such as availability of and access to land, land tenure, and differences in modes of agricultural production. Again, Brazil's regional diversity is important. Traditionally, high rural fertility in Brazil suggests that children have been an important asset to rural families; research on subsistence farmers in the Northeast has revealed that even very young children contribute to household production (Almeida, 1977).

A number of hypotheses have been suggested about the effects of recent socioeconomic changes in Brazil on rural fertility differences. One is that increased scarcity of land in more settled areas has reduced the value of children as farm laborers and made it more difficult for children to acquire a farm through inheritance. Research based on data from the 1970 population and agricultural censuses indicated that fertility was lower in more settled regions of Southeastern Brazil and higher on the agricultural frontier. However, the link between fertility and land availability was also conditioned by institutional factors, particularly Brazil's unequal distribution of land (Merrick, 1978); rural fertility in Northeastern Brazil was much less responsive to land scarcity as a consequence (Merrick, 1981).

Paiva (1982) has argued that the proletarianization of rural labor (the shift of farm labor out of smallholder status into wage labor as a result of the consolidation of land into larger holdings) has contributed to Brazil's recent fertility decline. He suggests that the effects of proletarianization in Brazil differ from the European experience described by Tilly (1978) and others, where fertility increased because the formation of new farm families was linked to having a plot of land.

These hypotheses will be discussed further in Chapter 4. The remainder of the present chapter explores differences in the average parity of currently married rural women in Brazil, using cross-tabulations that control for age and other socioeconomic variables. Subsamples for rural women were extracted from the 1970 census and 1976 survey data files. Since the 1976 survey did not include rural areas in the Northern and Central-Western regions of Brazil, the data on rural women are restricted to the Northeastern, Southeastern, and Southern states. Regional breakdowns follow the grouping adopted in Chapter 2, with the first consisting of the Northeast, the second including the states of Rio de Janeiro and Sao Paulo (labeled RJ-SP), and the remaining states (Minas Gerais, Espirito Santo, Parana, Santa Catarina, and Rio Grande do Sul) constituting a third group labeled "other." In Chapter 2, unadjusted total fertility rates for rural areas of these three groups of states showed that while fertility was lowest in Rio and Sao Paulo in 1970, fertility decline between 1970 and 1976 was most rapid in the "other" group, which fell between RJ-SP and the Northeast in level of socioeconomic development.

The same pattern appears when average parity is broken down by region, with controls for age and education. Table 34 presents data on the mean number of children ever born for currently married rural women in the three regional groups, with women grouped according to whether they had no education or reported any years of schooling completed. Average parity in 1970 was uniformly higher in the Northeast, with no apparent difference between those with none and those with some education. In 1970, the latter category accounted for only 26 percent of women in the region; this proportion increased to 39 percent in 1976, at which time differences by educational attainment also became observable. For example, there was only 0.1 difference for women aged 25-29 in 1970, but a .8 difference in 1976. In the other two regions, half of the women reported having some education in 1970, with the proportion rising to 65 percent in RJ-SP and 67 percent in the "other" group in 1976. In 1970, average parity was lower for rural women with some education in both regions, and this differential widened in 1976: for women aged 25-29, the differential was .4 in 1970 for the "other" group, increasing to 1.0 in 1976; for RJ-SP, it increased from .8 to 1.0. This indicates a more rapid fertility decline in the former region, which is consistent with the findings reported in Chapter 2.

To what extent does variation in other socioeconomic characteristics of rural women relate to differences in average parity? Table 35 presents the percentages of currently married rural women according to three characteristics; two of these (work status and migration status) were also examined for urban women, while the third (proletarianization) was defined to explore the hypothesis that shifts of the rural population into wage labor contributed to recent fertility declines. To measure proletarianization, women were grouped according to whether

TABLE 34 Mean Number of Children Ever Born for Currently Married, Rural Women by Region, Educational Attainment, and Age, 1970 and 1976: Brazil

	Education					
	Northeast		RJ-SP		Other	
Age Group	None	Some	None	Some	None	Some
1970						
20-24	2.48	2.28	2.18	1.84	2.36	1.85
	(.06)	(.09)	(.16)	(.09)	(.07)	(.06)
25-29	3.91	3.79	4.08	3.26	3.83	3.38
	(.08)	(.13)	(.20)	(.14)	(.09)	(.07)
30-34	5.72	5.57	5.04	4.25	5.40	4.69
	(.12)	(.16)	(.22)	(.18)	(.12)	(.10)
35-39	6.86	6.79	6.47	5.31	6.51	5.99
	(.13)	(.23)	(.26)	(.26)	(.13)	(.15)
40-44	7.46	8.25	6.77	6.01	6.89	6.62
	(.17)	(.32)	(.30)	(.35)	(.16)	(.17)
N (unweighted)	4,111	1,435	741	742	2,939	2,939
Percent (weighted)[a]	74.1	25.9	50.3	49.7	50.0	50.0
1976						
20-24	2.46	1.97	2.18	1.67	2.27	1.59
	(.08)	(.08)	(.14)	(.05)	(.09)	(.04)
25-29	4.12	3.29	3.80	2.83	3.78	2.78
	(.09)	(.10)	(.16)	(.08)	(.10)	(.06)
30-34	5.77	5.49	5.00	4.03	5.11	4.19
	(.12)	(.14)	(.21)	(.12)	(.14)	(.08)
35-39	7.13	7.07	6.03	4.64	6.51	5.43
	(.14)	(.19)	(.23)	(.14)	(.14)	(.11)
40-44	8.41	7.25	6.74	5.56	6.98	6.16
	(.18)	(.25)	(.21)	(.22)	(.17)	(.14)
N (unweighted)	3,143	1,987	823	1,916	1,913	3,572
Percent (weighted)[a]	61.3	38.7	35.1	64.9	33.3	66.7

Note: Standard errors of means in parentheses.

[a] Percentages refer to distribution within each region.

Source: Tabulations of subsamples of census and survey data files.

TABLE 35 Percent of Currently Married, Rural Women in Proletarian Households, Percent Working, and Percent Migrant, by Age and Region, 1970 and 1976: Brazil

Age Group and Status	Region					
	Northeast		RJ-SP		Other	
	1970	1976	1970	1976	1970	1976
Working						
20-24	6.5	15.2	2.8	6.9	5.7	19.8
25-29	9.2	16.6	4.8	15.4	6.6	22.8
30-34	8.9	24.0	3.2	13.2	6.6	26.9
35-39	8.0	24.0	5.0	20.6	5.6	28.5
40-44	9.2	26.4	3.8	19.3	7.5	27.5
Migrants						
20-24	8.6	11.3	23.7	32.3	22.7	21.5
25-29	8.8	10.9	22.0	25.2	19.5	16.7
30-34	6.9	8.6	20.5	25.2	17.9	17.4
35-39	6.2	5.1	14.6	16.1	14.7	13.1
40-44	6.7	5.9	18.0	14.9	13.2	10.3
Proletarian						
20-24	25.0	38.9	64.8	81.0	25.7	46.1
25-29	25.4	37.1	58.6	74.1	26.1	41.6
30-34	23.9	36.0	53.0	67.3	22.8	37.7
35-39	21.3	31.7	51.1	60.5	24.8	38.9
40-44	20.6	31.1	48.8	66.0	21.3	32.4

Source: Tabulations of subsamples of census and survey data files.

the head of the household in which they resided was a wage laborer or not, with the former considered proletarian. Migrant status and work status were defined as they were for urban women: women who had resided in their present municipality for 5 years or less were considered migrants, and work status was established according to the census and survey data. The earlier caution about differences in the way these sources define labor force participation is particularly important here, since a higher proportion of rural than urban women fall into the grey area defined by the census as not working and by the survey as working.

The proportion of rural women reported as working was below 10 percent for all of the age groups in all of the regions in 1970, ranging from 3 to 5 percent in Rio and Sao Paulo to 6 to 9 percent in the other two regions. When these figures are compared to the 1976 data, substantial increases are indicated. While it is impossible to tell how much these increases represent definitional differences, it does appear that increases may have been greater for women over age 30. It is also difficult to judge whether the lower rates in RJ-SP represent true differences in work status or some sort of regional variation in reporting.

In the case of migration, the highest proportion of women reported as migrants in both 1970 and 1976 is found in Rio and Sao Paulo, and the lowest in the Northeast. There is a slight increase in the migrant proportion in both regions between 1970 and 1976. As would be expected, migration rates are higher among women in their twenties than among those in their thirties. Rates in the "other" region are somewhat lower than those in the RJ-SP in 1970, but drop slightly between 1970 and 1976.

Regional differentials in socioeconomic characteristics are greatest in the proportion of women in proletarian households. In 1970, the shift to wage labor among household heads had progressed furthest in Rio and Sao Paulo, with the highest proportions being reported for younger women; these figures ranged from 65 percent for women aged 20-24 to 49 percent for those aged 40-44. The proportions were about equal in 1970 in the other two regions, ranging from 20 to 26 percent. Between 1970 and 1976, the greatest percentage point increases in proletarianization occurred in the "other" region, though the highest level of proletarianization continued to be that of RJ-SP. In the latter, the percentage ranged from 81 percent for women aged 20-24 to 66 percent for those 40-44, compared to 46 and 32 percent, respectively, in the former. This suggests that proletarianization may have been a factor in the lower fertility observed in Rio and Sao Paulo in 1970, as well as in the more rapid fertility decline observed in the "other" region between 1970 and 1976.

To what extent are these differences in socioeconomic characteristics reflected in average parity? Table 36 presents the mean number of children ever born by age and region for women in proletarian and nonproletarian households. Neither 1970 nor 1976 results suggest that average parity is significantly lower among the former group. Indeed, their averages are more often higher than lower;

TABLE 36 Mean Number of Children Ever Born for
Currently Married, Rural Women Aged 20-44, by Region
and Proletarian Status, 1970 and 1976: Brazil

	Region					
	Northeast		RJ-SP		Other	
	Proletarian					
Age Group	No	Yes	No	Yes	No	Yes
1970						
20-24	2.4	2.6	1.8	2.1	2.1	2.0
25-29	3.8	4.0	3.4	3.7	3.6	3.6
30-34	5.6	6.0	4.5	4.7	5.1	4.8
35-39	6.8	7.0	5.8	6.6	6.3	6.2
40-44	7.6	7.7	6.5	6.6	6.8	6.8
1976						
20-24	2.2	2.3	1.8	1.7	1.8	1.8
25-29	3.8	3.8	2.8	3.2	3.0	3.2
30-34	5.6	5.8	4.0	4.5	4.4	4.7
35-39	6.9	7.5	5.0	5.3	5.6	6.0
40-44	8.0	8.3	5.5	6.5	6.5	6.5

Source: Tabulations of census and survey data
files.

they are consistently higher in RJ-SP, where the proportion of proletarian women in the total is highest. This is puzzling in view of the relationship between fertility levels and the level of proletarianization at the regional level. It suggests that the effect of proletarianization on fertility may operate through a complex of other variables whose effects are manifested in such regional differences, or that proletarianization itself may be a manifestation of changes in another variable or set of variables.

One such important variable may be work status. Table 37 presents average parity for working and nonworking women by age and region. The table suggests that average parity was slightly lower for working women in the Northeast and "other" regions in 1970, but not in Rio de Janeiro and Sao Paulo; there were so few working women in the latter two states in 1970 that none of the averages for that group were significantly different from those of nonworking women. In 1976, the pattern of differences between working and nonworking women was even less clear: there were still no differences in RJ-SP, while working

TABLE 37 Mean Number of Children Ever Born for Currently Married, Rural Women Aged 20-44, by Region and Work Status, 1970 and 1976: Brazil

	Region					
	Northeast		RJ-SP		Other	
	Working					
Age Group	No	Yes	No	Yes	No	Yes
1970						
20-24	2.4	2.5	2.0	1.6	2.1	1.9
25-29	3.9	3.4	3.6	4.1	3.6	3.3
30-34	5.7	5.5	4.7	3.0	5.1	4.3
35-39	6.9	6.1	6.0	5.1	6.3	5.5
40-44	7.6	7.4	6.5	7.9	6.9	5.8
1976						
20-24	2.3	2.0	1.8	1.9	1.8	1.7
25-29	3.9	3.3	3.1	2.8	3.2	2.9
30-34	5.6	5.9	4.3	4.6	4.4	4.6
35-39	7.2	6.8	5.2	5.1	6.0	5.3
40-44	8.2	7.8	6.2	6.1	6.6	6.4

Source: Tabulations of census and survey data files.

women showed slightly lower averages for all but the age 30-34 group in the other two regions. The lack of any difference in the RJ-SP group and the reduction in the "other" group between 1970 and 1976 suggest that the effect of work status on fertility differences is reduced as proletarianization increases. Another potential covariate is migration; however, tabulations of average parity by migration status revealed no significant differences, and the results are not presented here.

This leads us back to education, which was the only socioeconomic characteristic of rural women for which a consistent and statistically significant pattern of differences in average parity was observed. It is tempting to conclude that education accounts for most of the differentials, as well as the changes in rural fertility observed between 1970 and 1976. A problem with the second point is that levels of educational attainment increased almost equally during that period in the RJ-SP and "other" regions, yet fertility decline was more rapid in the latter. Either the evidence is only circumstantial that relative increases in proletarianization in that region were also greater, or there may have been interaction between the education and proletarianization variables, and others as well. Since further presentation of data in tabular form would be an awkward way to address this issue, that task is undertaken in the next chapter using multiple regressions.

CONCLUSIONS

The purpose of this chapter was to examine evidence on the spread of contraceptive use to women in lower and middle socioeconomic classes who accounted for much of the acceleration in the decline of Brazilian marital fertility in the early 1970s, focusing on changes in the socioeconomic characteristics of these women that could have increased their motivation to control fertility. Because there are no nationally representative data on contraceptive use or socioeconomic characteristics, data on contraceptive use from recent state-level surveys were pieced together, while changes in socioeconomic variables and their relation to differences in average parity were examined based on 1970 census and 1976 PNAD survey data files.

Analysis of the proximate determinants of fertility in Chapter 1 identified increased use of contraception (or contraception combined with abortion) as a key factor in Brazil's accelerated fertility decline in the 1970s. Baseline data that would permit measurement of the extent to which this increase represented the spread of fertility control among lower- and middle-income groups are lacking; however, data from contraceptive surveys taken later in the decade show significant percentages of contraceptive use among these groups. This, along with evidence in Chapter 2 showing that these groups experienced the most rapid fertility decline during the decade, supports the conclusion that their use of fertility control had indeed increased. While Contraceptive Prevalence Surveys show that differences in contraceptive use between higher and lower income and education groups remained, the percentage of use among the latter was far from negligible. Survey data also show that organized family planning programs contributed to a reduction in socioeconomic class differentials in contraceptive use in a number of Northeastern states.

This occurred during a period when significant changes in socioeconomic conditions affecting the status of women were taking place in Brazil. The proportion of women reporting no education was reduced, and there were significant increases in the proportion reporting higher levels of educational attainment in both urban and rural areas. Increased proportions of married women were also reported as working, though it is difficult to determine to what extent this reflects differences in the way census and survey data defined labor force participation. Increased ownership of consumer durables was observed among women in urban households, while rural households were becoming increasingly reliant on wage labor, or proletarianized.

Such changes are consistent with a number of hypotheses about the reasons for increased motivation to control fertility. Increases in educational attainment represent a powerful modernizing force, and the relationship between differences in average parity and education noted in this chapter is clearly very strong. However, this relationship was complicated by significant collateral changes relating to increased economic pressures on low-income urban households and increases in rural proletarianization. The multivariate regression analysis in the next chapter permits further examination of hypotheses linking differences in average parity to these variables, as well as a decomposition of changes in average parity from 1970 to 1976 as they relate to changes in population composition and in the impact of the different variables on fertility.

CHAPTER 4

ANALYSIS OF FERTILITY DETERMINANTS AT THE NATIONAL LEVEL

This chapter uses multivariate regression analysis to explain how changes in average parity among married women in Brazil relate to their changing socioeconomic characteristics during the accelerated fertility decline of the early 1970s. In so doing, it attempts to provide a more systematic assessment of the hypotheses presented in the last two chapters, supported by tabular evidence, about socioeconomic differences in fertility decline in Brazil and the forces behind those differences.

The decision to focus on variability in the average parity of married women was based on several considerations. First, fertility was measured according to average parity rather than the last birth reported because of the questionable reliability and comparability of the latter in studying changes over time among different socioeconomic groups. Second, analysis of the proximate determinants of the decline in the total fertility rate between 1970 and 1976 indicated fertility control by married women to be the major factor involved; this conclusion was also supported by evidence on the diffusion of contraception among new regions and income groups. Third, accelerated fertility decline coincided with a number of important socioeconomic changes that could have had an impact on the motivation to control fertility, including increases in female educational attainment and possible aggravation of inflationary pressures on the economic resources of low- and middle-income households. The last two points suggested a working hypothesis about the acceleration of fertility decline: that it was triggered by the convergence of two sets of forces--increased availability of effective means of contraception and the emergence of socioeconomic conditions conducive to smaller family norms.

Because there is a lack of nationally representative data combining information on contraceptive use and socioeconomic characteristics, the analysis in this chapter is limited to the second set of forces. The principal question addressed is the extent to which the effects on reproductive behavior of such modernizing forces as increased household income and female educational attainment (as measured by average parity) combined with other factors affecting household behavior, particularly those reflecting such major structural dimensions of the Brazilian economy as inflation and income distribution. Differential patterns of change among rural and urban areas suggested a division of the chapter into separate sections for these groups, though work on the latter was even more restricted by data limitations.

URBAN WOMEN

As noted earlier, the acceleration of fertility decline in Brazil coincided with a period during which lower- and middle-income urban households were raising their consumption expectations and beginning to realize them through increased purchases of housing and other consumer durables, including televisions and automobiles, with most purchases made on the installment plan. Unequal treatment of wages and credit obligations in Brazil's indexing system made it more difficult for families to keep up with payments, and even to purchase basic necessities during periods of high inflation. As was suggested earlier, this, combined with increased knowledge of and access to contraception, may have reduced family-size desires. This explanation does not compete with a modernization framework, but extends it to incorporate other structural changes.

Among the research questions that need to be addressed are the following: (1) What measures in the available data files can be used as appropriate indices of the modernizing forces and economic pressures discussed above? (2) How should the relationship between these measures and average parity be specified? Are the relationships linear? Should interactions be taken into account? (3) Can the analysis be pushed beyond explanation of differentials in average parity in 1970 and 1976 to an assessment of the sources of change in fertility during that interval? In other words, do declines in average parity reflect changes in the composition of the population of married women according to modernizing characteristics, or is it more a case of changes in the parameters that reflect the impact of these variables on parity? The latter are likely to reflect structural changes, and one of the tasks here will be to incorporate in the specification variables for which such changes would be indicative of the specific structural forces hypothesized above, that is, increased economic pressures on household resources.

It is important to recognize that questions in censuses and large-scale surveys do not provide a great deal of conceptual precision for the measurement of modernization and its influence on fertility. Most of the measures in this chapter have appeared in the presentation of tabular evidence in earlier chapters; these include income and education, as well as age. A new variable that attempts to measure households' relative economic positions has also been added.

Table 38 lists the variables that have been selected for the analysis of data on urban women. Variable labels and a summary of variable definitions are shown. Average parity (CEB), the dependent variable, is listed first. In accounting for variation in this variable, the amount of exposure to the risk of conception needs to be controlled. This risk is associated with marital duration and maternal age. Data on age at marriage are provided only in the 1976 data file; maternal age is a less satisfactory substitute, particularly at earlier ages when there is greater variability because the marriage is recent. To maintain comparability between 1970 and 1976, regressions were run using maternal age (AGE) as a control for exposure to risk. Women were first separated into three broad age categories, with AGE used as a control variable for each: (1) 20-24, (2) 25-34, and (3) 35-44. To test the sensitivity of results to marital duration (MDUR), the 1976 data were then run using the AGE control variable.

The next two variables on the list relate to modernization. It has become fairly standard practice in analytical approaches influenced by household economic theory to use women's average educational attainment (MED) and their own and their husband's earnings (HINC) as variables in analyzing differences in average parity (see Schultz, 1976). Women's earnings and educational attainment reflect the opportunity costs of childrearing vis-a-vis other uses of their time, while the earnings of husbands and wives measure their available resources for childrearing and other activities. Theoretically, the effect

TABLE 38 Variable Labels and Definitions, Urban Women: Brazil

Variable	Definition
CEB	Average parity: number of live children ever born as reported in 1970 census and 1976 PNAD survey.
AGE	Mother's age: in years.
MED	Mother's education: natural logarithm of the number of years of school completed, defined as follows: MED=log (years +1), so that log (0 years)=0.
HINC	Monthly earnings of the head of household: natural logarithm of amount in 1970 cruzeiros.
MDUR	Duration of marriage in number of years for currently married women.
GAP	Estimated log of head's monthly earning (PINC) minus log of observed earnings (HINC). PINC = p(HED, EXP, TAX), where: HED = years of school completed by head. EXP = head's age - years of school completed - 6. TAX = natural logarithm of value added tax per capita of state in which woman resides.

on the number of children should be negative for cost factors and positive for resource factors; in fact, however, both often turn out to be negative because increasing income is usually accompanied by changing attitudes about family size, including a preference for quality rather than quantity of children.

Tabular evidence in earlier chapters indicated that differences in average parity in Brazil negatively correlated with both income and education. However, the question was raised of whether parity changes between 1970 and 1976 mainly reflected changes in the educational and income levels of married women of reproductive age, or whether other variables related to inflation and income distribution also contributed to fertility decline. The available census and survey data files provide only a few threads of evidence on the latter. Increased ownership of televisions, particularly among low-income households likely to have purchased them on credit, suggests that such factors could have been operative; increased female labor force participation suggests that economic pressures might have contributed to the delay or termination of childbearing.

However, exploratory attempts to incorporate television ownership and female labor force participation in the specification of the relationship between female educational attainment, husband's earnings, and average parity yielded unsatisfactory results. The problem was in identifying the endogenous effects of the employment and earnings of women in reproductive ages on their fertility, vis-a-vis the exogenous influence of those women's education and their husbands' earnings. The data files did not provide other exogenous variables that could be used to estimate fully identified parameters for female employment and earnings. Consequently, the analysis was limited to estimation of reduced-form coefficients; that is, only exogenous variables were included on the right-hand side of the regression equation.

In view of this, and to permit continued pursuit of a specification that would capture the effect of the relative economic position of a woman's household (as well as possible changes in that position) on her fertility, an approach based on the concept of relative income was adopted. A household's income is relative in that it may be greater or less than the income stream that would be expected on the basis of that household's human capital endowments. A gap between observed and expected income, if it existed, would indicate whether a household was more or less vulnerable to outside economic pressures such as inflation. The approach is consistent with Leibenstein's (1974) point about the relationship between income and fertility: that while the overall relationship may be negative, it may be positive within specific reference groups, with higher fertility among higher-income households within a particular group.

This approach was operationalized by first estimating the expected earnings of husbands using standard earnings equations, and then determining what each husband's earnings would be given his particular characteristics. The estimates were based on husband's earnings rather than household income for simplicity's sake (estimates could then be based on the characteristics of one individual without consideration of household size and structure as well as other income sources). Some of the limitations of this approach are offset by the fact that the analysis was restricted to married women with husbands present who were living in single-family households.

Earnings are measured in logarithms of 1970 Cruzeiros per month. The difference between reported (HINC) and estimated (PINC) earnings provides a measure of the gap described above. Variables in the earnings equation include husband's education in years of schooling completed (HED); husband's experience (current age minus years of schooling minus six [EXP]); and an index of the level of industrial output in the state of residence, which consists of the amount of value-added tax on manufacturing per capita in the state (TAX). The latter variable was added as a control for regional differences in labor market conditions, which are known to vary widely in Brazil. Earnings equations were estimated for 1970 and 1976, with the following results:

1970: PINC = 3.837 + .149 HEDUC
       (85.3)   (74.5)
      + .0008 EXP + .249 TAX
        (1.1)   (31.1) $R2 = .38$

1976: PINC = 4.013 + .158 HEDUC
       (77.2)   (79.0)
      + .011 EXP + .232 TAX
        (10.9)   (25.8) $R2 = .37$

Values of the t-statistic are shown in parentheses beneath regression coefficients. A new variable (GAP) was defined as the difference between PINC and HINC.

Other variables omitted from the analysis of individual-level data studied in this chapter were infant and child mortality. Mortality measures for use in analysis of individual records can and have been derived from these data files (Merrick, 1981); however, the process of transforming ratios of surviving children to children ever born into a normally distributed, jointly dependent variable would require controlling these ratios for length of exposure to risk of mortality using parity progression ratios. It was impossible to specify a statistically meaningful causal relation between fertility and mortality in such circumstances.

Unweighted means and standard deviations of the variables used in the regression analysis of differences in average parity are presented in Table 39. The data are broken down according to the three broad age categories described above. Exploratory analysis of the relationship between MED and CEB suggested a nonlinear specification.

TABLE 39 Means[a] (standard deviations) of Variables Used in Analysis of Differences in Average Parity for Urban Women, 1970 and 1976: Brazil

Year and Variable	Age		
	20-24	25-34	35-44
1970			
CEB	1.78	3.47	5.00
	(1.51)	(2.43)	(3.51)
MED	1.31	1.29	1.17
	(0.79)	(0.83)	(0.84)
AGE	22.19	29.52	39.17
	(1.37)	(2.85)	(2.84)
HINC	5.60	5.76	5.75
	(0.92)	(1.06)	(1.21)
GAP	0.11	-0.01	-0.04
	(0.72)	(0.81)	(0.97)
N	2,749	7,532	6,494
1976			
CEB	1.45	2.89	4.61
	(1.21)	(2.07)	(3.11)
MED	1.67	1.59	1.38
	(0.71)	(0.78)	(0.81)
AGE	22.26	29.38	39.29
	(1.37)	(2.76)	(2.76)
HINC	6.13	6.31	6.27
	(1.02)	(1.07)	(1.11)
MDUR	3.20	8.23	16.74
	(2.26)	(4.51)	(5.94)
GAP	0.09	-0.04	-0.02
	(0.86)	(0.75)	(0.92)
N	2,939	7,691	6,491

[a]Unweighted sample means.

Consequently, MED was defined as the logarithm of a woman's years of schooling completed plus one, so that the logarithm of zero years of schooling would equal zero. As indicated above, HINC is also measured in logarithms.

Since GAP is the residual of the estimated value of HINC, it has a zero mean for the total study population, but varies slightly from zero in specific age categories. Current earnings of husbands of younger women averaged slightly higher than their estimated earnings, while the average GAP for older women fell slightly below zero. It should also be noted that there are significant negative correlations (.7 to .8) between HINC and GAP; this indicates a tendency for current earnings to be lower than expected earning among husbands with lower earning levels, and for current earnings to exceed expected earnings by larger amounts among husbands with higher earnings. A check of outliers in the earnings equations indicated that these high zero order correlations were a statistical artifact produced by cases at extremes of the income distribution: overestimation of earnings when husbands reported zero earnings and underestimation when they reported very high earnings. These correlations disappeared when extreme cases were omitted; however, it was decided not to exclude such cases from the analysis of fertility differentials because the impact of the differential between HINC and PINC was of interest over the entire range of the income distribution.

The data in Table 39 on average marital duration (MDUR) in 1976 suggest that analysis of fertility differentials among younger women is likely to be quite sensitive to differences in exposure to the risk of conception because of the selectivity within that age group toward women who married early. The average age at marriage for women aged 20-24 in 1976 was 19.1 years, compared to 21.1 years for women aged 25-29. Relative variation in MDUR is also greater among younger women: the coefficient of variation for that group was 71 percent compared to 55 percent for 25-34 and 35 percent for 35-44. Caution is suggested in interpreting results for the youngest age category when MDUR cannot be controlled.

Analysis of Urban CEB Differentials in 1970 and 1976

Results of ordinary least squares regression analysis of differences in CEB for women grouped by broad age categories are presented in Tables 40 (1970) and 41 (1976). Three alternative regression equations were estimated for each data set. In each equation, the AGE variable was included in an attempt to control for length of exposure to risk of conception within the broader age groups; an additional equation substituting MDUR for AGE in the last alternative is also shown for 1976. Logarithms of both MED and HINC were employed after initial tests revealed nonlinearity in the relation between these variables and CEB. An education-income interaction term was also introduced to determine whether the slope of CEB with respect to income shifted with increases in education.

Interpretation of regression coefficients for MED and HINC is facilitated by the logarithmic specification, which makes them equally proportional to elasticities (the percentage change in CEB for each one percent change in MED or HINC). Dividing either coefficient by the mean of CEB gives the elasticity. Comparison between elasticities calculated from the first regression equation for each of the age groups in Tables 40 and 41 and averages for groups of lower- and higher-income countries reported by Schultz (1976) suggests that the responsiveness of CEB to changes in MED and HINC among urban Brazilian women was at an intermediate level, and that it moved in the direction of higher-income countries from 1970 to 1976. Schultz found that elasticities of average parity with respect to both mother's education and father's earnings became increasingly negative as the level of development increased.

This same tendency is observed in the Brazilian data. Elasticities for MED are greater (more negative) for younger women, and increase from 1970 to 1976. The results for HINC fall more clearly within the range of Schultz's higher-income countries. A summary of the results is as follows:

Age Group	MED		HINC	
	1970	1976	1970	1976
20-24	-.30	-.38	-.08	-.07
25-34	-.22	-.31	-.07	-.05
35-44	-.20	-.23	-.07	-.09
Lower (Schultz)	-.17 to -.06		+.05	
Higher (Schultz)	-1.1 to -.19		-.11 to +.28	

TABLE 40 Regression Analysis, Average Number of Children Ever Born (CEB), Married Urban Women, 1970: Brazil

Age Group	CONSTANT	MED	HINC	AGE	GAP	M*H[a]	R^2 (MSE)	F (P>F)
20-24								
(1)	1.841 (5.6)	-0.542 (14.3)	-0.145 (4.4)	0.232 (11.9)			0.15 (1.95)	163.7 (.0001)
(2)	-0.607 (1.2)	-0.424 (10.0)	0.407 (7.6)	0.236 (12.2)	-0.365 (6.1)		0.16 (1.93)	133.8 (.0001)
(3)	-0.274 (0.5)	-0.618 (3.2)	-0.466 (5.7)	0.236 (12.2)	-0.383 (6.2)	0.036 (1.8)	0.16 (1.93)	107.3 (.0001)
25-34								
(1)	0.064 (0.2)	-0.765 (21.7)	-0.265 (9.5)	0.201 (22.4)			0.17 (4.91)	520.5 (.0001)
(2)	2.846 (8.1)	-0.513 (13.1)	-0.797 (12.1)	0.199 (22.5)	-0.746 (14.0)		0.19 (4.79)	449.6 (.0001)
(3)	3.727 (8.4)	-1.017 (6.5)	-0.965 (14.0)	0.199 (22.6)	-0.797 (14.4)	0.092 (3.3)	0.19 (4.78)	362.3 (.0001)
35-44								
(1)	5.672 (9.4)	-1.022 (18.1)	0.362 (9.2)	0.066 (4.6)			0.11 (11.09)	263.1 (.0001)
(2)	10.442 (6.5)	-0.611 (9.7)	-1.292 (17.0)	0.067 (4.8)	-1.194 (14.2)		0.14 (10.76)	253.1 (.0001)
(3)	12.308 (15.8)	-1.743 (7.5)	-1.640 (15.9)	0.067 (4.7)	-1.348 (15.0)	0.203 (5.0)	0.14 (10.68)	208.4 (.0001)

Note: t statistics are in parentheses.

TABLE 41 Regression Analysis, Average Number of Children Ever Born (CEB), Married Urban Women, 1976: Brazil

Age Group	CONSTANT	MED	HINC	AGE	GAP	M*H[a]	R^2 (MSE)	F (P>F)
20-24								
(1)	-1.137 (3.3)	-0.552 (17.3)	-0.097 (4.4)	0.184 (12.2)			0.16 (1.27)	186.4 (.0001)
(2)	0.334 (0.9)	-0.400 (11.0)	-0.381 (9.6)	0.187 (12.6)	-0.377 (8.6)		0.18 (1.24)	161.5 (.0001)
(3)	-0.098 (0.2)	-0.288 (1.7)	-0.341 (4.7)	0.187 (12.6)	-0.372 (8.3)	0.019 (0.6)	0.18 (1.24)	129.3 (.0001)
(4)[b]	3.043 (9.1)	-0.414 (3.0)	-0.387 (6.6)	0.322 (42.3)	-0.241 (6.6)	0.045 (11.9)	0.47 (0.81)	506.8 (.0001)
25-34								
(1)	-0.754 (3.0)	-0.887 (28.2)	-0.143 (6.5)	0.203 (27.3)			0.23 (3.40)	758.2 (.0001)
(2)	1.659 (5.6)	-0.657 (18.8)	-0.599 (15.6)	0.206 (28.0)	-0.615 (14.4)		0.25 (3.31)	635.9 (.0001)
(3)	2.729 (6.4)	-1.178 (7.8)	-0.787 (12.0)	0.207 (28.1)	-0.651 (14.9)	0.088 (3.5)	0.25 (3.30)	512.0 (.0001)
(4)[b]	6.538 (20.0)	-1.300 (9.9)	-0.822 (14.4)	0.244 (59.3)	-0.519 (13.6)	0.154 (7.1)	0.43 (2.52)	1441.2 (.0001)
35-44								
(1)	5.403 (9.8)	-1.040 (19.6)	-0.422 (11.5)	0.085 (6.5)			0.14 (8.70)	360.6 (.0001)
(2)	9.659 (15.6)	-0.678 (11.7)	-1.253 (18.4)	0.097 (7.6)	-1.082 (14.4)		0.17 (8.45)	323.3 (.0001)
(3)	13.004 (17.1)	-2.437 (10.2)	-1.842 (17.8)	0.099 (7.8)	-1.263 (16.0)	0.295 (7.5)	0.18 (8.37)	278.1 (.0001)
(4)[b]	14.164 (25.0)	-2.546 (11.3)	-1.882 (19.4)	0.168 (30.2)	-1.179 (16.0)	0.330 (9.0)	0.27 (7.51)	483.2 (.0001)

Note: t statistics are in parentheses.
[a] Interaction term: MED*HINC.
[b] Marital duration (MDUR) substituted for age.

At 1970 mean levels of MED and CEB, the 48 percent increase in the average number of years of schooling achieved by women in the 25-34 age group (recalling that MED = log [years of school + 1]) would account for an 11 percent decline in CEB. While these results suggest that Brazilian experience during the early 1970s was consistent with patterns observed among lower-middle income countries, the elasticities of CEB with respect to father's earnings appear to lean more toward the negative values characteristic of higher-income countries than do those for MED.

One reason for this could be the earnings gap hypothesis discussed above: that the effects of earnings on CEB can be positive within a given reference group even if the overall relation between CEB and HINC is negative. The second set of regression equations, which incorporates the GAP variable, confirms this. The regression coefficient for GAP is negative, implying that the more husband's estimated earnings (PINC) exceed actual earnings (HINC), the lower is the average observed CEB. In a society like Brazil in which income differentials are associated with a variety of sociocultural factors that could influence reproductive behavior, it makes sense to look for the effect of income on fertility within rather than between specific reference groups.

Similar considerations raise the question of whether an interaction with sociocultural factors associated with differences in educational attainment affects the regression results for MED and HINC. The third set of regression equations includes an interaction term. This term is statistically significant in both 1970 and 1976 for women in the 25-34 and 35-44 age groups because of the large sample size; addition of the variable affects only the third digit of R-square. The term's positive sign indicates that with increases in MED, the negative impact of HINC on CEB is attenuated, as is the effect of MED as HINC increases. This is what one would expect given the variety of sociocultural influences described earlier.

As noted above, the variable AGE was included in all three variants of the regression equations as a control for differences in the risk of exposure to conception within each of the broader age groups. Marital duration is a better measure of such risk, but was not included in the 1970 census. However, it was incorporated in the 1976 survey, and equation (4) in Table 41 substitutes MDUR for AGE to provide some measure of the effect of using AGE as the measure of exposure to risk. As one would expect, AGE appears to be least satisfactory for younger women, for whom both absolute and relative variation in CEB was more sensitive to MDUR than AGE. It is interesting to note that while the coefficients for MED and HINC increased in negative magnitude with the addition of MDUR, the impact of GAP was reduced; this suggests that the effect on CEB of the relative status captured by GAP may be tied to marital duration. Among younger women whose husband's earnings fall below the expected level, lower CEB could be the result of longer intervals between marriage and first birth, a point that deserves further exploration.

Concern about MDUR is warranted because of its implications for interpreting changes in CEB from 1970 to 1976. The extent of this concern will depend on one's confidence in the conclusions derived earlier from census and survey data: that average ages at marriage and first birth did not change substantially between 1970 and 1976, and that most of the decline in total fertility can be attributed to a decline in marital fertility rather than to changes in the proportions married. The issue is less important to determining how much changes in socioeconomic status contributed to declines in CEB than to examining how those changes were translated into declines via the proximate determinants of fertility.

Sources of Change in CEB from 1970 to 1976

Regression analyses of differences in CEB also can be used to identify sources of change in CEB from 1970 to 1976. As noted earlier, an important question is whether such change resulted from a redistribution of women according to socioeconomic characteristics or from a shift in the parameters relating these characteristics to CEB. One approach is to evaluate the regression coefficients reported in Tables 40 and 41 using sample means, and then examine changes in the contribution of each variable to the level of CEB for the two dates. With two sets of regression results, there are three ways that one can proceed: forward using 1970 coefficients with means for both dates, backward using 1976 coefficients with both sets of means, or by comparing means and coefficients for each date. Changes in the average value of CEB could be the result of changes in educational attainment or other variables included in the regressions, changes in regression coefficients, or shifts in conditions that are not measured, but are reflected in the constant term. The first two variants of this approach hold the coefficients constant, but will give different results to the extent that coefficients have changed; by definition there is no change in the constant term. The third variant allows for change in the constant, but confuses changes in composition with shifts in coefficients. An alternative approach is to reestimate coefficients and include both a dummy variable for time to capture shifts in the constant term, and interaction terms for time and each of the variables in the regression to measure changes in regression coefficients. The new estimators can then be evaluated at both sets of sample means to determine the contribution of changes in composition to observed changes in the level of CEB. Both of these approaches have been attempted.

Table 42 presents the first approach: the first column represents changes with the 1970 regressions; the second column represents changes with the 1976 regressions; and the third column shows the difference between the evaluation of 1970 regressions with 1970 means and the 1976 regressions with 1976 means. The third set of regressions in Tables 41 and 42 (with the interaction term) was used for the two older age categories where interactions were significant. The total of changes in each group of coefficients adds to the estimated change in CEB for that group; by definition, the estimated change in CEB equals the actual change in the last column.

In the first two variants, estimated changes exceed the actual in all cases, especially using the 1970 coefficients and in the case of older women; this suggests some combination of change in coefficients and in the constant term. Changes in the average level of husbands' earnings appear to have had a greater impact than maternal education, more so in 1970 than in 1976, which suggests an attenuation in the importance of the earnings effect. An important fraction of the negative effects of MED and HINC is offset by the positive MED*HINC interaction term. Compared to MED and HINC, changes in the GAP variable had little effect; in fact, a slight narrowing of the average GAP contributed a slightly positive impetus to average CEB. Shifts in age composition also raised CEB for older women.

The third variant is useful mainly in illustrating how the combined effects of changes in composition and in coefficients relate to changes when coefficients are held constant. For example, the effect of changes in the HINC coefficient and the average level of HINC would have contributed to an increase of .562 in CEB among women aged

TABLE 42 Changes in Contribution of Independent Variables to Levels of CEB, 1970 and 1976: Brazil

Age Group and Variable	1970 Regression Coefficients	1976 Regression Coefficients	Combined Coefficients
20-24			
CONSTANT	0	0	0.914
AGE	0.014	0.011	-1.072
MED	-0.152	-0.143	-0.112
HINC	-0.220	0.208	-0.094
GAP	-0.006	-0.006	+0.005
CEB	-0.351	-0.335	-0.332
25-34			
CONSTANT	0	0	-0.998
AGE	-0.021	-0.022	+0.206
MED	-0.309	-0.357	-0.564
HINC	-0.566	-0.462	0.562
GAP	0.027	0.022	0.021
INTERACTION	0.245	0.236	0.210
CEB	-0.624	-0.583	-0.563
35-44			
CONSTANT	0	0	0.696
AGE	0.008	0.011	1.261
MED	-0.379	-0.530	-1.340
HINC	-0.938	-1.054	-2.213
GAP	-0.027	-0.026	-0.029
INTERACTION	0.409	0.595	1.029
CEB	-0.929	-1.004	-0.363

25-34 had there not been offsetting changes in MED and the constant. Since both types of change are clearly operative, the alternative approach to decomposition using reestimated coefficients with dummy variables for interactions with time should be helpful, particularly for the 25-34 age group.

Table 43 presents estimates of the regression coefficients using the combined 1970 and 1976 data files. Four additional variables have been added: a dummy for time, and one interaction term each for time and MED, HINC, and GAP. These four variables should account for changes in the constant term and in coefficients for those three variables. These regressions confirm what Table 42 suggested about changes in coefficients for women in the middle and upper age categories. For women in the 25-34 age group, the negative effect of husband's earnings is

TABLE 43 Regression Analysis and Test for Interactions, Merged 1970 and 1976 Data Files: Brazil

	Age Group		
Variable	20-24	25-34	35-44
CONSTANT	-0.103 (0.3)	3.628 (9.8)	11.704 (18.6)
MED	-0.425 (11.1)	-1.017 (7.0)	-1.740 (7.9)
HINC	-0.398 (8.3)	-0.965 (15.2)	-1.641 (16.9)
AGE	0.212 (17.6)	0.203 (35.6)	0.083 (8.7)
GAP	-0.363 (6.7)	-0.797 (15.6)	-1.348 (15.9)
INTERACTION	--	0.092 (3.6)	0.203 (5.3)
TIME	-0.057 (0.2)	-0.781 (1.5)	1.970 (2.5)
HINC*TIME	0.002 (0.0)	0.183 (1.9)	-0.205 (1.4)
MED*TIME	0.035 (0.6)	-0.150 (0.7)	-0.666 (2.0)
GAP*TIME	0.027 (0.4)	0.147 (2.1)	0.068 (0.6)
INTERACT*TIME	--	-0.007 (0.2)	0.088 (0.6)
R^2 (MSE)	0.18 (1.58)	0.23 (4.05)	0.16 (9.65)
F (F>P)	159.6 (.0001)	459.0 (.0001)	248.1 (.0001)

attenuated. This shows up in the HINC*TIME coefficient, as well as in INTERACTION*TIME; the MED*TIME coefficient is not significant. For women aged 35-44, there is a significant increase in the constant term and a decline in the impact of education.

When the regression results for the merged files are used to decompose change, the results are consistent with those reported in Table 42 in the relative impact of the variables. The main point that stands out in Table 44 is that the decline in the negative impact of husband's earnings over time for women aged 25-34 results from a change in the value of the regression coefficient, as does the rather large increase in the impact of earnings for women aged 35-44. This, plus changes in the constant

TABLE 44 Decomposition of Changes in Average Parity from 1970 to 1976 Using Regression Coefficient for Merged Data: Brazil

	Age Group		
Variable	20-24	25-34	35-44
MED	-0.124	-0.308	-0.378
HINC	-0.217	-0.567	-0.939
AGE	0.013	-0.022	0.009
GAP	0.006	0.027	-0.027
INTERACTION	--	0.246	0.413
TIME	-0.057	-0.781	1.970
MED*TIME	0.059	-0.243	-0.922
HINC*TIME	0.021	1.162	-1.130
GAP*TIME	-0.003	-0.006	-0.002
INTERACT*TIME	--	-0.068	-0.772
CEB - ESTIMATED[a]	-0.331	-0.559	-0.402
CEB - OBSERVED	-0.332	-0.563	-0.363

Note: Interaction term not significant; see text.
[a]Totals may vary due to rounding.

term (as reflected in the change attributed to TIME), suggests that some important structural shifts accompanied the changes in composition by MED and HINC and contributed to declines in CEB.

What is puzzling is that these shifts do not show up in the GAP variable, which, despite its importance in explaining differentials in CEB, does not appear to contribute much to changes in CEB between 1970 and 1976. One reason for this could be that changes in the average level of GAP are not the appropriate place to be looking for the effects of changes transmitted through that variable. GAP was introduced to measure the effect of inflationary conditions and changes in the distribution of earnings on the economic position of households. Therefore, changes in the average level of GAP should be less relevant than changes in its distribution.

Table 45 examines changes in the distribution of GAP between 1970 and 1976 and indicates the possible impact of such changes on CEB. The table shows the percent of women in each age category, broken down by deciles of family income, residing in families whose husband's earnings fall more than one standard deviation from the mean level of GAP for that age group. The table also shows in parentheses the relative weight (as a percent of all women in the age group) of these women in total CEB. These data suggest that for certain groups (e.g., ages 25-34 in middle-income deciles) there may have been a greater dispersion of GAP in 1976. However, the table also shows that this increase in dispersion was probably not great enough to have made a major difference in changes in the average level of CEB over the period under study. In this connection, it is important to note that the relative earnings effect expressed in GAP does appear to make a difference in the explanation of differentials in CEB in both 1970 and 1976. The point is that GAP (and the structural changes it measures, perhaps quite inadequately) does not appear to account for much of the change in CEB between 1970 and 1976.

Thus our assessment of the components of changes in CEB from 1970 to 1976 indicates that increases in the educational attainment of married women in Brazil and increases in their husbands' earnings contributed significantly to the decline of average CEB. At the same time, structural change is not ruled out. Clearly, the role of that change is suggested by the significant and somewhat erratic shifts in the values of the regression coefficients for HINC, as well as changes in the constant terms in regres-

TABLE 45 Percent of Women with GAP Greater than One Standard Deviation from Mean, 1970 and 1976: Brazil

Age Group and Year	Income Deciles			All Groups
	1-3	4-6	7-10	
20-24				
1970	29.8 (3.6)	6.5 (2.5)	3.4 (1.7)	7.8
1976	21.5 (3.4)	5.5 (2.1)	2.6 (1.2)	6.7
25-34				
1970	35.3 (3.8)	4.4 (1.4)	3.6 (2.0)	7.2
1976	32.2 (4.1)	8.9 (2.8)	2.9 (1.6)	8.5
35-44				
1970	31.4 (3.1)	5.8 (1.5)	2.3 (1.5)	6.1
1976	34.3 (3.3)	12.7 (3.4)	3.8 (2.4)	9.1

Note: The relative contributions of each group to total children ever born, expressed as a percent of all women in the age group, are shown in parentheses.

sions for the 25-34 and 35-44 age groups. It is also clear that the conceptual limitations of census and multipurpose national sample survey data do not permit a detailed pursuit of the nature of these shifts.

RURAL WOMEN

Prior to 1970, fertility rates among rural Brazilian women were constant or rising at the national level. Regional declines in the South and Southeast were offset by constant or increasing rates in the Northeast and Frontier areas. The impact of this sluggishness in rural fertility decline on overall fertility rates was offset by declines in the share of rural areas in total population; rapid out-migration from rural areas more than offset the higher rural rate of natural increase. With the advent of a decline in natural increase in rural areas, the rural population declined absolutely during the 1970s.

The rural exodus that has characterized the last three decades of Brazilian demographic experience was triggered by a combination of social, economic, and political forces, many of them longstanding features of rural Brazilian society. One of the most basic of these is the combination of a limited supply of good land and increasing population pressure; droughts and infertile soil have plagued areas with a high concentration of rural population, particularly in the Northeastern states. A second force is the unequal distribution of land, with substantial proportions of rural families being forced to eke a subsistence out of minifundia holdings of fewer than five hectares. A third is that there has been increased consolidation of land holdings accompanying the commercialization of Brazilian agriculture; this process has received additional stimulus from the energy crisis and Brazil's resultant need to raise foreign exchange through agricultural exports and increase production of alcohol as a substitute for petroleum imports. This lack of opportunity in rural areas, combined with hopes of paid employment and urban amenities, has motivated Brazil's rural-urban migration.

While migration was the primary demographic response to adverse socioeconomic conditions among the masses of Brazil's rural population, other demograhic processes were affected, including fertility and family formation. Chapter 3 suggested several hypotheses about how such changes might be affecting rural fertility in Brazil. All focus in one way or another on the role of children as both immediate productive resources and longer-term investments for rural families, and on how changes in rural socioeconomic and institutional conditions could have affected this role.

One hypothesis relates to land availability. As the amount of land available to farm families in more densely settled areas is reduced, several forces that could motivate not only out-migration, but also lower fertility are set in motion. For families remaining in agriculture that wish to transmit land to their children through inheritance, large numbers of children will lead to an uneconomical subdivision of plots; this can be avoided only by having fewer children, forcing children to start their own families later, or encouraging the children's migration. The value of children as immediate productive resources will also be affected to the extent that smaller plots reduce the need for child labor.

The influence of these forces on reproductive behavior is mediated by institutional factors and by the availability of new land in other areas. Research on land availability and fertility in rural Brazil using data from the 1970 censuses of population and agriculture found that fertility was lower in more densely settled regions of Southeastern Brazil and higher in areas of new rural settlement in the Central-Western region (Merrick, 1974). An extension of that research to Northeastern Brazil and to the frontier settlements in the Amazon region did not reveal similar patterns (Merrick, 1981). Several reasons for this were suggested: Amazon settlement really did not get underway until after 1970, and the very unequal distribution of access to land in the Northeast was not as conducive to the pattern observed in the South, here a higher proportion of family farms were owner-operated.

Research with 1970 data also revealed the very severe limitations of population census data for dealing with links between rural demographic changes and socioeconomic and institutional factors affecting those changes. These limitations were overcome to some extent by combining population census data with information from the agricultural census. Analysis of changes during the 1970s will have to await the availability of detailed information from the 1980 censuses of agriculture and population. Unfortunately, the PNAD surveys taken during the 1970s do not provide the geographic detail required for linking them to results of the 1975 agricultural census; moreover, the PNAD sample does not include rural areas of the Central-West and Amazon regions, so that the potential positive effects on fertility of frontier settlement in those regions during the 1970s cannot be examined.

Some features of the relationship between fertility decline in rural Brazil during the 1970s and socioeconomic change in the areas included in the PNAD surveys can be studied. One of these relates to an institutional factor mediating the response to increasing economic pressures, such as scarcity of land and consolidation of land in larger holdings, on the demographic responses of farm families. This factor is rural proletarianization, or the shift from an owner-operator and farm family labor mode of production to wage labor. As noted earlier, European experience, as well as evidence from Southern Brazil, indicates that lower fertility is more likely to result from a scarcity of land when farm families own their land and reduced fertility allows them to maintain control of the land. Rural proletarianization weakens this motivation. As noted in Chapter 3, Paiva (1982) disagrees with this interpretation for Brazil. He argues that proletarianization reduces the value of children as farm laborers and provides incentives for reduced fertility, including increased market work for both women and children. The potential value of market work would be increased by education, and by a shift toward quality rather than quantity of children.

The data with which to evaluate these two interpretations of Brazilian experience are scant. Tabular evidence presented in Chapter 3 indicated that average parity was indeed lower in regions with higher levels of proletarianization (measured according to the proportion of rural household heads reported as employees); in the same tables, however, average parity was higher rather than lower for proletarian households within those regions. While one must be careful to avoid the fallacy of composition, one must also be careful about bias arising from the location of families when their characteristics have been measured in census and survey data. For rural areas, those data detect only that proportion of the proletarianized population remaining at the time interviews were conducted; those who moved (either to urban areas or to other rural areas) and who may well have had lower fertility would not be included.

Another aspect of change in rural fertility relates to the socioeconomic differentials observed in Chapter 2. While these differentials were not as great as those observed in urban areas, the data presented in Chapters 2 and 3 indicated that rural women with some education had lower fertility than those with no education, and that the proportion of rural women with some education increased from 1970 to 1976. Also, rural women with no education as a percent of all women aged 15-49 declined from about 21 percent to about 13 percent, a result of some combination of increases in educational attainment among rural women, out-migration, and possible underrepresentation of less-educated rural women in the PNAD survey. Such evidence suggests that the role of education should not be neglected in examining rural fertility differences.

Analysis of Rural CEB Differentials in 1970 and 1976

As indicated above, neither the 1970 census nor the 1976 PNAD survey provides many meaningful measures of concepts relevant to the analysis of changes in rural fertility in Brazil. The multivariate analysis that follows is presented primarily to illustrate how the relationships between differences in average parity and socioeconomic variables described for urban women compare to the case of rural women. No pretense is made of even approximating a comprehensive explanation of changes in rural reproductive patterns based on these data.

Table 46 lists the variables included in the analysis. Average parity (CEB) is the dependent variable, and education of women (MED) is included in logarithmic form as it was for urban women. Census and survey measures of income and earnings had so little conceptual content for the rural population that they were quickly abandoned. Husband's education (HED) has been substituted as a proxy measure of earnings potential, but no attempt was made to calculate the gap between actual and potential earnings. Two additional dummy variables were employed: one for residents of Northeastern states (NE), included to pick up the effects of regional differences in economic and social structure not reflected in education, and one to indicate if the household was proletarian (PROL), based on whether or not the husband's status was reported as employee or paid farm laborer.

Unweighted means and standard deviations of these variables are shown in Table 47. Average CEB declined by 12 percent for married women aged 20-24, 6 percent for

TABLE 46 Variable Labels and Definitions, Rural Women: Brazil

Variable	Definition
CEB	Average parity: number of live children ever born as reported in 1970 census and 1976 PNAD survey.
AGE	Mother's age: in years.
MED	Mother's education: natural logarithm of the number of years of school completed, defined as follows: MED=log (years +1), so that log (0 years)=0.
HED	Father's education: natural logarithm of the number of years of school completed, defined as follows: HED=log (years +1), so that log (0 years)=0.
NE	Northeast: dummy variable equal to one for residents of northeastern states.
PROL	Proletarian: dummy variable equal to one when employment status of father is rural wage labor.

TABLE 47 Means[a] (standard deviations) of Variables Used in Analysis of Differences in Average Parity for Rural Women, 1970 and 1976: Brazil

Year and Variable	Age Group		
	20-24	25-34	35-44
1970			
CEB	2.21 (1.70)	4.42 (2.71)	6.79 (3.82)
MED	0.52 (0.66)	0.53 (0.67)	0.41 (0.61)
HED	0.53 (0.66)	0.56 (0.67)	0.49 (0.64)
AGE	22.07 (1.42)	29.17 (2.87)	39.01 (2.79)
NE	0.45 (0.49)	0.43 (0.50)	0.43 (0.50)
PROL	0.31 (0.46)	0.30 (0.46)	0.26 (0.44)
N	2,456	4,880	4,108
1976			
CEB	1.95 (1.50)	4.14 (2.57)	6.73 (3.62)
MED	0.90 (0.75)	0.78 (0.74)	0.61 (0.70)
HED	0.84 (0.74)	0.76 (0.73)	0.65 (0.71)
AGE	22.17 (1.42)	29.26 (2.85)	39.21 (2.89)
NE	0.32 (0.47)	0.33 (0.47)	0.31 (0.46)
PROL	0.48 (0.50)	0.43 (0.49)	0.38 (0.48)
N	2,344	5,247	4,615

[a]Unweighted sample means.

those aged 25-34, and less than 1 percent for those aged 35-44. Relative variation in average CEB was somewhat lower for rural than for urban women. For women in the 25-34 age group, the coefficient of variation (ratio of the standard deviation to the mean) was 0.61 in 1970 compared to 0.7 for urban women. In 1976, relative variation increased, and was close to the level observed for urban women. There was a greater proportional increase in average education for women than for men, with the greatest increase occurring among ages 20-24. The Northeast was represented less in 1976 because of a smaller sampling fraction for that region in PNAD (as well as possible underrepresentation in the sample). The proportion of women in proletarian households increased for all three age groups, again with the greatest increase among younger women.

Multivariate regression results for 1970 are presented in Table 48, and those for 1976 in Table 49. Separate regressions were run for each of the three broad age categories, with a control for age within each category as well. Three regressions were selected for each group: the first includes, in addition to AGE, the education variables MED and HED; the second adds the dummy variable for the Northeastern states (NE); and the third includes the dummy variable for proletarian households (PROL). Since both MED and HED enter in log form, their regression coefficients are again proportional to elasticities (which are derived by dividing the coefficients by the sample mean value of CEB).

A summary of the elasticities of CEB with respect to average MED and HED is as follows:

Year	20-24		25-34		35-44	
	MED	HED	MED	HED	MED	HED
1970	-.16	-.06	-.10	-.02	-.04	-.01
1976	-.16	-.10	-.15	-.06	-.07	-.08

Compared to the results for urban women, the responsiveness of CEB to increases in MED is one-third to one-half as great for rural women, and the increase in responsiveness from 1970 to 1976 is smaller. Compared to results for the range of countries reported by Schultz (1976), results for older rural Brazilian women are close to the bottom of the range of elasticities for lower-income countries (-.17 to -.04) and for younger women near the top.

Although addition of the dummy variable for residence in Northeastern states (the second set of equations) does not add significantly to the amount of variance explained,

TABLE 48 Regression Analysis, Average Number of Children Ever Born (CEB), Married Rural Women, 1970: Brazil

Age Group	CONSTANT	MED	HED	AGE	NE	PROL	R^2 (MSE)	F (P>F)
20-24								
(1)	-4.317 (8.46)	-0.352 (5.62)	-0.163 (2.56)	0.308 (13.31)			0.09 (2.634)	84.5 (.0001)
(2)	-4.399 (8.58)	-0.335 (5.28)	-0.136 (2.11)	0.308 (13.32)	0.120 (1.65)		0.09 (2.632)	64.1 (.0001)
(3)	-4.415 (8.61)	-0.335 (5.27)	-0.136 (2.08)	0.307 (13.29)	0.129 (1.76)	0.083 (1.17)	0.10 (2.632)	51.6 (.0001)
25-34								
(1)	-4.342 (11.67)	-0.470 (6.90)	-0.162 (2.40)	0.312 (24.65)			0.13 (6.421)	239.8 (.0001)
(2)	-4.598 (12.22)	-0.440 (6.42)	-0.087 (1.24)	0.314 (24.82)	0.338 (4.25)		0.13 (6.398)	185.0 (.0001)
(3)	-4.645 (12.27)	-.436 (6.36)	-0.091 (1.28)	0.314 (24.85)	0.344 (4.23)	0.090 (1.13)	0.13 (6.398)	148.3 (.0001)
35-44								
(1)	0.721 (0.87)	-0.346 (2.98)	-0.229 (2.06)	0.162 (7.65)			0.02 (14.32)	28.6 (.0205)
(2)	0.097 (0.12)	-0.290 (2.49)	-0.086 (0.75)	0.168 (7.95)	0.679 (5.38)		0.03 (14.23)	28.8 (.0393)
(3)	0.085 (0.10)	-0.289 (2.48)	-0.086 (0.75)	0.168 (7.96)	0.681 (5.36)	0.027 (0.20)	0.03 (14.23)	23.1 (.0273)

Note: t statistics are in parentheses.

TABLE 49 Regression Analysis, Average Number of Children Ever Born (CEB), Married Rural Women, 1976: Brazil

Age Group	CONSTANT	MED	HED	AGE	NE	PROL	R^2 (MSE)	F (P>F)
20-24								
(1)	-2.803 (6.10)	-0.339 (7.22)	-0.238 (5.03)	-0.237 (11.49)			0.11 (2.009)	100.3 (.0001)
(2)	-3.017 (6.51)	-0.318 (6.78)	-0.194 (3.94)	0.242 (11.69)	0.235 (3.45)		0.12 (2.000)	78.5 (.0001)
(3)	-3.021 (6.49)	-0.320 (6.78)	-0.194 (3.94)	0.241 (11.68)	0.236 (3.42)	0.005 (0.08)	0.12 (2.000)	62.8 (.0001)
25-34								
(1)	-4.495 (13.55)	-0.650 (12.42)	-0.362 (6.85)	0.322 (28.72)			0.20 (5.325)	428.1 (.0001)
(2)	-4.768 (14.34)	-0.621 (11.88)	-0.268 (4.95)	0.322 (28.89)	-0.519 (7.22)		0.20 (5.273)	337.2 (.0001)
(3)	-4.861 (14.51)	-0.617 (11.80)	-0.266 (4.91)	0.323 (28.96)	0.540 (7.44)	0.140 (2.17)	0.21 (5.270)	270.9 (.0001)
35-44								
(1)	1.009 (1.43)	-0.555 (6.40)	-0.731 (8.48)	0.167 (9.36)			0.07 (12.251)	111.6 (.0001)
(2)	0.304 (0.43)	-0.468 (5.44)	-0.546 (6.27)	0.171 (9.69)	1.204 (10.43)		0.09 (11.97)	112.9 (.0001)
(3)	0.222 (0.31)	-0.462 (5.36)	-0.541 (6.20)	0.171 (9.72)	1.219 (10.47)	0.105 (0.99)	0.09 (11.97)	90.5 (.0001)

Note: t statistics are in parentheses.

the regression coefficient is significant for the two older age groups. This indicates an interaction between education and residence rather than an additive effect. Tests for the interaction suggested that MED slopes were lower in the Northeast, though so few rural women in that region reported any education that it was difficult to judge the significance of the results.

The third set of equations attempted to assess the impact of proletarianization on average CEB. The results were consistent with the tabular results in Chapter 3, which suggested that CEB was slightly higher in proletarian rural households. When other variables were controlled, however, this difference was significant only for women in the 25-34 age group in 1976. These results confirm the point made earlier that an adequate test of the proletarian hypothesis will require a more precise measurement of the process of proletarianization that captures present and previous residence and occupational status, as well as a richer depiction of the institutional forces underlying that process.

Changes in Rural CEB from 1970 to 1976

The change in average CEB from 1970 to 1976 that can be accounted for in the regression analysis results from increased educational attainment. In this connection, it should be recognized that most of the observed change is not explained by changes in the variables included in the regressions. It is hoped that the case study data reported in Part II of this report will provide richer insight into the nature of changes in rural fertility than do aggregate census and sample survey data.

CONCLUSIONS

Most of the variance in average parity that can be explained by application of multivariate regression analysis to data on individual married women from the Brazilian census and PNAD survey relates to modernization variables--education and average earnings. Most of the change that can be accounted for between 1970 and 1976 relates to increases in these two variables. The attempt to incorporate a variable measuring the relative economic position of urban households indicated that there was a positive association between fertility and relative economic status; that is, CEB was higher on average for women whose husbands' current earnings exceeded the level of earnings that would be expected given their education and other characteristics. However, decomposition of changes in CEB from 1970 to 1976 did not show that a change in GAP contributed to fertility decline.

These regression results do not suggest that increased modernization was the only reason for the change in Brazilian fertility. Changes in regression coefficients and in constant terms in the regression equations suggested that a variety of unmeasured factors could account for the unexplained variance. Measures that were available in the census and survey data provided little insight into the nature of such changes, whether related to increased access to contraception through public or private channels, or to institutional changes associated with shifts in the Brazilian model of socioeconomic development.

It should also be recognized that average parity is a poor measure of fertility for purposes of accounting for change. It is a cumulative variable, and comparisons of averages for different groups at different dates measure the result of a demographic process rather than the process itself. As noted above, it would have been better to use current fertility as measured by births reported for the year prior to the interview; however, as reported in Chapter 2, the performance of that measure inspired more confidence in its robustness for work with subgroups of the population. Attempts to derive other measures (such as the length of the first open birth interval) from these data files proved equally unrewarding.

Data limitations curtailed even further the analysis of differences and the decomposition of changes in the average parity of rural women. The main finding for these women was that increased educational attainment contributed most to the explanation of variance, though only a limited portion of the total variance was explained by the regressions. Some doubts were raised about the hypothesis that proletarianization contributed to fertility decline; however, caution was suggested about the validity of using data on rural women classed as proletarian at the time of the interview to test this hypothesis, rather than using the experience of the proletarianization process.

It was also impossible to link what the census and survey data reported about the demographic characteristics of individual rural residents and their families to economic characteristics of their farms and institutional features of their localities. For this reason, the study could not explore hypotheses relating fertility decline to changes in land availability, reduced need for child labor, and increased nonfarm economic activity for rural women and children. The census and survey data files did include questions on school attendance that merited further study. Information on child labor was included in agricultural censuses, but not in the demographic censuses and surveys. If Brazil is ever to conduct a fertility survey patterned after the World Fertility Survey, it would focus ideally on these elements of rural socioeconomic structure, as well as those aspects of change in urban areas that are not covered by currently available census and survey data.

PART II FERTILITY DETERMINANTS AT THE LOCAL LEVEL

CHAPTER 5

THE NIHR: PURPOSE AND METHODOLOGY

As noted in the Introduction, the discussion in this and the following chapters parallels Part I, but with a local- rather than a national-level focus. There are, of course, advantages to be gained from both: the national-level analysis permits aggregate conclusions and hypotheses, however tentative; the local-level data examined in the following pages provides another, complementary perspective on those perceptions. These chapters examine the purpose and methodology of the NIHR; levels and trends in the total fertility rate for the nine local contexts studied; and the effects of nuptiality, marital fertility patterns, the proximate determinants, and socioeconomic factors, specifically income, on fertility for the nine contexts. The final chapter shows that the national-level and the local-level conclusions are consistent.

The NIHR was conducted between May 1975 and March 1977 by Centro Basileiro de Analise e Planejamento (CEBRAP) in Sao Paulo, under the financial auspices of the International Development Research Centre (IDRC, Canada), the Population Council (USA), and Financiadora de Estudos e Projectos (FINEP, Brazil). It consists of a series of local case studies based on a view of population dynamics as part of the overall structural dynamics of society, with economic determinants (manpower requirements, forms and degrees of accumulation, property patterns, etc.) having a decisive influence. However, this dominance of socioeconomic factors over population dynamics does not operate in an obvious way. Therefore, rather than simply assuming such relations, it is essential to examine analytically and empirically how they are established. Although structures condition behavior, and behavior only exists through the actions of individuals (with their aspirations, motivations, forms of personality, individually calculated interests, etc.), the mediation between structures and action is essential. If the mediations are not taken into account, the analysis must inevitably become static. The result is the deduction of rigid prescriptions for action from structural patterns, or, at the opposite extreme, the dissolution of social conditioning factors into the subjectivity of the individual agents, so that the only way to understand human reproduction is to take a purely psychological approach. The NIHR perspective takes the role of social institutions--the Church, private enterprise, the educational system, the medical system, and so on--as being crucial to such mediation. The way population practices and values are actually realized, and population policies defined, depends on how population is seen in the context of these institutions, and how, within each one, interests and values concerning the family, number of children, procreation, and family planning are articulated.

The NIHR began by choosing the areas of Brazil that would represent as purely as possible the different forms in which the production is organized. A two-dimensional typology of the areas was then developed according to their dominant forms of production and their place in the process of development.[2] In the former category, three modes were distinguished, each of which might predominate in a given area, although in combination with the others: the capitalist mode, a system of small autonomous producers, and rural servitude. The capitalist form was subdivided into monopolistic and competitive; for the small autonomous producers, the distinction was between rural and urban. The second dimension, place in the process of development, was based on the assumption that development tends to concentrate economic activities and population in certain areas, and to disperse them in others. The former were classed as "concentration areas," which are invariably urban; the latter were labeled "dispersion areas," which as a rule comprise extractive or agricultural activities, with the formation of frontiers at the edges of an overexpanding transportation system. This classification also left room for certain areas, labeled "interstitial," which fall between the types described above, and which tend to lose activities and population; these areas may be either urban or rural.

These two dimensions could produce a total of 15 possible types. However, four of these were discarded as meaningless: the monopolistic and interstitial capitalist area; simple commodity production with an urban location in a dispersion area; simple commodity production with a rural location in a concentration area; and rural servitude in a concentration area. The monopolistic capitalist area undergoing dispersion was also discarded since it was considered highly rare in its pure state in Brazil; moreover, within a given gradient, it might appear in some regions classified as competitive-capitalist in a dispersed form. Finally, rural servitude in an interstitial form was also omitted since this combination might be found, at least partially, in regions defined as simple commodity production with a rural location and interstitial form.

The next stage of analysis consisted of making the nine remaining possibilities correspond to actual regions in Brazil. Regions were distributed both spatially and, whenever possible, according to the dual classification. The results are shown in Table 50; the contexts selected are described in detail in the Appendix. The nine areas chosen cover seven municipalities (for the sake of convenience, the rural and urban categories in the system of autonomous producers are represented by the rural and urban areas of the same municipalities, thus yielding nine area types and only seven municipalities). These municipalities are distributed over six states: Sao Paulo, Rio Grande do Sul, Pernambuco, Espirito Santo, Para, and Piaui. The map of Brazil (see page 14) gives an idea of this geographical distribution.

For each of the nine chosen areas, two types of study were performed: a macro-structural study covering the whole population of the area, and following this, a survey based on a probabilistic sample of the population in the same area.

The aim of the macro-structural study was to acquire as complete as possible a knowledge of the dynamics of the population, its socioeconomic structure, and the area's social institutions from its foundation to the present. The three components of population dynamics considered were natality, mortality, and migration. The socioeconomic factors considered essential to the study's objectives were the area's landowning structure, product mix, and predominant types of activity; the number of persons engaged in work and the types of occupations (present and previous); the duration and type of land occupation; production values and forms of appropriation of surplus; and production techniques. The study of institutions focused

TABLE 50 Nine Contexts Defined in Terms of Modes of Production and Type of Involvement in the Development Process: Brazil

Modes of Production	Insertion in Development Process		
	Concentration	Dispersion	Interstitial
Capitalism			
Monopolistic	Sao Jose dos Campos (Sao Paulo - SP)	--	--
Competitive	Recife (Pernambuco - PE)	Sertaozinho (Sao Paulo - SP)	Cachoeiro do Itapemirim (Espirito Santo - ES)
System of Autonomous Producers			
Urban	Santa Cruz do Sul (Rio Grande do Sul - RS)	--	Parnaiba (Piaui - PI)
Rural	--	Santa Cruz do Sul (Rio Grande do Sul - RS)	Parnaiba (Piaui - PI)
Rural Servitude	--	Conceicao do Araguaia (Para - PA)	--

on their role in individual reproductive decision making. The institutions considered included the economic production unit, the family, the health care system, the educational system, religious and political institutions, and the mass media. The sources of information used were secondary: censuses (demographic, industrial, and agricultural); other specialized publications containing statistical data; historical monographs; papers on research carried out previously in the same region; direct observation with qualified informants; focused interviews with people who had lived in the region for a long time; and in-depth interviews with members of the population in general.[3]

The second stage of the NIHR consisted of a fertility survey conducted in each of the nine areas, shaped by the findings of the macro-structural study. That initial study helped delineate the sample by revealing, for example, the production relations prevailing in the area; the rural proletariat and its spatial distribution, both in the countryside and on the urban outskirts of a municipality; the annual cycle of each region's range of major products, coupled with the rainy and dry seasons; and the seasonality of harvests requiring harvest workers. In-depth interviews among the population in general were another important aid in designing the survey. The sampling procedure proposed for the survey was three-stage equiprobability: the primary sampling unit was a census tract, the secondary unit a block, and the tertiary unit a household. Whenever possible, appropriate sampling fractions were determined to ensure that each household in a given region had the same probability of belonging to the sample.

A household was understood as a group of people linked by kinship, affinity, or economic relations and living under the same roof. Each was given a questionnaire consisting of three modules.

The first, known as the household module, contained information on all the members of the household, identifying them through their relation to the head of the household, as well as their age, sex, marital status, level of schooling, occupation (type of activity, position, and periodicity), monthly earnings, and consumption. In addition, there was information on help given to or received from other members of the group not living in the household, and on the division of labor within it. In rural areas, additional questions concerned the different arrangements for land tenure, types of harvest, number of animals, agricultural implements, and the like. During the interview, this information was given by any adult considered a qualified informant and a member of the household group.

The second module, a life history, was designed to obtain fundamental quantitative data for a study of reproduction strategies. Unlike most fertility studies, the NIHR was not limited to women between ages 15 and 49 in stable marital unions.[4] Any member of the household group was eligible for this module, as well as for the third, described below.[5] Some clarification is required concerning the inclusion of males in this survey. Although rarely carried out in practice, the need for this inclusion has been pointed to with some frequency in the literature since the husband's role in decision making within the family, his position on the use of contraceptives, and so on are important determinants of reproductive behavior.[6] In the NIHR, inclusion of males is justified not only for these reasons, but also for others resulting from the theoretical approach adopted: since the NIHR set out to link the forms of production to modes of reproduction, the agent most closely linked with the production process was especially important. One individual was selected at random from each household for application of the life history module and referred to thereafter as the Ego. The Ego's life history was followed from birth to the present. Information was gathered on migration, education, and occupation, as well as on the composition of and changes in the Ego's family group. The module also contained a detailed reproductive history, beginning with the menarche (for women) or earliest sexual relation (for men) and continuing up to the menopause or andropause, respectively, with information gathered on unions, duration and result of pregnancies, use of contraceptives, breastfeeding, surviving children, dates of death of nonsurvivors, and so on. If the Ego then had previous or current marital unions, the life history of the spouse was gathered in equal detail from the beginning of the union. Information given by Ego was also used to reconstruct, in less detail, the spouse's life history at three points prior to the union--at birth, age 10, and age 18.

Finally, the third module, also answered by the Ego, was aimed at obtaining transversal material to explain a number of actual practices involving the relationship between institutions and reproductive behavior. These included the existence of distinct plans or strategies regarding reproduction, help given to and received from children, and the like.

In conclusion, it should be emphasized that the NIHR was not intended as a representative national sample. Its samples are representative only in relation to the area or municipality from which they were selected. Given the characteristics of the study, it would be practically meaningless to aggregate the nine contexts to provide estimates of national-level demographic parameters. Thus the discussion that follows, while parallel to that of Part I in many ways, is quite different in focus, and serves as a complement to that analysis.

CHAPTER 6

THE TOTAL FERTILITY RATE: LEVELS AND TRENDS

Before proceeding with an analysis of the total fertility rate based on NIHR data, it is worth clarifying some points with regard to these data. The NIHR surveys were performed with the aim of covering 400 households in each area except Sao Jose dos Campos and Recife, where 800 households per area were included. As mentioned above, the information unit was any adult. However, for purposes of the following analysis, the unit will be taken as a woman, and some comments should be made in this connection.

First, it is worth noting that the information on a woman's reproductive history (contained in the life-history module) was given by the woman when she was the selected adult, or by her mate when he was selected, whether his wife was alive or not. Thus, the samples do not refer only to cohorts of women who survived until the survey, and it is not necessary to make the usual assumption that the fertility experience of women who did not survive is faithfully represented by the experience of those who did. With this in mind, whenever the reproductive history of an adult is considered, the woman may have been in any one of the following situations:

1. alive and single
2. alive and married
3. alive and separated
4. alive and widowed
5. dead and married while alive

Situations 1, 3, and 4 could only occur if the woman was the informant; situation 5 could only occur if a man was the informant; and situation 2 could occur in either case.

Second, the fact that the investigation also included single women avoided the problem of completeness involved in leaving out all childbearing experienced by women who declared they were single at the time of the survey. At the same time, it meant that, in general, the premarital experience of women ever married at the time of the survey was not eliminated.

Third, it should be stressed that in this investigation there was no cut-off age for asking questions on fertility history. Thus the data were not truncated, as usually happens when histories are not obtained for women over age 50. This means that fertility rates could be calculated for almost all age groups and for a distant past, although it must be remembered that memory problems may introduce certain difficulties.

The total fertility rates (Table 51) were established for three different points in time: 1965, 1970, and 1975. For each of these periods, the rates were calculated on the basis of the total number of women alive at that time, regardless of marital status. Thus if a woman was alive, for instance, in 1965, she was not necessarily alive in 1970 or after. Moreover, when the informant (Ego) was a husband separated from his wife during the year for which the fertility rate was calculated, this case was eliminated, since there was no way of knowing that woman's situation with regard to the number of children between the year of separation and the year of reference for calculating fertility. A further clarification is required concerning the dates of the surveys. For seven out of the nine areas, the surveys were conducted in 1976 or 1977; thus, the data for births in 1975 present no problems as to the calendar year. However, in Sao Jose dos Campos, the survey was performed from May to December 1975, and in Santa Cruz do Sul-Urban from November 1975 to July 1976. A correction was thus necessary for these two areas since the women in both were not exposed for the whole year. For Sao Jose dos Campos, the number of births in 1975 was multiplied by the factor 1.530, and for Santa Cruz do Sul-Urban by 1.045.

The first observation to be made when analyzing Table 51 is that there is some consistency between these results and those of Table 2 from Part I of this report. Indeed, the 1970 rate for Sao Jose (4.83) was consistent with that for Sao Paulo State (4.07), especially given that more than 70 percent of the latter's population was urban in 1970. Similarly, for Parnaiba-Rural, Parnaiba-Urban, and Recife, located in Northeast Brazil, total fertility as reported in Table 51 varied from 8.42 to 5.45 in 1970; the Table 2 value for the Northeast (7.58) is within this

TABLE 51 Total Fertility Rates, Nine Contexts, 1965, 1970, and 1975: Brazil

	Total Fertility Rate			Percent Decline		
Context	1965	1970	1975	1970, 1965	1975, 1970	1975, 1965
Parnaiba-Rural	8.42 (221)	7.92 (253)	8.89 (258)	5.94	+12.25	+5.58
Sao Jose dos Campos	5.83 (413)	4.83 (534)	4.03 (592)	17.20	16.56	30.87
Recife	5.45 (405)	5.38 (509)	4.90 (571)	1.28	8.92	10.09
Conceicao do Araguaia	7.18 (204)	7.26 (273)	6.46 (319)	+1.11	11.02	10.03
Parnaiba-Urban	8.21 (221)	7.76 (272)	6.09 (289)	5.48	21.52	25.82
Sertaozinho	5.74 (224)	5.67 (249)	3.68 (275)	1.22	35.10	35.89
Cachoeiro	4.68 (208)	3.48 (261)	2.97 (302)	25.64	14.66	36.54
Santa Cruz-Rural	7.28 (221)	6.07 (273)	4.52 (278)	16.62	25.53	37.91
Santa Cruz-Urban	4.35 (243)	2.54 (271)	2.92 (277)	41.61	+14.96	32.87

Note: Numbers in parentheses are number of women.

range. It should also be noted that in 1970, 58 percent of the northeastern population lived in rural areas. Finally, for Conceicao do Araguaia, a frontier area, Table 51 shows a total fertility rate of 7.26 for the same period; this is very similar to the Table 2 rate for Frontier States of 7.08.

There was a very large variation in fertility from one context to another, and this variation increased over time. In 1965, the maximum variability was about 4 children per woman, rising to 5.4 in 1970 and 6.0 in 1975. The extreme cases were always Santa Cruz do Sul-Urban, with the lowest total fertility rate, and Parnaiba-Rural, with the highest. Figure 5 (on page 37) highlights the enormous differences in fertility between these two contexts: the reproductive pattern of Santa Cruz-Urban is more like that of a European country with low fertility, while that of Parnaiba-Rural resembles a natural-fertility pattern. A further point, which also confirms the theoretical approach of the NIHR, is that the rural contexts do not necessarily have higher fertility rates than the urban contexts.

In analyzing the trends for each context, it can be seen that from 1965 to 1970, with the exception of Conceicao do Araguaia, all areas show a decline. This decline was most marked in Santa Cruz-Urban (42 percent), Cachoeiro (26 percent), Sao Jose dos Campos (17 percent), and Santa Cruz-Rural (17 percent); Parnaiba-Urban and -Rural had a slight decline of around 5 to 6 percent; and Recife and Sertaozinho had a fall of only 1.2 percent. For 1970 to 1975, the decline was much steeper, except for Parnaiba-Rural and Santa Cruz-Urban. However, the total fertility rate for the latter area in 1975 should be taken with reservations, since fluctuations in the sampling process made the specific fertility rate for women between 15 and 19 very high in 1975. For the same period, the percentage decline was consistently high, ranging from 9 percent to 35 percent; this explains the acceleration in Brazil's fertility decline of an average 24 percent. The decline in contexts located in North and Northeast Brazil--Recife, Parnaiba-Urban and -Rural, and Conceicao do Araguaia--accelerated over the 1970-75 period, rising from 9 percent to 22 percent. In 1970-75, Sao Jose dos Campos maintained the same level of decline as for 1965-70--around 17 percent. Cachoeiro showed deceleration in 1970-75 with a decline of only 15 percent, as compared to its 26 percent decline for the preceding period. For the 10 years from 1965 to 1975, it is very clear that there was a fall of over 30 percent in Sao Jose, Sertaozinho, Cachoeiro, and Santa Cruz-Urban and -Rural; Recife and Conceicaco do Araguaia maintained a fall of 10 percent; and only Parnaiba-Rural showed markedly high rates.

Another approach to changing fertility levels from 1965 to 1975 is to examine parity for women in the different contexts. Table 52 shows some of this information. To reduce the fluctuation in the sample due to the small number of cases, only average parity based on that of the 25-29 and 30-34 age brackets was calculated, with the aim of reflecting the average number of children up to 30 years of age. The drop for 1970-75 was also fairly steep--around 17 percent--for most areas, thus corroborating earlier findings.

TABLE 52 Mean Parity $1/2$ $(P_{25-29} + P_{30-34})$, 1965, 1970, and 1975: Brazil

Context	1965	1970	1975	$\frac{1970}{1965}$%	$\frac{1975}{1970}$%
Santa Cruz-Urban	2.32	1.99	1.65	14.22	17.08
Santa Cruz-Rural	2.92	3.16	2.80	+8.22	11.39
Cachoeiro	2.99	2.57	2.09	14.05	18.68
Sao Jose dos Campos	3.13	3.02	2.48	3.51	17.88
Recife	3.27	3.09	2.72	5.50	11.97
Sertaozinho	3.54	3.47	2.91	1.98	16.14
Conceicao do Araguaia	3.93	4.25	4.34	+8.14	+2.12
Parnaiba-Urban	4.44	4.33	3.58	2.48	17.32
Parnaiba-Rural	4.68	4.70	4.42	+0.43	5.96

The central question posed by the data reported above is why contexts with very different social and economic structures show such similar rates of decline, while more similar contexts show such different rates. The discussion that follows explores this question by examining the role of nuptiality and marital fertility in the fertility declines observed at the local level (Chapters 7 and 8); the role of the proximate determinants (Chapter 9); and the role of socioeconomic factors, specifically family income (Chapter 10).

CHAPTER 7

NUPTIALITY

As will be seen in the next chapter, a decline in marital fertility was the primary determinant of the fertility declines noted above. This conclusion parallels that of the national-level analysis in Part I. Before analyzing marital fertility, however, it is important to examine some other determinants related to nuptiality--the type of union and the initial, mean, and final age at marriage--that can contribute to a rise or fall in fertility.

TYPE OF UNION

Distribution of Types of Union

Table 53 shows the distribution of ever-married women from the NIHR according to type of union in three periods of time--1960, 1970, and 1975. Before this table is analyzed, some points must be made about the various types of union. During the colonial and imperial periods in Brazil, marriages were performed by the Catholic Church. In 1890, however, civil marriage was legally instituted as the only valid form of marriage. Since then, those who follow some kind of religion have continued to conduct religious marriages, either exclusively or as a complement to legal marriage. Two other types of union are present in Brazilian society: consensual union and permanent union. Both of these are also known as free unions since they are not limited by any type of binding connection, civil or religious. Both consensual and permanent unions are defined as stable: in the former, the couple live in the same house; in the latter, they do not.

Comparing the nine NIHR contexts (Table 53), for a fixed time period, say 1975, there is a great difference in the types of union, ranging from the situation in which practically all unions were legal (Santa Cruz do Sul-Urban) to the opposite extreme, in which less than 30 percent of couples legalized their unions (Parnaiba-Rural). It is also noteworthy, in the same line of thought, that in Parnaiba-Urban and -Rural, and in Conceicao do Araguaia, the category Religious Only accounted for a large number of unions; in the other contexts, free union was more common than religious union, even reaching one-third of all unions in Recife. This diversity among contexts found for 1975 can also be seen for earlier periods from at least 1960 onward, as the data in Table 53 clearly show. Indeed, in 1960 the proportion of legal unions varied from 29.9 percent in Parnaiba-Rural to 92.5 percent in Santa Cruz-Urban; between these extremes, there were intermediate figures such as 52.0 percent in Parnaiba-Urban, 63 percent in Araguaia, and 66.6 percent in Recife. What is noteworthy here, however, is that for all contexts, the main change over the 15 years analyzed consisted of a gradual decline in religious as compared with free unions. In certain contexts, this decline was smaller, as in Sao Jose and Santa Cruz-Urban; in others it was greater, as in Parnaiba-Urban and -Rural, and in Recife. In Sertaozinho, the fall in the number of religious unions was not sufficient to account for the increase found for free unions, but was partly due to a reduction in the relative weight of legal unions; the same can be said of Conceicao do Araguaia.

This relative increase in free unions as a result of a fall in either religious or legalized unions is also shown in Table 54, based on the findings of the 1960 and 1970 censuses and the 1978 PNAD (National Household Sample Survey). It should be observed that in these sources, free unions include only consensual unions; there is no explicit mention of permanent unions. From this it can be concluded that the latter have been incorporated in either the consensual or single category. Indeed, the 1970 census defined single women as follows: "those women who have not entered into any civil or religious, or civil and religious marriage, and do not live in a stable consensual union."

The data in Table 54 also lend some validity to the findings from the NIHR shown in Table 53 (which are dependent on sample fluctuations given the small number of cases): there is a great deal of similarity between the contexts (Table 53) within a particular region and the results for that same region (Table 54); in other words,

TABLE 53 Percent Distribution of Ever-Married Women, by Type of Marital Union, Nine Contexts, 1960, 1970, and 1975: Brazil

	Type of Union		Other			Total Number of Women
Context	Religious Only	Civil and Religious and Civil Only	Permanent	Consensual	Total	
Sao Jose dos Campos						
1960	3.2	89.9	0.4	6.4	6.8	249
1970	2.0	89.7	1.1	6.1	7.2	442
1975	1.4	89.8	2.5	6.1	8.6	557
Santa Cruz-Urban						
1960	4.1	92.5	0.0	3.5	3.5	172
1970	3.3	93.9	0.0	2.8	2.8	245
1975	2.9	92.0	0.7	4.3	5.0	276
Cachoeiro do Itapemirim						
1960	3.4	89.0	0.8	6.8	7.6	118
1970	2.1	89.7	1.5	6.7	8.2	194
1975	1.7	90.8	2.1	5.5	7.6	238
Santa Cruz-Rural						
1960	5.8	84.7	1.2	8.1	9.3	171
1970	4.8	86.3	1.8	6.3	8.1	269
1975	3.7	87.6	2.3	6.4	8.7	298

Parnaiba-Urban						
1960	39.2	52.0	4.1	4.1	8.2	169
1970	35.7	52.7	3.8	7.6	11.4	235
1975	32.8	53.3	3.4	10.4	13.8	268
Parnaiba-Rural						
1960	55.9	29.9	4.9	9.2	14.1	184
1970	55.1	28.5	4.9	11.0	16.3	263
1975	52.1	30.0	5.9	11.9	17.8	286
Sertaozinho						
1960	3.0	91.1	0.0	6.0	6.0	168
1970	2.2	90.4	1.3	6.1	7.4	230
1975	2.2	85.5	3.0	9.0	12.0	270
Conceicao do Araguaia						
1960	32.8	63.0	0.8	3.4	4.2	119
1970	35.0	55.4	0.4	8.9	9.3	234
1975	32.6	53.8	0.3	13.3	13.6	301
Recife						
1960	9.2	66.6	6.1	18.4	24.5	227
1970	6.3	68.3	8.3	16.8	25.1	363
1975	5.2	64.2	9.9	20.3	30.2	462

TABLE 54 Percent Distribution of Ever-Married Women, by Type of Marital Union, 1960, 1970, and 1978: Brazil

Context	Type of Union		
	Religious Only	Civil and Religious and Civil Only	Consensual
Brazil			
1960	20.2	73.4	6.4
1970	14.4	78.6	8.1
1978	8.1	81.2	10.7
Sao Paulo			
1960	5.1	92.1	2.8
1970	3.1	92.8	4.1
1978	1.7	90.3	8.0
Southern States			
1960	9.6	86.8	3.6
1970	6.2	89.7	4.1
1978	3.5	90.0	6.5
Minas Gerais/ Espirito Santo			
1960	17.9	78.9	3.2
1970	10.8	85.2	4.0
1978	5.0	89.0	6.0
Northeastern States			
1960	42.5	48.1	9.4
1970	33.1	57.6	9.3
1978	21.5	64.1	14.4

Source: Altmann and Wong (1981b).

Sao Jose dos Campos is similar to Sao Paulo, Santa Cruz do Sul to the Southern Region, and Parnaiba to the Northeastern Region. It is also noteworthy that Table 54 shows, both for the country as a whole and for the four regions, a marked increase in free unions between 1960 and 1978.

Marriage strategies can also be understood in light of the various types of union in which interviewees found themselves. Considering the nine contexts as a whole first of all, it can be seen that out of a total of 2,234 unions, the great majority--88 percent--were first unions. Of these, 71 percent were legal unions, while half of the remaining 30 percent were religious and the other half free (Table 55). It is evident that, with divorce impossible in Brazil at the time, a new civil marriage was impossible, so that among second unions, permanent and consensual unions were more frequent. Thus legal unions among second unions refer to cases where the

TABLE 55 Distribution of Unions According to Order and Type: Brazil

Type of Union	1st Union		2nd Union		3rd Union		Total	
	No.	Percent	No.	Percent	No.	Percent	No.	Percent
Religious Only	294	15.0	38	16.8	5	11.9	336	15.0
Civil and Religious and Civil Only	1,397	71.0	45	19.9	7	16.7	1,149	64.9
Permanent	116	5.9	39	17.3	9	21.4	164	7.3
Consensual	160	8.1	104	46.0	21	50.0	285	12.8
Total Number of Women	1,967	100.0	226	100.0	42	100.0	2,234	100.0
Total Percent of Women	88.0		10.1		1.9		100.0	

first legal union ended in widowhood, or the first religious or free union ended in separation.

It is immediately noteworthy that at the start of their married lives, 14 percent of women (or of men or of partners) preferred no binding connection, and 6 percent did not even choose the bond of living together. This type of preference is a focal point of the discussion in the present chapter. First, the chapter analyzes whether this kind of behavior is more common in more recent than in older unions. Next, it examines whether even the conventional rural/urban distinction differentiates this behavior. Finally, these issues will be elaborated by examining each context individually.

Table 56 shows the distribution of the total of 1967 first unions of ever-married women according to when the union occurred, that is, women married by 1960, between 1961 and 1970, and after 1970. As can be seen, more than half were older unions--before 1960--while 29.1 percent took place between 1961 and 1970; the rest were more recent unions. It is interesting to note that the preference for legal unions remained at the same level: about 71 percent of first unions were legal, irrespective of when they were initiated. Religious unions, however, gradually lost their relative position, falling from 18.4 percent for older unions to 7.3 percent for those initiated after 1970; there was also a concomitant rise in permanent and consensual unions, which together accounted for 21.3 percent of more recent unions. In other words, the points made in the analysis of Tables 53 and 54 are supported by using as a reference point whether the union is recent or not, that is, the different marriage cohorts.

A breakdown of the total sample from the nine contexts into urban and rural shows first that within both groups there is considerable similarity in the temporality of first unions. Indeed, 52 percent and 51 percent of women were married before 1960 in urban and rural contexts, respectively; for both contexts 29 percent were married between 1961 and 1970. On the other hand, some very interesting differences can be seen in both contexts in regard to types of unions and timing. As regards the preference for religious union as the first union, in urban contexts, this preference declined drastically over time, from 14.0 percent to 2.6 percent, a drop of 5.4 times (see Table 57); in the rural areas, the drop was only 1.8 times. For more recent rural marriages, religious unions represented about the same proportion (13.8 percent) as that for marriages that took place at least

TABLE 56 Distribution of Ever-Married Women by Type of First Union, for Three Marriage Cohorts: A (until 1960), B (1961-70), and C (1971-76), and for Nine Contexts: Brazil

Type of First Union	A No.	A Percent	B No.	B Percent	C No.	C Percent	Total No.	Total Percent
Religious Only	187	18.4	80	14.0	27	7.3	294	15.0
Civil and Religious, and Civil Only	273	71.1	409	71.9	265	71.4	1,397	71.0
Permanent	40	3.9	42	7.4	34	9.2	116	5.9
Consensual	67	6.6	38	6.7	45	12.1	150	8.1
Total Number of Women	1,017	100.0	569	100.0	371	100.0	1,967	100.0
Total Percent of Women	52.0		29.1		18.9		100.0	

TABLE 57 Distribution of Ever-Married Women by Type of First Union, for Three Marriage Cohorts: A (until 1960), B (1961-70), and C (1971-76), for Five Urban and Four Rural Contexts: Brazil

Type of First Union	Urban Contexts				Rural Contexts			
	A	B	C	All	A	B	C	All
Religious Only	14.0	6.0	2.6	9.6	25.2	26.6	13.8	23.4
Civil and Religious, and Civil Only	75.3	78.1	75.9	76.3	64.2	61.9	59.8	62.7
Permanent	5.1	7.7	10.0	6.8	2.0	6.7	7.2	4.4
Consensual	5.4	8.0	11.5	7.4	8.4	4.5	19.0	9.4
Total Number of Women	625	348	229	1,202	292	221	152	765
Total Percent of Women	52.0	28.9	19.1	100.0	51.2	28.9	19.9	100.0

15 years ago in urban contexts (14.0 percent). Moreover, in the rural contexts, the preference for legal unions also fell in relative terms, although less drastically. At the same time, there was a moderate rise (and a steeper one than in the urban contexts) in permanent and consensual unions as a percentage of all first unions; this reached 26.2 percent of initial preferences for more recent unions.

The next step in the analysis was to investigate how these findings operated within each context, that is, to see how the preferences for the various types of union among the total first unions developed over time. To this end, Table 58 shows the distribution of ever-married women according to the type of union, for the same three marriage cohorts. It may be noted immediately that in all contexts, there was a progressive increase in permanent and consensual unions; only Santa Cruz-Urban showed any stabilization in the proportions of permanent unions, while only in Cachoeiro did consensual unions show an increase in proportions, followed by a decrease.

In this comparison of contexts, it is highly interesting to note that in the country's poorer areas analyzed here--Parnaiba and Conceicao do Araguaia--religious unions represented a noteworthy alternative among unions occurring before 1960; indeed, they competed with legal unions in Parnaiba-Urban and overtook them in Parnaiba-Rural. A number of different reasons may explain this. First, work relations, above all in the countryside, then offered no protection in the form of social security for individuals or their families; thus no documents were required on family structure, birth of children, and so on. Another reason, somewhat related to the first, may be the fact that no property was owned that could be divided for inheritance. It is also worth mentioning the possible absence of civil registries at that time in certain areas of the country, whereas churches have always been universally present. Then, too, the continuation of the custom of religious marriage, which is so deep-seated in Northeast Brazil, represented a resistance to the new relative prominence granted the Catholic Church by the Republic. Finally, religious marriage as a first union can be seen as a forerunner of legalized union.

The relative decline of religious unions in these contexts may be due to changes in all or some of these elements. One change is undeniable: access to registries became easier with improved communications. Moreover, the fact that a legalized union entitled one to social secur-

TABLE 58 Distribution of Ever-Married Women According to Type of First Union, for Three Marriage Cohorts: A (until 1960), B (1961-70), and C (1971-76), Nine Contexts: Brazil

First Union Type	Cachoeiro			Santa Cruz-Urban			Sao Jose dos Campos			Sertaozinho			Santa Cruz-Rural		
	A	B	C	A	B	C	A	B	C	A	B	C	A	B	C
Religious Only	4.8	0.0	0.0	3.9	1.1	2.3	4.0	2.3	0.0	1.7	0.0	2.0	6.3	1.9	1.2
Civil and Religious and Civil Only	88.7	90.6	88.6	94.4	97.7	88.1	92.0	89.9	87.4	91.4	89.6	66.7	82.8	85.6	75.0
Permanent	0.8	2.3	8.6	0.0	0.0	0.0	1.8	5.5	8.1	1.1	3.9	3.9	1.7	8.6	14.6
Consensual	5.6	7.0	5.7	1.9	2.1	9.0	2.2	2.3	4.4	5.7	6.5	27.4	9.1	3.8	8.3
Total Number of Women	124	85	70	179	89	42	274	218	135	174	77	51	175	104	48

First Union Type	Recife			Parnaiba-Urban			Conceicao do Araguaia			Parnaiba-Rural		
	A	B	C	A	B	C	A	B	C	A	B	C
Religious Only	11.4	3.3	2.0	45.5	35.0	18.7	31.8	40.3	22.3	59.4	58.7	23.2
Civil and Religious and Civil Only	66.1	67.0	55.8	46.6	50.0	64.6	61.4	51.3	53.2	26.1	23.9	50.0
Permanent	8.6	13.7	18.4	4.8	7.5	8.3	0.7	0.8	2.1	5.8	8.7	8.9
Consensual	13.9	15.9	23.8	3.2	7.5	8.3	6.1	7.6	22.3	8.7	8.7	17.8
Total Number of Women	280	182	147	189	80	48	132	119	94	207	92	56

ity certainly represented a stimulus. For example, in Parnaiba, the Social Security Office performs a most important role in the life of wage-earners (Loyola, 1978), many of whom are laid off for sickness due to nervous exhaustion. They then register with the Social Security Office and, as they themselves put it, "stay on the shelf" for months or even years receiving benefits. A new supply of labor is therefore recruited to replace those laid off. When some of these fresh workers are in turn laid off sick, some who have previously been laid off are reemployed, and so on. Thus, each family group always has the possibility of one of its members being either laid off and receiving a portion of his or her wage from the government, or employed and receiving the full wage. Although this situation may seem strange, it represents an attempt to overcome the problem of poverty in the region, or to "redistribute poverty."

At the other extreme low proportions of religious unions are observed in most contexts, except unions initiated before 1960 in Recife, where this type of union still represented 11 percent of the total (Table 58). In Cachoeiro and Sao Jose dos Campos, this proportion was already low, falling to zero for more recent unions.

As for legal unions, Cachoeiro practically maintained a stable pattern (around 90 percent); Santa Cruz-Urban and -Rural, which accounted for the highest level of legal unions, saw an increase of this type of union from the first to the second cohort, mainly because of a drop in the relative importance of religious unions. In these two contexts, the decline in the relative weight of legal unions among more recent unions can be explained directly by an increase in free unions. It should be remembered that Santa Cruz do Sul is made up largely of European immigrants, mostly of German origin, who developed family-based agricultural activities and later specialized in tobacco growing. This led the urban part of the municipality to develop an industrial complex based on the processing of tobacco. The prominance of legal unions can be linked not only to cultural factors, but also to issues of property ownership and inheritance. One possible explanation of any decline in the proportion of legal unions may therefore be removal of the latter stimulus by the breaking up of these properties, already small, over the years. In Sao Jose dos Campos, where much of the working population is employed on a wage-earning basis by large and medium-sized companies, it could only be expected that legalized unions would account for a high percentage of the total number of unions.

The Role of Consensual Unions

To understand Brazilian marriage strategies, it is essential to examine the role of consensual unions more closely. Consensual union may be an option for living together when there is no stimulus for legalized union, as discussed above. To this reason should be added the far from negligible cost of a civil marriage.[8] In Parnaiba, for example, one can clearly observe the phenomenon of "marriage by seduction" (Loyola, 1978) as a strategy to avoid spending money on a civil, or even a religious, marriage. This represents a method used by women--above all those from the poorer groups within the population--to guarantee a union in a context where the male-female ratio in the 15-49 age group was only 84:100 in 1960 and 1970. Once the girl had been "seduced," her family summoned the "seducer" and demanded that he remain with the girl "to correct his error," but without a dowry or any wedding feasts or ceremonies, as a pseudo-punishment.

Consensual unions are also a solution to separations following legal or even religious unions. Indeed, up until 1978,[9] dissolutions of legal unions, even when formalized before a judge (desquite), made new civil unions impossible. The Catholic Church also does not permit a second religious union, since this bond is indissoluble according to the law of God. Thus, the only way to marry again was through a free union.

Consensual union may also result from a change in values that sees legal bonds as unnecessary. This may be especially important among the younger groups of the population, as part of a general questioning of traditional norms and values. Women's liberation has made women both more economically independent and more disposed to express their sexuality, again leading to a preference for free unions.

The preference for consensual union may reflect a definitive decision, or it may represent a preliminary stage in conjugal life prior to a legal and/or religious union. It is also probable that pregnancy may contribute to legalization in large Brazilian metropolises. However, the size of the cities included in the NIHR, such as Recife and Sao Jose dos Campos, together with the time covered by the survey (which stopped at 1977), made it impossible to support this conclusion empirically.

The issue raised here can be clarified by a brief analysis of consensual unions for each of the nine contexts. To this end, the following classification has been developed:

(1) consensual union as the only union
(2) consensual union following a legal union
(3) consensual union following a religious union
(4) consensual union prior to a legal union
(5) consensual union prior to a religious or permanent union

The study was made based on the three above-mentioned marriage cohorts, with results as shown in Table 59.

It should be noted at the start that the small number of cases for each context, except Recife, permits a merely illustrative analysis of each situation. It must also be remembered that marriage strategies are a dynamic process; thus a woman living in a consensual union at a given moment has a certain probability of legalizing it or of entering a religious union at any subsequent moment.

Sao Jose dos Campos is one context where the great majority of consensual unions represented a second or third union following a civil marriage. It thus illustrates situations (2) and (3). Out of the total of 42 cases, 16 occurred before 1960, a further 16 between 1961 and 1970, and the remaining 10 after 1970. For older consensual unions, 68.7 percent occurred as the only marriage solution after a legal union. This proportion fell to 56.3 percent for the following cohort, while for more recent unions it was 60.0 percent. The 6 cases out of 42 in which consensual union preceded a civil union took place before 1971. Of these, 3 cases involved the legalization of a consensual union, with 2 cases taking place after the birth of a child; in the other 3 cases, the legal union was with a different person. Situation (1) represented 9 cases, or 21.4 percent of the total; these 9 cases were equally distributed over the three marriage cohorts.

Parnaiba-Rural illustrates a certain balance between the types of consensual unions, with the greatest incidence for situations (4) and (5) (34.5 percent). As noted above, religious union has always been highly valued in this region, one of Brazil's poorest. Thus there were 6 cases in which a consensual union preceded a legal union and 13 in which it preceded a religious union. Of these 6 former cases, 5 were unions legalized with the same person, with 3 of these occurring after the birth of children. Of the 13 cases where religious unions followed consensual unions, 50 percent were with the same person, with the bearing of children an associated factor. In Parnaiba-Rural, it is also worth noting that 21 of the 55

TABLE 59 Distribution of Consensual Unions by Different Types, Nine Contexts: Brazil

Contexts	Consensual Union			Total Number of Women
	Only Type of Union C_1	Before a Legal and/or Religious Union C_2	After a Legal and/or Religious Union C_3	
Sao Jose dos Campos	21.4	16.7	61.9	42
Parnaiba-Rural	30.9	34.5	34.6	55
Parnaiba-Urban	39.4	24.3	36.3	33
Conceicao do Araguaia	45.6	11.1	26.7	45
Recife	50.0	19.8	30.1	146
Santa Cruz-Urban	58.3	0.0	41.7	12
Sertaozinho	75.0	6.3	18.7	32
Santa Cruz-Rural	80.8	11.6	7.6	26
Cachoeiro do Itapemirim	82.3	0.0	17.7	17

consensual unions began before 1961, meaning that they had already lasted at least 16 years; only 3 of these had occurred following a legal and/or religious union.

The picture presented by Parnaiba-Urban is to some extent parallel. Of the consensual unions prior to another union (24.3 percent), 6 cases preceded legal unions and only 2 preceded religious unions. Of the 6 former cases, 5 were with the same person, with legalization occurring after the birth of one or more children.

Santa Cruz-Rural and Sertaozinho were the contexts that showed the highest proportions of consensual unions as the only union (situation (1)); in both contexts, most of these unions occurred before 1961. Consensual union as a strategy preceding another type of union (situations (4) and (5)) was most infrequent. It was also infrequent as a solution following a separation, perhaps because the separation rates in these two rural contexts were among the lowest for the whole NIHR (12.4 percent and 18.5 percent, respectively for Santa Cruz and Sertaozinho, as compared, for example, with 34.4 percent and 39.5 percent, respectively, for Parnaiba-Rural and Recife). In Sertaozinho, there were 2 cases in which consensual union preceded a legal union, with legalization associated with the birth of a child; in Santa Cruz-Rural, there were 2 such cases.

However small the number of consensual unions in Santa Cruz-Urban and Cachoeiro, where the numerical results were subject to considerable sample fluctuation, it should be noted that these contexts showed a very similar absence of consensual unions as a stage prior to a legal union. This may simply indicate that not enough time had passed for these unions to be converted into legal marriages since, as seen above, religious unions were extremely rare in these two urban contexts. However, from the data for Cachoeiro, it can be seen that of the 14 consensual unions as only unions, 7 had already occurred by 1961, while the other 7 had occurred during the past 15 or 16 years. Thus, this is not a recent practice. The situation was analogous in Santa Cruz, where for 7 cases, 3 were older and 4 had occurred over the preceding 15 years.

The context with the highest number of consensual unions was Recife, which represents 36 percent of the total for these unions. Table 60 shows how the different consensual situations were distributed in Recife for three distinct marriage cohorts. These figures show that the first two marriage cohorts behaved in a very similar way: consensual union as the only union had a greater weight,

TABLE 60 Distribution of Consensual Unions, by Type for Three Marriage Cohorts, Recife: Brazil

	Marriage Cohort		
Consensual Union	A	B	C
Only Type of Union	44.2	42.5	61.1
Before a Legal and/or Religious Union	28.9	27.5	5.6
After a Legal and/or Religious Union	26.8	30.0	33.3
Total Number of Women	52	40	54

from 42 percent to 44 percent, while the remaining 60 percent was equally divided between the other two situations. In other words, almost 30 percent of consensual unions preceded a legal and/or religious union. For the more recent cohort, the situation is the same as regards consensual union after a nonfree union. It can therefore be seen that around 30 percent of consensual unions, irrespective of the marriage cohort, represented a solution to the problem of separation. As for consensual union preceding a nonfree union, this percentage fell considerably for the last cohort, with a resulting rise in the percentage of consensual unions as only union. This suggests that there had not been enough time for a consensual union initiated between 1971 and 1977 to be transformed into a legal and/or religious marriage. Examining the 17 cases of consensual unions preceding a legal union for the three cohorts, it can be seen that in 8 cases, legalization occurred with the same person and following the birth of a child; in 2 cases, legalization was not associated with the birth of a child.

Type of Union and Fertility

The mean number of children born in consensual unions, while lower in most instances than the means for religious and legal unions, is still significant in all nine contexts, as can be clearly seen from the data in Table 61. Except for Cachoeiro de Itapemirim and Santa Cruz do Sul-Urban, the mean number of children born per woman was greatest for women in religious only unions, followed by those in legal unions, and, lowest of all, those in consensual unions. Unfortunately, the small size of the samples makes it impossible to break down each type of union by its duration.

For this reason, although a central point of this report is variation among the contexts, it is useful to combine them in order to increase the sample size and be able to control for the duration of the union, which enhanced the study of the influence on fertility of the type of union. Table 62 shows the mean number of children for those women who had had only one union and were still married at the time of the interview. This group was chosen to avoid the problems raised by combining all the children born of different unions that might have occurred within the same period. As can be seen, there is a clear decline in the mean number of children from only religious to permanent unions for the first two marriage cohorts.

TABLE 61 Mean Number of Children Ever Born Alive by Ever-Married Women, by Type of Marital Union, Nine Contexts, 1975: Brazil

Context	Type of Union		
	Religious Only	Civil and Religious and Civil Only	Consensual
Cachoeiro de Itapemirim	2.2	3.1	3.2
Santa Cruz do Sul-Urban	3.5	2.5	3.5
Sao Jose dos Campos	4.2	3.4	1.2
Sertao Zinho	5.8	4.3	2.6
Santa Cruz do Sul-Rural	5.8	3.9	2.3
Recife	4.4	3.5	2.1
Parnaiba-Urban	5.6	5.3	3.1
Conceicao do Araguaia-Rural	4.1	3.9	2.3
Parnaiba-Rural	6.0	5.3	2.7

TABLE 62 Mean Number of Children Ever Born, for Currently Married Women (first marriage), by Type of Union and Three Marriage Cohorts, Nine Contexts: Brazil

	Marriage Cohorts						
Types of Union	Until 1960 A		From 1961-70 B		From 1971 on C		All Cohorts
Religious Only	4.6	(181)	4.4	(128)	1.9	(46)	4.2
Civil and Religious and Civil Only	4.3	(922)	3.2	(708)	1.5	(464)	3.3
Consensual	3.9	(46)	2.9	(47)	1.6	(79)	2.5
Permanent	3.4	(32)	2.7	(40)	1.6	(45)	2.5

Note: Numbers in parentheses are number of women.

However, the difference between the fertility of women who had only religious unions and those who had civil and/or religious unions tended to increase considerably for unions between 1961 and 1970. It should be noted that any conclusion about the most recent marriage cohort must be regarded with caution since this period covers 6 years at the most, and may thus include unions that lasted a very short time; in this period, a difference of, say, one year makes a considerable difference as regards fertility.

AGE AT MARRIAGE

It is valuable for the study of nuptiality and fertility to estimate some nuptiality parameters, such as initial, mean, and final age at marriage. The information used for this purpose concerns the proportion of nonsingle women and the average parity per age bracket for 1965, 1970, and 1975. The method used to adjust nuptiality patterns to the empirical data was that suggested by Coale (1971), with r_2 defined as the ratio of nonsingle women aged 15-20 to those 20-25, and r_3 the ratio of nonsingle women aged 20-25 to those 30-35. Initial age at marriage was confined to the 10-14 age bracket. The small number of cases in each context once again made it difficult to interpret the results, as shown by the data in Table 63. Indeed, these estimates fluctuate considerably from one period to another within a single context, thus restrict-

TABLE 63 Estimates for Nuptiality Parameters Using Coale's Method, Nine Contexts: Brazil

Context	Initial Age at Marriage			Mean Age at Marriage			Final Age at Marriage		
	1965	1970	1975	1965	1970	1975	1965	1970	1975
Sao Jose dos Campos	13.91	11.83	14.90	18.97	21.27	23.50	31.71	45.05	45.19
Santa Cruz do Sul-Urban	13.26	11.85	12.59	23.33	23.96	21.96	48.72	54.16	45.58
Santa Cruz do Sul-Rural	--	10.85	11.90	--	20.28	21.43	--	44.05	45.45
Parnaiba-Urban	12.04	10.92	13.62	19.68	19.10	18.48	38.96	39.71	30.72
Parnaiba-Rural	--	10.00	12.69	--	19.54	18.10	--	43.60	46.46
Sertaozinho	--	--	10.18	--	--	18.53	--	--	39.50
Conceicao do Araguaia	--	--	13.73	--	--	18.99	--	--	32.25
Cachoeiro do Itapemirim	13.83	14.35	11.69	21.46	19.49	20.32	40.71	32.44	42.05
Recife	--	12.99	12.78	--	19.86	23.44	--	37.15	50.32

Note: -- indicates sample size too small to calculate.

ing any analysis of trends. This effect of fluctuations in the samples is reduced by working with data for all the women in the household rather than just one woman per household, as has been the case until now in this discussion. In fact, this leads to a substantial increase in the size of the samples for each context; unfortunately, however, it is only feasible for the year of the investigation, for which information on all members of the household is available. Table 64 shows mean age at marriage calculated by Hajnal's method (1953), on the basis of information about single women in the households by age bracket. As can be seen, the findings for 1975-77 are generally very similar to those for the various regions of Brazil (see Table 7) in 1976; this suggests that the quality of the data is acceptable and that the fluctuations observed in Table 57 were in fact due to the small number of cases. Moreover, the effect of migration must also be present as a disturbing element in this type of analysis. All the contexts were indeed subject to migratory influxes of varying intensity and duration, affecting the contingents of men and women apt to marry.[10]

With these reservations in mind, it can be seen that the highest initial age at marriage in 1975 was found in Sao Jose dos Campos (14.9 years) and the lowest in Sertao-

TABLE 64 Mean Age at Marriage (Hajnal method), Nine Contexts: Brazil

Context	Mean Age at Marriage
Sao Jose dos Campos	23.74
Santa Cruz do Sul-Urban	25.22
Santa Cruz do Sul-Rural	23.37
Parnaiba-Urban	23.39
Parnaiba-Rural	23.47
Sertaozinho	23.42
Conceicao do Araguaia	19.64
Cachoeiro de Itapemirim	23.95
Recife	23.26

zinho (10.2 years). These extremes seem consistent with the mean for Brazil in 1976, estimated by Altmann and Wong (1981b), at 13.3 years. For the Northeastern region, the age found was 12.7 years, very close to the values for Recife (12.8) and Parnaiba-Rural (12.7). For 1970-75, even taking all the above reservations into account, it can be seen that, in general, there was a certain increase in the initial age at marriage. As regards the final age at marriage, an important index of nuptiality and closely related to the "marriage market," the larger urban centers and metropolises were the regions that most favored late marriage; this applies to Recife, Sao Jose dos Campos, and Santa Cruz do Sul-Urban, contexts in which final ages were highest in 1975. With some exceptions, it can also be said that the final age at marriage generally increased between 1970 and 1976.

It should be observed, on the other hand, that the contingent of women who remain single after a given age depends, among other things, on the availability of men "exposed to the risk" of forming a union. In 1970, the sex ratio varied considerably in the 15-49 age bracket for all the areas studied. If the information at the level of municipalities from the 1970 census is used, the sex ratios per 1,000 women aged 15-49 were as follows: Sertaozinho, 1,115; Sao Jose, 1,040; Santa Cruz, 970; Cachoeiro, 960; Parnaiba, 953; Recife, 785. The proportions of women still single in the 30-39 age bracket, as shown by the data at the household level, were, in the same order, as follows: 7.4 percent, 8.8 percent, 9.1 percent, 12.3 percent, 12.5 percent, and 14.8 percent. In other words, the higher the sex ratio, the lower the proportion of still single women.

Given the reservations mentioned above, it may be concluded from this descriptive analysis that, despite the different levels in the parameters for the various contexts, initial age at marriage is rising, mean age at marriage is also increasing, and final age at marriage has also risen. What is far less clear from these data is the timing of the changes, which makes it difficult to draw firm conclusions about how they affect fertility levels. In any case, as indicated in the following chapters, the primary factor involved in Brazil's accelerated fertility decline is declining marital fertility, traceable to changing patterns of contraceptive use.

CHAPTER 8

MARITAL FERTILITY

The total fertility rates analyzed up to this point reflect the effect of unmarried women; that is, they depend on a larger or smaller proportion of still-unmarried women in the various age brackets. In the 30-39 age bracket, the figure may be as high as 15 percent. Moreover, as noted above, this proportion varies from one context to another. Marital fertility as measured by the total marital fertility rate, the topic of the present chapter, by definition avoids this effect. Table 65 shows total marital fertility rates for 1970 and 1975. In 1970, they varied from 3.70 to 9.61, and in 1975 from 2.96 to 9.64. In both cases, the lowest figure is for Santa Cruz do Sul-Urban, and the highest for Parnaiba-Urban and -Rural. As can be seen, except for Parnaiba-Rural, marital fertility declined in all contexts between 1970 and 1975. The largest decline was registered for Sertaozinho (as noted above in the comparison of total fertility rates). In those populations where birth control is not practiced, the natural marital fertility pattern after 25 years of age is shown by a convex curve that drops slowly until age 35, and then falls abruptly to reflect the steep decrease in the proportion of fertile women. On the other hand, in populations that voluntarily control fertility, the rapid decline in marital fertility rates at early ages results in greatly reduced levels of fertility at the age of 30, giving the curve a concave shape. Thus, the decline in world fertility levels involves a transition from a structural pattern represented by a convex curve to a new pattern represented by a concave curve. In Brazil, this transition can be seen in both high-fertility and low-fertility regions.

This transition can be seen from Figure 6 (see page 40) by comparing the marital fertility curves representing

TABLE 65   Total Marital Fertility Rates, Nine Contexts, 1970 and 1975: Brazil

Context	Total Marital Fertility Rate		Percent Decline $\frac{1975}{1970}$
	1970	1975	
Parnaiba-Rural	9.41 (228)	9.64 (243)	+ 2.44
Sao Jose dos Campos	6.35 (417)	5.26 (520)	17.25
Recife	7.26 (386)	6.37 (472)	12.31
Conceicao do Araguaia	8.17 (231)	7.09 (292)	13.26
Parnaiba-Urban	9.61 (231)	7.46 (245)	22.45
Sertaozinho	6.69 (223)	4.72 (248)	29.42
Cachoeiro	5.32 (197)	4.16 (250)	21.76
Santa Cruz-Rural	6.68 (225)	5.98 (245)	10.46
Santa Cruz-Urban	3.70 (218)	2.96 (234)	20.02

Note: Numbers in parentheses are number of women.

the six contexts with highest and lowest fertility levels in the NIHR. The curve for Brazil as a whole represents the middle point in the transition from a high level--as in the case of Parnaiba-Rural (with a roughly convex curve)--to a low level--as in the case of Cachoeiro de Itapemirim (with a distinctly concave curve). These differing marital fertility patterns reflect varying distances from a natural-fertility pattern. Such distances occur in a typical manner and, according to Coale, can be measured through the parameter "m," known as the degree of fertility control, or how far fertility practice has moved away from natural fertility as a result of the use of contraceptives and abortion.

The degrees of control estimated for the nine regions in 1970 and 1975 are shown in Table 66. As can be seen, in both 1970 and 1975, the greatest degrees of control were in Santa Cruz do Sul-Urban and Cachoeiro de Itapemirim; in 1975, the value for the latter was higher than for the former. The lowest levels of control were in Parnaiba-Urban and -Rural and Conceicao do Araguaia. The evolution over time of these parameters shows that there was a clear increase in fertility control for all regions.

TABLE 66 Values for the Fertility Control Measure (m) Estimated by Coale's Method, 1970 and 1975: Brazil

Context	1970	1975
Sao Jose dos Campos	0.7495	1.1792
Santa Cruz do Sul-Urban	1.9284	1.3880
Santa Cruz do Sul-Rural	0.0451	0.6624
Parnaiba-Urban	-0.2444	0.2220
Parnaiba-Rural	0.0486	0.2361
Sertaozinho	--	1.2004
Conceicao do Araguaia	--	0.1487
Cachoeiro de Itapemirim	0.6604	1.4547
Recife	0.0520	0.6721

Note: -- indicates sample size too small to calculate.

The exception was Santa Cruz do Sul-Urban, which already had fairly high levels, where the degree of control fell from 1.9 to 1.4. This decrease was probably the main factor leading to that region's increase in the total fertility rate from 2.5 to 2.9 children between 1970 and 1975.

The variations in fertility levels between 1970 and 1975 can be clarified by comparing them with the nuptiality parameters and degrees of control for the same period. In the case of Sao Jose, for example, the drop in fertility was from 4.8 to 4.0 children between 1970 and 1975; this is associated with an increase in the degree of control from 0.7 to 1.2, and with an increase in mean age at marriage and initial age at marriage from 21.2 to 23.5 and 11.83 to 14.90 years of age, respectively.

CHAPTER 9

THE PROXIMATE VARIABLES

The factors that directly influence fertility and together determine its level--the so-called proximate variables--can be grouped as follows, according to Bongaarts (1983):

a) exposure to regular sexual relations
   - proportion of married women
b) prevalence of deliberate control of marital fertility
   - use and efficiency of contraceptives
   - prevalence of induced abortion
c) determinants of natural marital fertility
   - duration of postpartum infecundity
   - fecundity
   - spontaneous intrauterine mortality
   - prevalence of permanent sterility

However, not all these factors have the same impact in determining discrepancies between natural fertility and the total fertility rates observed in a given context. In fact, the proportion of married women, the use and efficiency of contraceptives, the prevalence of induced abortion, and the duration of postpartum infecundity account in general for over 95 percent of those discrepancies; the effects of the remaining three factors are difficult to measure in such studies as fertility surveys. Postpartum infecundity depends in turn on the length of sexual abstention following delivery and on the duration of breastfeeding. In Latin America, prolonged abstinence is not as common a practice as it is in some African and Asian countries. As can be seen in Table 67, in the NIHR, a limited number of women declared they abstained. On the other hand, what does still exist among some groups of women of rural origin is "postpartum quarantine" or "re-

TABLE 67 Currently Married Women Aged 15-49 Currently Using Contraception, by Types of Methods, Nine Contexts: Brazil

Methods Used	Sao Jose dos Campos	Santa Cruz-Urban	Santa Cruz-Rural	Parnaiba-Urban	Parnaiba-Rural	Sertao-zinho	Cachoeiro de Araguaia	Cachoeiro de Itapemirim	Recife
Foam/Cream/Jelly	1.8	1.7	--	3.6	2.9	1.6	4.2	3.5	9.7
Diaphragm	--	--	--	--	--	--	--	--	--
Rhythm	11.9	11.2	29.3	14.5	8.8	4.0	5.7	7.6	13.5
Coitus Interruptus	4.3	--	5.2	1.8	--	20.6	1.4	0.7	4.3
Condom	8.3	1.7	0.2	1.8	--	1.6	--	0.7	2.2
IUD	1.4	--	--	--	--	--	1.4	1.3	0.5
Pill	60.8	75.0	44.8	36.4	29.4	60.3	38.0	57.2	30.7
Sterilization	8.3	10.4	16.4	30.9	55.9	8.7	46.5	27.6	37.1
Abstention	1.4	--	2.3	5.5	2.9	3.2	1.4	0.7	0.5
Other	1.8	--	--	5.5	--	--	1.4	0.7	1.5
Total	100.0	100.0	100.0	100.0	100.0	100.0	100.0	100.0	100.0
Number of Cases	278	116	133	55	34	126	71	145	186

clusion," referring to a period when diet, bodily hygiene, and sexual practices are carefully controlled. Given these complications, in this section the duration of postpartum infecundity is measured exclusively by the duration of breastfeeding.

In the terms of the Bongaarts index, described in Chapter 1, the values for the marriage rate, C_m in each of the nine NIHR contexts were the following:

Cachoeiro de Itapemirim	0.648
Santa Cruz-Urban	0.710
Sao Jose dos Campos	0.657
Sertaozinho	0.842
Santa Cruz-Rural	0.698
Recife	0.651
Parnaiba-Urban	0.766
Conceicao do Araguaia	0.777
Parnaiba-Rural	0.832

The subsections below discuss the NIHR in relation to the other three primary proximate determinants: noncontraception use (C_c), postpartum infecundability (C_i), and abortion (C_a).

CONTRACEPTIVE USE

Contraceptive Prevalence

The NIHR registered greatly varying levels of contraceptive use in the various contexts. Parnaiba-Urban and -Rural--an area which, as noted in the Appendix, has been occupied for a long time and now has a practically stagnant economy--was shown to have the lowest fertility rates consistently, and it is this area which registered the lowest proportion of contraceptive use. These proportions are far from negligible, however: indeed, of every five women in Parnaiba-Rural who were married at the time of the survey, one was using some contraceptive method. In Conceicao do Araguaia, this proportion reached almost 30 percent, while in the other contexts it was over 50 percent. If these proportions are compared with those obtained by the Contraceptive Prevalence Surveys (CPS), described in Chapter 1 of this report, there is a high degree of consistency among some of the available results. For the state of Piaui, except for the capital, the CPS showed a contraceptive use rate for 1979 of around 28.8

percent, very close to the value obtained by the NIHR for Parnaiba-Urban (27.7 percent), as shown in column 1 of Table 68. The CPS rate for Recife in 1980 was 51.5 percent using contraceptives, while the NIHR rate was 57.5 percent. Similarly, in Santa Cruz do Sul-Urban, the CPS showed 63.0 percent of married women using contraception; this value was very close to that found by Etges (1976), in 1975 for Rio Grande do Sul (64.6 percent). On the other hand, attention should be paid to the very high rates found in the NIHR for Sao Jose dos Campos (74.9 percent) and Sertaozinho (69.2 percent), when compared with the data for Sao Paulo found by Nakamura et al. (1979), in 1978 (63.4 percent for the municipality of Sao Paulo, and 58.6 percent for the rest of the state). Even when the NIHR rates were estimated as an average of age-specific use rates (column 2, Table 68), Sao Jose still had a high rate of 71.9 percent, and the rate for Sertaozinho remained unaltered. Since there is as yet no reason to suppose that these two contexts constitute special cases in the use of contraceptives as compared with other parts of Sao Paulo state, it is probable that the NIHR has overestimated the proportions of contraceptive use. For the purposes of all the following calculations, therefore, the proportions of contraceptive use for Sao Jose and Sertaozinho adopted were, respectively, 63.4 percent and 58.6 percent.

TABLE 68 Currently Married Women Aged 15-49 Currently Using Contraception, Nine Contexts: Brazil

Context	Currently Using (percent)	Average of Age-Specific Use Rates	Number of Cases
Sao Jose dos Campos	74.9	71.9	475
Santa Cruz-Urban	63.0	60.6	219
Santa Cruz-Rural	58.3	54.3	242
Parnaiba-Urban	27.7	27.7	220
Parnaiba-Rural	20.7	19.6	207
Sertaozinho	69.2	69.3	224
Conceicao do Araguaia	29.6	29.1	274
Cachoeiro do Itapemirim	69.9	64.5	229
Recife	57.5	52.0	348

The data used as a basis for calculating average age-specific use rates showed that control was differential according to age but existed for all ages. Evidently, when observing this fact by age bracket, caution should be the rule given the extremely small number of women in each bracket. To provide a more complete idea of what may be happening in the urban areas of Brazil, the information on all five urban contexts has been combined by age bracket. As was done in Chapter 8, this is a device to increase the size of the samples, for as already stressed at the outset, it is contrary to the very objective of the NIHR to aggregate situations as distinct as these. The relevant figures are thus the following:

Age	Percent Use
15-19	48.1
20-24	62.0
25-29	71.6
30-34	71.6
35-39	64.3
40-44	53.1
45-49	26.8
Mean value	56.8

In other words, 48 percent of young couples living in urban areas are already regulating fertility. The maximum use rate is in the 25-29 and 30-34 age brackets, with the proportion falling thereafter. Proceeding the same way for the rural contexts, a lower overall mean value of 45.5 percent is obtained. For the different age brackets, the rural use rates are as follows:

Age	Percent Use
15-19	30.7
20-24	50.4
25-29	55.8
30-34	53.4
35-39	46.9
40-44	44.0
45-49	37.5
Mean value	5.5

Contraceptive Methods

Table 67 shows the methods used by those women who were resorting to contraception. Such devices as the IUD and diaphragm were practically absent from all nine contexts. There were four main methods: rhythm, coitus interruptus, the pill, and female sterilization. In Santa Cruz-Urban, Cachoeiro, and Sao Jose dos Campos, 85.4 percent, 84.8 percent and 78.1 percent of women, respectively, used highly efficient methods (the pill or sterilization, with the highest proportion for the pill). In Conceicao do Araguaia and Parnaiba-Rural, 84.5 percent and 85.4 percent of women, respectively, were using the pill or tubal sterilization (with a higher proportion for the latter). The remaining five contexts showed proportions for use of these two methods ranging from 61 percent to 69 percent; in Recife, female sterilization took the place of the pill. In sum, the more traditional methods have already lost ground to more modern and efficient methods. One interesting fact is the 8.3 percent figure for use of the condom in Sao Jose dos Campos, whereas this method has practically disappeared in the other contexts; this may reflect the presence of large numbers of immigrants who had arrived in Sao Jose over the years immediately preceding the survey. Similarly, the high proportion of women using the rhythm method in Santa Cruz-Rural may be explained by the fact that most of the population is of German extraction, and thus influenced by the European tradition. The fact that vaginal methods only appeared significantly in Recife is another noteworthy point.

Although the NIHR samples were small and the proportions of women sterilized at the time of the survey were therefore subject to considerable sample fluctuations, the growth of this practice can also clearly be seen in the results of the CPS, as reported in Chapter 1. One noteworthy fact about the age distribution of married women who were sterilized at the time of the NIHR (Table 69) is that in Cachoeiro, Conceicao do Araguaia, and Parnaiba-Rural, 50 percent or more were age 34 or younger, while in Araguaia, 15 percent had not yet reached the age of 25. What is surprising in all this is the fact that female sterilization is illegal in Brazil. The Medical Code of Ethics, Chapter VI, "On Medical Responsibility," article 52, states:

TABLE 69 Age Distribution of Currently Married, Sterilized Women Aged 15-49, Nine Contexts: Brazil

Age Group	Santa Cruz-Urban	Sertaozinho	Parnaiba-Urban	Recife	Cachoeiro do Itapemirim	Conceicao do Araguaia	Santa Cruz-Rural	Parnaiba-Rural	Sao Jose dos Campos
15-19	0.0	0.0	0.0	0.0	0.0	0.0	0.0	0.0	0.0
20-24	0.0	0.0	0.0	1.4	2.5	15.2	4.5	5.3	13.0
25-29	0.0	9.1	5.9	26.1	22.5	27.3	18.2	26.3	8.7
30-34	16.7	9.1	29.4	18.8	20.0	24.2	13.6	26.3	8.7
35-39	41.7	27.3	23.5	39.1	35.0	6.1	22.7	31.6	39.2
40-44	8.3	18.2	23.5	11.6	17.5	15.2	27.3	5.3	13.0
45-49	33.3	26.3	17.7	2.9	2.5	12.1	13.6	5.3	17.4
Number of Women	12	11	17	69	40	33	22	19	23

Sterilization is condemned, but may be practised in exceptional cases, when there is a precise indication approved by two medical doctors consulted in conference.

Aside from the few cases in which a woman's health problems lead to the advisability of sterilization, the marked increase in tubal sterilization among Brazil's female population may be the result of two factors.

The first is a consequence of the misuse of caesareans over recent years; this has been stimulated by the INAMPS (National Health and Welfare Service) through higher remuneration for this kind of operation than for normal delivery. Official data show that from 1971 to 1980 in Brazil, the proportion of caesareans to total deliveries rose from 14.6 percent to 29.3 percent. The rates for Sao Paulo over the same period rose from 17.5 percent to 36.0 percent, and similar increases occurred in practically all the Brazilian states.[11] A study performed in Ribeirao Preto, Sao Paulo state, concerning standards of assistance for deliveries showed that in 1972, 1973, and 1974, 18.1 percent, 23.0 percent, and 24.1 percent of hospital deliveries, respectively, were caesareans (<u>Boletin de la Oficina Sanitaria Panamerican</u>, 1978). Recent data on Greater Sao Paulo and Greater Recife permit a comparison between the type of delivery of the latest and penultimate children born to mothers who gave birth over the last 8 months (Berquo, 1981). The results for Greater Recife show that 14 percent of deliveries of the penultimate child were caesareans, while the rate is 27 percent for the latest child. In addition, 11 percent of these mothers gave birth by caesarean in both cases. For greater Sao Paulo, 21 percent of deliveries were caesareans for the penultimate child and 31 percent for the latest, while 17 percent of these mothers had given birth by caesarean in both cases. It is well known that any woman who has already had two or three caesareans is a sure candidate for sterilization. The policy adopted by INAMPS has thus increased women's chances of being sterilized. Nowadays, in fact, doctors receive the same remuneration whether a delivery is normal or caesarean; nevertheless, it seems that the doctors themselves have grown accustomed to caesarean deliveries and thus continue persuading pregnant women to accept them, with a continuing effect on sterilization levels.

The second factor which may determine the marked increase in tubal sterilization is linked to the non-official family planning programs underway in Brazil. As noted in Chapter 3, physicians in private practive have been making more frequent use of public facilities to perform sterilizations even though use is not officially promoted. If this were not so, given the legislation mentioned earlier, these results would not be occurring and affecting even very young women, as seen in the data shown here.

Bongaarts' Index of Contraception

In calculating the Bongaarts contraception index (C_c = 1 - S x E x U), described in Chapter 1, the values for "U" are already available in the second column of Table 68. Values for "E" in any given context are calculated by adding the products of the values in Table 63 and the weights which correspond to each of the methods in accordance with its efficiency:

Methods	Contraceptive Efficiency
Foam/Cream Jelly	0.87
Diaphragm	0.88
Rhythm	0.82
Condom	0.91
IUD	0.96
Pill	0.98
Sterilization	1.00
Abstention	1.00
Other	0.90

Values for "E" thus calculated are shown in Table 70. If "U", "E", and "S" are replaced in the formula for C_c by their respective values, the results obtained are as shown in Table 71.

As can be seen, the degree of control is greatest in Cachoeiro de Itapemirim, followed by Sao Jose and Santa Cruz do Sul-Urban. The lowest values of C_c are for Conceicao do Araguaia and Parnaiba-Urban and -Rural. In other words, these results confirm the findings obtained when "m" was calculated by Coale's method. The relation between the values for C_c and total fertility is also very clear: that is, the lower the value for C_c, the lower the total fertility rate.

TABLE 70 Estimates (in percent) for Use Efficiency of Contraceptives (e), for Currently Married Women, Nine Contexts: Brazil

Method	Parnaiba-Urban	Parnaiba-Rural	Sertaozinho	Conceicao do Araguaia	Cachoeiro do Itapemirim	Recife	Sao Jose dos Campos	Santa Cruz do Sul-Urban	Santa Cruz do Sul-Rural
Abstention	5.50	2.90	3.20	1.40	0.70	0.50	1.40	0.00	2.30
Sterilization	30.90	55.90	8.70	46.50	27.60	37.10	8.30	10.40	16.40
Oral	35.77	28.81	59.09	37.24	56.06	30.09	61.78	73.50	43.90
IUD	0.00	0.00	0.00	1.34	1.25	0.48	2.36	0.00	0.00
Condom	1.64	0.00	1.46	0.00	0.64	2.00	7.55	1.55	0.18
Diaphragm	0.00	0.00	0.00	0.00	0.00	0.00	0.00	0.00	0.00
Foam/jelly/cream	3.13	2.52	1.39	3.65	3.05	8.44	1.60	1.50	0.00
Rhythm	11.89	7.22	3.28	4.67	6.32	11.07	9.80	9.18	24.03
Others	6.57	0.00	18.54	1.26	1.26	4.77	4.90	0.00	4.68
Values of e	95.3	97.35	95.66	96.06	96.88	95.26	97.69	96.13	91.76

TABLE 71 Index of Contraception, Nine Contexts: Brazil

Context	Value of C_c
Cachoeiro do Itapemirim	.312
Sao Jose dos Campos	.316
Santa Cruz-Urban	.360
Sertaozinho	.381
Santa Cruz-Rural	.450
Recife	.457
Parnaiba-Urban	.710
Conceicao do Araguaia	.693
Parnaiba-Rural	.791

Postpartum Infecundability

Before the 1960s, almost no studies on breastfeeding in Brazil were carried out. Rea (1981) presents a table, reproduced here (Table 72), which gives a good idea of the Brazilian breastfeeding situation. These data show considerable variability depending on the region and living standard. The author does, however, emphasize that comparison in this case should be approached with caution since the information and/or methodologies involved are mostly heterogeneous.

As noted in Chapter 5, the phenomenon of early weaning exists in today's Brazil, as it also does in a number of other Latin American countries (Lesthaeghe et al. 1981). On the local level, a recent study conducted by UNICEF/INAM/CEBRAP (Berquo et al. 1981) in the metropolitan areas of Sao Paulo and Recife showed a very low average time for breastfeeding for mothers in both areas. Unbiased estimates of the average duration of natural breastfeeding can be made using the calculation technique known as the current status method, based on the proportions of children in each age group who were being breastfed at the time of the interview (Jain and Bongaarts, 1981). The average time for Greater Sao Paulo was 3

TABLE 72 Percent of Breastfed Children at 4 Months of Age, by Various Studies: Brazil

Location	Year	Percent	Remarks
Recife (PE)	1968	5.8	>3 months
Sao Paulo (SP)	1971	72.0	immigrants
Sao Paulo (SP)	1973	31.6	low-income
Ribeirao Preto (SP)	1974	39.3	
Salvador (BA)	1974	38.9	
Rio de Janeiro (RJ)	1974	25.0	
Pelotas (RS)	1974	16.0	
Icapara (SP)	1975	78.8	3 months, rural
Vale do Ribeira	1975	75.0	3 months, rural
Salvador (BA)	1975	45.0	>3 months
Getulina and Guaiembe (SP)	1975	89.5	Japanese extraction, 3 months
Campinas (SP)	1976	35.3	
Austin (RJ)	1977	54.0	
Paulinea (SP)	1977	40.0	
Sorocaba (SP)	1978	30.0	>3 months
Botucatu (SP)	1978/79	50.7	3 months, medical post, school
Sao Paulo (SP)	1979	41.9	low-income
Sao Mateus (SP)	1980	13.0	working-class district
Greater Sao Paulo (SP)	1981	38.0	
Greater Recife (PE)	1981	25.0	

Source: Rea (1981).

months, and for Greater Recife 2.2 months. Even considering that this study included mothers of children no more than 8 months old at the time of the interview and thus truncated the distribution with regard to higher breastfeeding times, these values are very low. Between the first and second month, 42 percent of children in Recife and 53 percent in Sao Paulo had already been weaned.

The fact that women in Recife breastfeed for less time than those in Sao Paulo had already been highlighted by Puffer and Serrano (1973) at the time of the Interamerican Study on Childhood Mortality, conducted between 1968 and 1970. This survey showed that of the children who died in their first year, the proportion breastfed for one month was 26.8 percent and 35.5 percent for the municipalities of Recife and Sao Paulo, respectively; the proportion of breastfed children who died at ages 6-11 months or over was 1.4 percent and 4.1 percent for Recife and Sao Paulo, respectively. Although the data presented by Puffer and Serrano refer to children who had already died at the time of the study and thus to some extent underestimated the breastfeeding times, they nevertheless indicate the regional differences involved.

In 1975, working with 593 families in the Vale do Ribeira (coastal region of Sao Paulo state) having a total of 1,005 children under 5 years, Rea (1981) found 14.6, 7.4, and 5.8 months to be the mean breastfeeding times, respectively, for mothers born in the Vale region, other regions of Sao Paulo state, or other states. For the NIHR contexts, the mean breastfeeding times were as follows:[12]

Cachoeiro de Itapemirim	8.5 months
Conceicao do Araguaia	8.5 months
Sertaozinho	7.3 months
Parnaiba-Rural	6.3 months
Sao Jose dos Campos	6.0 months
Santa Cruz-Rural	5.5 months
Parnaiba-Urban	4.8 months
Santa Cruz-Urban	4.2 months
Recife	3.3 months

On the basis of these values, Bongaarts' index of postpartum infecundability (C_i) was calculated. In the NIHR survey, as usually occurs in surveys of this kind, there are no reliable data on the postpartum amenorrhea period, that is, on "i." For this reason, the model put forward by Bongaarts (1983) was used, which establishes an exponential relation between "i" and the mean duration of breastfeeding, here represented by B:

$$i = 1.753 \exp(.1396B - 0.001872B^2).$$

If B is replaced by the values found for mean breastfeeding times, the values shown in Table 73 are obtained for "i" and C_i. Since C_i is 1 in the complete absence of lactation or of postpartum abstinence and tends toward zero as the duration of postpartum infecundity increases, it can be seen that Cachoeiro and Conceicao do Araguaia showed the highest intervals for postpartum amenorrhea, while Recife showed the lowest.

TABLE 73 Values of "i" and C_i, Nine Contexts: Brazil

Context	Value of "i" in Months	Value of C_i
Cachoeiro do Itapemirim	5.0	0.850
Conceicao do Araguaia	5.0	0.850
Sertaozinho	4.4	0.873
Parnaiba-Rural	3.9	0.892
Sao Jose dos Campos	3.8	0.897
Santa Cruz-Rural	3.6	0.906
Parnaiba-Urban	3.3	0.918
Santa Cruz-Urban	3.0	0.928
Recife	2.7	0.942

ABORTION

The information on abortion in the NIHR covers both spontaneous and deliberate abortion, for the same reasons as those alleged in the majority of surveys on human reproduction: the questionable credibility of replies to questions intended to identify the two separately when the survey itself has not been specifically designed to study abortion. With the information available, total abortion rates (TAR) were calculated (Table 74). These rates were extremely variable from one context to another. The rate for Santa Cruz-Urban was only 9.2 percent of that for Parnaiba-Rural. In Santa Cruz-Urban and -Rural, abortion was practiced little, with Cachoeiro next in frequency. Sao Jose, Sertaozinho, and Recife had much higher and very similar rates. Parnaiba had the highest rate of all, though lower for urban than for rural women. To calculate C_a, the total fertility rates were taken from Table 51 and values for "u" from Table 62. Values for C_a (Table 74) were all very high, and close to 1. Thus, although this practice is underway in Brazil and involves many thousands of women, in overall calculations of fertility control it is of secondary importance.

TABLE 74 Total Abortion Rates (TAR) and Bongaarts' Abortion Rate (C_a), Nine Contexts: Brazil

Context	TAR	C_a
Cachoeiro do Itapemirim	0.719	0.963
Santa Cruz-Urban	0.068	0.985
Sao Jose dos Campos	0.462	0.931
Sertaozinho	0.454	0.942
Santa Cruz-Rural	0.104	0.987
Recife	0.478	0.947
Parnaiba-Urban	0.617	0.953
Conceicao do Araguaia	0.263	0.983
Parnaiba-Rural	0.735	0.967

CHAPTER 10

SOCIOECONOMIC FACTORS: FAMILY INCOME

As pointed out in Chapter 5, the fertility rates observed for each of the nine NIHR contexts varied considerably. Succeeding chapters showed that, at least at this level of analysis, a variety of reproduction strategies have been adopted by the populations of the different contexts. The present chapter incorporates into the analysis the socioeconomic variables. Among these, family income appears to have distinctive importance and is the focus of the discussion that follows.

The analysis below is limited to the urban contexts since it addresses only monetary income. Families have been classified in four categories, depending on their per capita monthly income at the time of the survey (between 1975 and 1977):

(1) up to one-half the minimum wage[13]
(2) between one-half and one minimum wage
(3) between one and two times the minimum wage
(4) over twice the minimum wage

This variable has been incorporated into the analysis according to its equivalent at the particular moment of the time of interview; this precaution was taken since the information concerned was not taken from the individual life histories, but from data included in the form dealing with the domestic group. Although this disparity makes interpretation of the results somewhat problematic, the present analysis is only preliminary; later research will be able to incorporate variables from the life histories.

The distribution of families according to income (Table 75) varies considerably from one context to the next. On the one hand, Santa Cruz, Cachoeiro, and Sao Jose dos Campos are somewhat similar, showing a degree of equili-

TABLE 75 Percent Distribution of Women Aged 15 Years
and Over, by Per Capita Monthly Income (in fractions of
one minimum wage), Five Urban Contexts, at Time of
Survey: Brazil

Context	Up to 1/2 Min. Wage	Between 1/2 and One Min. Wage	Between One and Two Times Min. Wage	Over Twice Min. Wage
Santa Cruz-Urban	21.0	30.9	24.0	24.0
Cachoeiro do Itapemirim	22.9	31.0	24.4	21.7
San Jose dos Campos	25.1	29.3	21.6	24.0
Recife	42.9	23.3	17.4	16.3
Parnaiba-Urban	70.3	16.5	5.9	7.2

brium among the four income groups, though the group between one-half and one minimum wage has a slightly greater relative weight. In the Northeast, however, this equilibrium gives way to an asymmetrical distribution with a heavy concentration in the lowest bracket. In Recife, 42.9 percent of the families sampled fell into the first income category; an even more striking picture is presented by Parnaiba, where 70.3 percent of the families sampled fell within the per capita income bracket defined as up to half the minimum wage. These data reflect the variations in economic development among the nine contexts described in the Appendix.

With regard to Recife, as pointed out in the Appendix, the city's labor force has been characterized over recent decades by intense fluctuations between employment, unemployment, odd jobs, and various kinds of urban underemployment. The evolutionary rate for hiring of employees and dismissals in the metropolitan region of Recife for the period 1978-79 gives some idea of this fluctuation: in industry, the number of workers hired fell from 170 to 166, while the number of those dismissed rose from 150 to 194; in the service branch, while there was a rise in hirings from 118 to 128, dismissals also rose, from 113 to 125 (FIDEPE, 1980). Moreover, there can be no doubt about the underpayment of the labor force as a determinant of the poverty that dominates the Northeast of Brazil; even in the metropolitan region, 24 percent of all occupied persons work 56 hours or more per week.

As will be remembered, the urban economy of Parnaiba is linked to a subsistence- or peasant-based economy centered on the large estates (latifundia), and mercantile or commodity relations have penetrated very little. The town is a collection and distribution center for products of plant extraction. It also has a small manufacturing branch that employs a very limited number of people--around 18 percent of the local labor force in full-time employment, while most of its production is put out to domestic or self-employed workers. As regards commerce, here, too, 95 percent of active workers are self-employed. Income from these activities is too low for subsistence, and it thus becomes necessary to combine extractive, industrial, and commercial activities and handicrafts. The bottom line of Table 75 clearly reflects this picture, characterized by a small contingent of families integrated into a formal market, with the majority engaged in occasional or irregular activities.

An analysis of female fertility for each of the five urban contexts and the four income groups yields some interesting observations. Table 76 shows the average number of children born to ever-married women 15 years of age or over who, at the time of the survey, came within a given income bracket.

This table shows, first, that in all the contexts surveyed, fertility decreases as per capita monthly income rises. In Santa Cruz do Sul, it makes little difference whether a woman belongs to the first or second income bracket; the greatest decrease is for families with per capita monthly income of over one minimum wage. In Sao Jose dos Campos, virtually the same picture holds true, although the coloring is somewhat more vivid. In Recife, however, it does make a difference in the average number of children whether a woman's family has a monthly income of between one-half and one minimum wage: compared with the first bracket, the decrease in fertility is around 30 percent. Unfortunately, it was impossible to assess the evolution of fertility for all four income groups in Parnaiba because of the extremely low number of women in the two higher brackets; for the two lower groups, however, there was a drop of 24 percent in the average number of children.

Second, the table shows that, even when a given income category is kept fixed, the various contexts show different levels of fertility: Santa Cruz do Sul and Parnaiba are at one extreme of a slope, especially as regards the first bracket, while Recife, Cachoeiro do Itapemirim, and Sao Jose dos Campos, with some small discrepancies among themselves, form an intermediate group. This variation in the average number of children per woman, which reaches its peak--2.49--for the poorest families, drops in a uniform manner until it reaches 0.32 for the bracket over

TABLE 76 Average Number of Children Born to Ever-Married Women Aged 15 and Over, by Per Capita Monthly Income (in fractions of one minimum wage), Five Urban Contexts: Brazil

Urban Contexts	(1) Up to 1/2 Min. Wage	(2) Between 1/2 and 1 M. W.	(3) Between 1 and 2 Times Min. Wage	(4) Over Twice M. W.	Percentage Decrease			
					(2)/(1)	(3)/(2)	(4)/(3)	(4)/(1)
Santa Cruz do Sul	3.37	2.96	2.29	1.74	12	23	27	50
Recife	4.28	3.05	3.33	1.87	30	10	43	56
Cachoeiro	4.39	3.38	2.47	2.06	21	27	16	53
Sao Jose dos Campos	4.97	4.23	2.94	1.94	16	32	35	62
Parnaiba	5.86	4.49	--	--	24	--	--	--
Maximum Difference	2.49	1.53	1.04	0.32				

twice the minimum wage. If Parnaiba is eliminated from the comparison (since the reduction in the variation may be influenced by the fact that Parnaiba is not represented in the two higher income brackets), the maximum difference between the contexts for the four brackets would then be, respectively, 1.60, 1.27, 1.04, and 0.32. In other words, the decrease in the variation between contexts as the per capita monthly income of the families rises is a persistent trend.

This trend may well reflect, among other things, the effect of the population's degree of involvement in the formal labor market. Such involvement requires more skill, reflected, for example, in a higher level of schooling; it also exposes people to a mass of information related to health, hygiene, sex, and reproduction. In Sao Jose dos Campos, for example, a survey of the big companies, mainly the multinationals, showed that social workers within the companies present the idea of planning to employees whose productivity is falling off; this planning includes the reduction of fertility. In their study of social institutions and reproductive behavior, Loyola and Quinteiro (1982:43) make the following point:

> . . . social institutions were observed to act basically along "controlist" lines, i.e., they induce or transmit, in an explicit or diffuse manner, the pattern of the small conjugal family, whose corollary is the idea of birth control. According to the viewpoint of the institutional agents, such a reproductive pattern is associated -- again at all points of the survey in general -- to economic and social problems (poverty, cost of living, social marginality, etc.) and appears as a solution offered to such problems in the short or long term.

However, as Loyola and Quintero note further (pp. 43-45), this institutional role varies significantly from one institution and from one context to another.

> Thus, to give one example of a contextual variation, the most general references to social problems can, in a large town in the South undergoing intense industrialization and with full employment (the case of Sao Jose dos Campos at the time of the survey), be translated into other, more specific references which basically concern the disorganizing effects on the social fabric of the excessively intense pace

of industrialization and immigration; in Parnaiba or Recife, they may take on the connotation of backwardness as compared with the South, while situations of unemployment and underemployment may be seen as non-residual realities which affect the population as a whole through their pathological consequences: abandoned minors, prostitution (Parnaiba and Recife), marginality and criminality (Recife).

Finally, it should be noted that, in addition to the basic criteria used to select the NIHR urban contexts--the prevailing form of organization of production and the social division of labor--or perhaps even as a result of these criteria, the contexts have specific features that may help to explain fertility levels. Thus in 1950, Santa Cruz do Sul, a region with a large population of German origin, already had a fertility rate considered low by Brazilian standards; moreover, family size in Santa Cruz has been highly influenced by property size, which has fallen gradually over the last few decades because of the successive sharing of inheritances among surviving children.

CHAPTER 11

CONCLUSIONS

DECOMPOSITION OF GENERAL FERTILITY RATES

The contribution of changes in age structure, marital status, and marital fertility to declines in general fertility rates in 1970-75 is shown for the nine contexts in Table 77. The standardization procedure used (see United Nations, 1979), taking 1970 as the base year, shows that the three factors play specific roles in reducing fertility in the different contexts and that distinct interaction effects are also present.

As can be seen, over the period considered, the decline in the general fertility rate varied a great deal from one context to another, as has already been observed with regard to total fertility rates. The largest fall, in Sertaozinho, was around 67.43 per 1,000 (174.70-107.27). At the other extreme was Santa Cruz-Urban (90.41-83.75), with 6.65 per 1,000. Cachoeiro de Itapemirim, Sao Jose dos Campos (154.49-140.20), Recife (174.85-162.00), and Conceicao do Araguaia (236.26-225.70) showed similar declines, which varied from 11 to 15 per 1,000; Parnaiba-Urban (227.94-185.12) and Santa Cruz-Rural (190.48-149.28) had larger declines of around 40 per 1,000. The only exception was Parnaiba-Rural (250.49-273.26), with a growth of 22.27 per 1,000 between 1970 and 1975.

In all the contexts where there was a reduction in the general fertility rate, except for Santa Cruz-Urban, the decline in marital fertility was the most directly responsible factor. In Cachoeiro, Recife, Sao Jose, and Araguaia, the decline can be totally explained by the reduction in marital fertility, and would have been even larger if age structure and marital status had not contributed to the attenuation of this reduction. In Cachoeiro, Recife, and Araguaia, the contribution of marital

TABLE 77 Changes in General Fertility Rates Due to Age Structure, Marital Status, and Marital Fertility, Nine Contexts, 1970-75: Brazil

	Santa Cruz-Urban	Conceicao do Araguaia	Recife	Sao Jose dos Campos	Cachoeiro de Itapemirim	Santa Cruz-Rural	Parnaiba-Urban	Sertaozinho	Parnaiba-Rural
Age structure	-5.05	7.24	9.12	11.15	2.21	13.59	10.69	-13.72	-14.67
Marital status	-2.90	13.25	11.23	8.42	6.64	-9.77	-8.08	1.52	13.78
Marital fertility	-5.36	-22.34	-25.95	-25.09	-20.85	-41.51	-34.25	-64.55	19.47
Interaction of age structure and marital state	-0.33	-3.06	-5.45	-2.58	-1.82	3.78	1.68	0.86	-5.55
Interaction of age structure and marital fertility	7.29	-5.66	-1.69	-4.88	-0.62	-7.92	-12.63	8.12	12.82
Interaction of marital status and marital fertility	-0.44	-0.57	-0.15	-1.51	-0.70	1.50	-0.44	0.34	-6.74
Interaction of age structure and marital fertility	0.01	1.46	0.46	0.20	0.65	-0.46	0.09	0.19	2.43
Total change in general fertility rate explained	-6.79	-10.98	-12.43	-14.33	-14.49	-40.79	-42.94	-67.62	21.54
Total change in general fertility rate observed	-6.65	-10.56	-12.86	-14.29	-14.47	-41.79	-42.82	-67.43	22.27

Note: Base year, 1970.

status to an increase in the general fertility rate surpassed that of the age structure of the female population; in Sao Jose, the opposite was the case.

It is interesting to note that in Parnaiba-Urban and Santa Cruz-Rural, even though, as already stressed, the major factor determining the decline was the fall in marital fertility, the change in the distribution of the female population according to marital status also contributed to the decline. The age structure of the female population, on the other hand, showed little change in the same period, thus favoring an increase in the general fertility rate.

In Sertaozinho, it was not only the fall in marital fertility, but also the change in the age structure of the population that contributed to the decline in the general fertility rate. In Santa Cruz-Urban, these two factors were almost equal in contributing to the small decline for that region.

Finally, the increase in the general fertility rate shown for Parnaiba-Rural was the result of an increase in the marital fertility rate, a more favorable distribution by marital status, and an age distribution which favored a drop in fertility.

DECOMPOSITION OF TOTAL FERTILITY

As seen above, Bongaarts' model for estimating the total fertility rate is expressed by the relation

$$\text{TFR} = 15.3 \times C_i \times C_c \times C_a \times C_m \quad (1).$$

In other words, the starting total fecundity rate of 15.3 is gradually reduced by the action of the various inhibiting factors. The first of these is postpartum infecundity, C_i, which when applied to 15.3 reduces it to the total natural marital fertility rate:

$$\text{TNMFR} = 15.3 \times C_i.$$

This in turn, when reduced through the effects of C_c and C_a, becomes the total marital fertility rate, or

$$\text{TMFR} = \text{TNMFR} \times C_c \times C_a.$$

Finally, the latter, when subjected to the effect of C_m, becomes the total fertility rate, or

$$TFR = TMFR \times C_m.$$

Table 78 shows the decomposed values for the different contexts studied. As can be seen, the values of C_i in Cachoeiro do Itapemirim and Conceicao do Araguaia caused the greatest reduction--around 15 percent--in the total fecundity rate owing to the effect of lactation. In Recife, this effect was the lowest of all--only 6 percent. The prevalence of deliberate control of marital fertility was undeniably the main factor accounting for the reduction in the natural marital fertility rate in all contexts. In Cachoeiro and Sao Jose dos Campos, this effect reached 70 percent, followed by Santa Cruz-Urban and Sertaozinho, where it was 65 percent. In Santa Cruz-Rural and Recife, it accounted for 61 percent and 57 percent, respectively, of the fall in the rate in question. The rate for Parnaiba-Rural was reduced by only 24 percent. It should be stressed that in all contexts, although in a differentiated manner, contraception was the factor directly responsible for the difference between the total natural marital and total marital fertility rates. As for the effect of the absence of marriages, it was very small in Parniaba-Rural and Sertaozinho, varying between 16 and 17 percent. In Parnaiba-Urban and Conceicao do Araguaia, this effect was about 22 percent, increasing to about 30 percent for Santa Cruz. In Sao Jose dos Campos and Recife 34 percent of the women were not yet married, and in Cachoeiro it was 35 percent, bringing the total marital fertility rate down from 3.91 to 2.53. In the other five contexts, this effect was practically uniform--between 21 percent and 24 percent.

FINDINGS AT THE NATIONAL/STATE AND LOCAL LEVELS

When the findings in Parts I and II of this report are compared, they are found to be complementary and mutually supportive. Both data sets clearly show an accelerated fertility decline in Brazil during the 1970s. Both indicate the importance of consensual unions in Brazilian nuptiality patterns, as well as the difficulties involved in gathering data on these unions; they also point to shifts in age at marriage. However, the national- and local-level analyses lead to the same conclusion: that the primary factor responsible for Brazil's accelerated fertility decline is declining marital fertility. This decline can in turn be traced, at both levels of analysis,

TABLE 78 Proximate Determinants of Total Fertility, Nine Contexts, 1975: Brazil

Measure	Cachoeiro do Itapemirim	Santa Cruz-Urban	Sao Jose dos Campos	Sertaozinho	Santa Cruz-Rural	Recife	Parnaiba-Urban	Conceicao do Araguaia	Parnaiba-Rural
Total Fecundity Rate	15.3	15.3	15.3	15.3	15.3	15.3	15.3	15.3	15.3
Postpartum Infecundity, C_i	0.950	0.928	0.897	0.873	0.906	0.942	0.918	0.850	0.892
Total Natural Marital Fertility Rate	13.0	14.2	13.7	13.4	13.9	14.4	14.0	13.0	13.6
Abortion, C_a	0.963	0.985	0.931	0.942	0.987	0.947	0.953	0.983	0.967
Contraception, C_c	0.312	0.360	0.316	0.381	0.450	0.457	0.710	0.693	0.791
Total Marital Fertility Rate	3.91	5.04	4.03	4.80	5.44	6.23	9.47	8.86	10.40
Nonmarriage, C_m	0.648	0.710	0.657	0.842	0.698	0.651	0.766	0.777	0.832
Total Fertility Rate (estimated)	2.53	3.58	2.65	4.04	3.80	4.06	7.25	6.88	8.65

to changing patterns of contraceptive use: increased prevalence, coupled with the use of more effective methods (the pill and sterilization). Among the other proximate determinants of marital fertility, postpartum infecundability has relatively little impact in Brazil, where the practice of breastfeeding is quite limited; abortion, shown in both data sets to be increasing, is nevertheless an indeterminate factor because of the usual data-gathering problems. Finally, both analyses point to a combination of factors--changes in relative income, increased educational attainment, and increased female labor force participation--as the main socioeconomic determinant of Brazil's changing patterns of contraceptive use: these factors are associated with increased desires for consumer durables, the diffusion of information on family-size limitation, and therefore an increase in conscious fertility control.

NOTES

1 The relationship between income and fertility levels is examined for the nine NIHR local contexts in Part II of this report.
2 For a further discussion of the typology used, see the Appendix. See also Lopes, (1975), Faria (1975), and Singer (1975).
3 These case studies, which have already been conducted in the nine areas, can be found in the series <u>Estudos de Populacao</u>, CEBRAP, 1975-81, Sao Paulo.
4 The justification for eliminating the usual age limits can be found in Berquo (1973).
5 When a member of the household group had any kind of marital union, previously or currently, and was under 18, he or she was also considered a candidate for sampling.
6 See internal document prepared for the Project by Patarra (1976).
7 Considering up to three as the maximum number of unions, since a negligible fraction surpassed that number.
8 Until November 1981, when the legal minimum wage was 8,464 cruzeiros in Sao Paulo state, the cost of a civil marriage was 1,650 cruzeiros; in Pernambuco (Northeast), these figures were 7,128 and 1,500 cruzeiros, respectively.
9 Divorce was made legal in 1978, and with it came the possibility of new legal unions.
10 CEBRAP is at present conducting a study of the migrations affecting the NIHR.
11 On this subject, see Brazil (1971-1980).
12 These values refer to a subsample of about 100 women from each context who had at least one child born alive in the last 5 years.
13 Legal minimum wage limits in force at the time of the survey: Santa Cruz-Urban, $603.60 cruzerios; Sao Jose dos Campos, $532.80 cruzerios; Cachoeiro do Itapemirim, $655.20 cruzerios; Parnaiba-Urban, $544.80 cruzerios; Recife, $602.40 cruzerios.

APPENDIX

THE NIHR CONTEXTS

PARNAIBA*

From the nineteenth century onward, Parnaiba was the main commercial entrepot for imports and exports in a primary-exporting economy (initially based on meat, and later on extractive products). Not only has it undergone the fluctuations and, finally, decline that are inherent in such economies, but it has also in recent decades been edged out of the main transportation and trading system by the increasing dominance of road over river and sea transportation. Beginning in the 1950s, this twofold process led to a major change in the region's economy, which entered a phase of stagnation. Nevertheless, the municipality retains the character of an extremely simple primary-exporting model, rooted in a peasantry that is practically unaffected by mercantile relations.

The 1970 data for the rural zone of Parnaiba depict a landowning structure in which the large estates, or latifundios, are of little commercial importance but are linked to a broadly based peasant agriculture.

The importance of peasant activities in this municipality is reflected in its agrarian structure, which can be seen in the distribution of land. In 1970, more than 80 percent of establishments (those under 5 hectares) occupied less than 5 percent of the area exploited by tenants and sharecroppers. Less than 1 percent (22

---

*Summarized by Maria Lucia Indjaian, from a text by Maria Andrea Loyola based on papers by Lopes and Brandt (1978).

establishments with over 50 hectares) represented almost half the total area.

Half the value of agricultural and livestock-breeding activities is attributable to farming and characteristically commercial activities, just under one-third to animal husbandry, and 12 percent to products of plant extraction. Cultivated areas are small on average, with four basic products (rice, beans, cassava, and corn) representing 82 percent of the municipality's agricultural production. The main commercial products are carnauba wax and cattle. A few establishments report some permanent crop production of a more commercial nature (banana, coconut, cashew, and mango), representing 8 percent of the overall value of agricultural production. Rice is the only widespread commercial commodity whose production can be characterized as peasant; its cultivation is aimed at obtaining a monetary supplement, and is in this way equivalent to the sale of leftovers from the grower's own consumption, seasonal employment, or craft activities.

The most widespread labor relation in the area is sharecropping. Ground rent varies depending on whether the land is handed over to the farmer already prepared for planting, and whether the owner supplies the seed; it may consist of a half, a third, or a quarter share of production. The most common case is payment of the ground rent alone in the form of a quarter share; this kind of tenant, known as a rendeiro, often does not live on the land in question, which is usually let to him for 2 years. He depends in many ways on the landowner, who represents the only channel for obtaining bank credit and even supplies of foodstuffs. The sale of products grown on the land will also depend on the landowner since they are often sold "on paper," that is, as a future harvest. Although this dependence may vary in degree, it restricts the alternatives of the great majority who possess neither land nor the conditions to acquire it. Another kind of tenant, the agregado*, usually lives on the estate and has the owner's permission to cultivate a small plot. In return, he provides payment in the form of services, which may or may not be of an economic nature.

---

*Agregado: a term usually applied to one who lives on a large estate and has the owner's permission to cultivate a small plot in return for payment in the form of services (which may or may not be economic in nature).

Parnaiba's urban economy is closely tied to this peasant economy. As in the past, the main roots of the urban economy are in the commercialization of extractive products. Of these, the most important is (and has been since the beginning of the century) carnauba wax, practically 100 percent of which is exported. In 1970, the value of foreign exports, consisting of carnauba wax and jaborandi, represented 90 percent of the total economic output. The babassu nut is distributed to the domestic market. At the present time, while the town acts as a reception center for products of plant extraction, it also contains a modest manufacturing sector. It remains a service center and a pole of demographic attraction. Its medical facilities are used by other municipalities 100 km away or more (some even in neighboring Maranhao and Ceara), while its commercial establishments often serve more distant townships. Despite the weakening of its economy, the town continues to be the focus of ongoing rural-urban migration, and over the last decade, its growth has increased. However, this is probably attributable more to the stagnation of the rural economy than to any dynamism in urban activities. In 1970, the urban area contained 60.87 percent of the population; 25 percent of this population was not native to the municipality, having migrated mainly from Ceara (42.25 percent) and Maranhao (28.60 percent).

The 1970 Demographic Census showed that 35.1 percent of occupied persons worked in the secondary sector and 62.4 percent in the tertiary. The 1970 Industrial Census reported the existence of 114 industrial establishments, which absorbed 589 persons. If this number is subtracted from the total of 3,237 persons habitually occupied in manufacturing activities according to the Demographic Census, that leaves 2,648 persons involved in occasional or irregular activities. This would seem to represent the reserve labor available to the town's industry for seasonal variations and turnover. The increase in the number of persons engaged in manufacturing activities (21 percent) signifies a proliferation of domestic or autonomous craft production rather than a growth of industry. There are only three industrial enterprises with more than 100 employees (Vegetex, Morais e Cia., and Tropical de Alimentos). Most of those occupied in the manufacturing sector, according to demographic censuses, work in craft and repair activities, as well as in civil construction, which is in fact mostly represented by craft activities.

The employment situation for commerce is similar to that for the industrial sector. The 1970 Commercial Census registered 1,025 wholesale and retail establishments employing 1,824 persons. The Demographic Census showed that 2,751 persons were habitually engaged in commercial activities. This discrepancy can be explained primarily by the seasonal nature of agriculture and extraction: trading in goods fluctuates with agricultural supply, and job opportunities vary as a result. It is probable that, as with industry, this seasonal variation entails modifications in the size of the autonomous sector, rather than a variation in demand for manpower. At present, Parnaiba can be seen as undergoing a rapid increase in the numbers of people occupied as "autonomous" or self-employed intermediaries in the circulation of commodities. Of the 1,824 persons registered by the Commercial Census, the Demographic Census classed 1,725 as being in this category. As regards local subsistence products, contrary to what might be expected of an economy based on small autonomous production, direct exchange does not predominate, but a multiple circuit based on buying and selling operations. As regards consumer products imported from other regions, the situation is more complex: although there are some wholesale firms, most of the large retail establishments seem to prefer to purchase their goods directly from larger markets, and to this end have representatives in or send buyers to Fortaleza, Rio, and Sao Paulo.

The low rates of pay common to several categories of employees and autonomous workers explains why they must resort to a combination of agricultural, extractive, craft, industrial, and commercial activities to ensure the minimum earnings needed for survival. In 1970, 47.8 percent of those occupied in industry earned less than $100 cruzerios (which then represented 80 percent of the legal minimum wage for the region). Among these workers, that proportion was greater for employees (49.9 percent), and less for autonomous workers (47.4 percent), and those in commerce (47.2 percent). In the service sector, the corresponding figures were 84.5 percent for employees and 74 percent for autonomous workers.

The public sector is a major factor accounting for employment levels in Parnaiba. The pace of public works has a considerable influence on variations in job levels, while welfare and government health service agencies seem to be responsible for much of the municipality's monetary income. This is why a situation characterized by the existence of large numbers of unemployed workers can continue, and why a large part of local commerce can survive. In 1970, 6,720 of the total urban labor force of 15,052 persons were calculated to have been laid off for health or other reasons according to the books kept at the Parnaiba branch of the INPS (Instituto Nacional de Previdencia Social--the governmental agency in charge of social security and the health services). Given the stagnation of the region's productive activities, it can be seen that much of the monetary circulation that enables small commerce to survive in Parnaiba is injected by the INPS, and secondarily by the FUNRURAL (Rural Workers' Welfare Fund). The employment situation will be significantly altered only if there are even greater injections of government resources than those currently maintaining an active local market.

A summary of the main demographic indicators for Parnaiba for the period 1940-70 is presented in Table A.1

CACHOEIRO DE ITAPEMIRIM*

The growth of the coffee trade was the main factor in the occupation of the territory now comprising the municipality of Cachoeiro de Itapemirim and its surroundings, in the south of Espirito Santo state. Settlement began in the early 1700s as a result of the hunt for gold in the Castelo mines and the setting up of the first sugar mills along the banks of the River Itapemirim; however, it was not until the middle of the nineteenth century that the expansion of the coffee trade in the states of Minas and Rio generated a definitive settlement of the Espirito Santo tablelands, where Cachoeiro de Itapemirim lies. This period was also decisive in reinforcing the strategic position occupied by Cachoeiro de Itapemirim since its foundation as a polarizing center for both the economic activities and communications in the south of the state. The coffee trade brought the Leopoldina railroad as far as Cachoeiro, which thus became an entrepot for the entire region's production on its way to the port of Rio de Janeiro, via Cachoeiro-Campos.

When the coffee trade began to decline, its place was taken by livestock breeding, mostly of dairy cattle. Cachoeiro was also to be a nucleus for the dairy

---

*Summary by Sales (1979).

TABLE A.1 Dynamics of the Population of Parnaiba (municipality[a]), 1940-70: Brazil

Year	Total Population	Rate of Growth (percent)	Decomposition of Natural Increase		Decomposition of Birth Rate	
			Crude Death Rate (per 1,000)	Crude Birth Rate (per 1,000)	General Fertility Rate (per 1,000)	Proportion of Women Aged 15-49 in Total Population (percent)
1940	42,062		25.0	49.8	189.0	26.3
1950	64,260	4.33	22.9	48.9	185.0	26.3
1960	76,469	1.75	20.6	49.9	197.0	25.3
1970	98,113	2.52	18.7	49.9	207.9	24.0

[a]The municipality covers the urban and rural population.

Source: Berquo and Jose (1978).

production of the state's southern region, particularly after the founding of the Cachoeiro de Itapemirim Dairy Cooperative in the 1940s and continuing to the present, when it absorbs the production from 18 neighboring municipalities. The major consequence of this shift to dairy cattle breeding is shown by Cachoeiro's declining rural population, which from 1950 to 1970 fell from 53,701 to 42,903; this represents a drop from 66.2 percent to 40.1 percent of the municipality's total population. Its urban population, however, has been constantly growing: in 1970, it reached 64,219, or 59.9 percent of the total, thus overtaking the rural population in relative terms.

This growth in Cachoeiro's urban population is certainly due mainly to the influx of migrants attracted to the town as the center of economic activities in the entire southern region of the state. However, this has not been the only result of the shift of population out of the municipality's rural areas. This migration has very probably reached not only Cachoeiro, but also, and above all, other rural areas in the same state or even other states with an emerging agricultural frontier; in fact, most of those who have migrated to the town of Cachoeiro have come from neighboring towns. Some data from field observation and secondary sources support this hypothesis. First, the main labor relation in the local coffee plantations is the half-share sharecropping system, with a predominance of small producers. This leads the producers naturally to look for other agricultural frontier regions when their own plantations undergo a crisis; prior to the decline in the coffee plantations, this had already been observed in the migration of small producers from the south to the central region of the state. Second, the municipality as a whole had a negative migratory balance for 1960-70. Given the urbanization level observed for the municipality during the same decade, it is probable that this balance would have been positive if a large proportion of those who emigrated from the countryside had gone directly to the town of Cachoeiro.

The initial industrial thrust in Cachoeiro at the beginning of the century was significant for the later consolidation of urban society there, as well as for its recent industrial growth, still based mainly on the exploitation of the municipality's natural resources. Although no quantitative data are available for the years following 1970, it seems undeniable that the town has undergone its most significant growth over the last 10 years because of the expansion of its dynamic industrial sector and the resulting increase in commerce and services in general. The influx of immigrants to the town can be seen in the expansion of the urban site itself, which has begun spreading out along the banks of the River Itapemirim toward the hills around the town. There has been intense civil construction work over the last 10 years, above all in the building of new housing estates throughout the town's outskirts.

Industrial Census data show a degree of stabilization in Cachoeiro's industrial sector between 1940 and 1960; from then up to 1970, there was a substantial growth both in the number of establishments and employees, and in the value of manufacturing operations. Of the various kinds of industry, those which grew most over this period were the extraction and production of nonmetallic minerals; the basic raw material in this field comes from the reserves of limestone and marble located in the municipality near the town of Cachoeiro. The largest and most diversified marble and granite producers, however, began operations or expanded out of already existing marble and granite cutting workshops in the late 1960s and early 1970s. Between 1970 (date of the last census) and 1979, when the field survey was carried out, the number of firms in this sector decreased (from 80 to 45 establishments), while at the same time the number of employees substantially increased (from 1,214 to 2,100). This would seem to indicate that during this period, the industrial sector underwent continuous vertical expansion, with the firms involved growing, diversifying production, and absorbing other existing workshops.

Along with this industrial sector, made up mostly of medium and large factories engaged primarily in exporting their products, Cachoeiro also has a large number of small factories, most of which are engaged in supplying local consumer needs. The great majority of industrialists are native to the municipality, while many of its large-scale enterprises arose as a result of individual initiative. The latter managed to expand their businesses into large factories, such as the present-day Itapoa de Calcados (footwear), or even local empires, such as the Itapemirim Group, whose main business is long-distance passenger transport, but whose activities also include a whole range of both service and industrial undertakings.

A summary of the main demographic indicators for Cachoeiro de Itapermirin for the period 1940-70 is presented in Table A.2.

TABLE A.2 Dynamics of the Population of Cachoeiro do Itapemirim (municipality), 1940-70: Brazil

Year	Total Population	Rate of Growth (percent)	Decomposition of Natural Increase		Decomposition of Birth Rate	
			Crude Death Rate (per 1,000)	Crude Birth Rate (per 1,000)	General Fertility Rate (per 1,000)	Proportion of Women Aged 15-49 in Total Population (percent)
1940	72,834		23.3	47.1	199.1	23.6
1950	81,082	1.08	21.7	44.9	194.7	23.0
1960	90,271	1.08	19.1	45.5	195.9	23.2
1970	107,122	1.73	16.9	41.5	175.1	23.7

Source: Berquo and Quintero (1979).

SAO JOSE DOS CAMPOS*

Within the framework selected by the NIHR, Sao Jose dos Campos represents the case of modern Brazilian capitalism powered by the forces of big oligopoly capital. Like the other towns in the Vale do Paraiba region, until the early years of the present century, Sao Jose had an economy based on coffee planting. Unlike the other towns, however, it did not slump when the coffee axis shifted to the western part of Sao Paulo state; rather it developed by replacing coffee partly with semisubsistence activities and partly with livestock and dairy cattle breeding. At the same time, being a point of rail, and later road, intersection, it served as an entrepot for goods being transported from the large urban centers to the coastal ports. It was in the 1950s, and especially in the 1960s, that Sao Jose began to take on the features of a modern Brazilian capitalist development because of the enormous industrial boom that took place at this time. This boom involved an industrialization process based on large-scale enterprise; above all, it was a "modern" process in that it was based on the expansion of oligopolies, or the so-called multinationals.

The distinctive marks of this process can be seen both in the forms of economic organization that arose and in the structure of local society: since industrialization was based on the investments of large firms with head offices outside the area, it operated through so-called "organizational policies" implemented by employees operating on site (executives, managers, personnel heads, technicians, and engineers). At the same time, the process of industrialization and modernization formed the workers into the "masses." This was in fact a caricature, however, for they kept one foot in their past as migrants and the other foot in the system of aspirations, which suffered drastic changes in the space of a few years.

Along with these characteristics, there arose an intermediary of great strength--the government and its agencies, and the weight of its "modernizing bureaucracy." Government action contributed to economic growth from 1950 onward, when the Centro Tecnico da Aeronautica (Air Force Technical Center) was set up. This was initially made up of technical and aeronautical engineering schools, but

---

*Summary by Maria Lucia Indjaian, based on Cardoso (1975).

later developed the nuclei of an aeronautics industry. A further contribution now being made by the state is the installation of huge facilities belonging to Petrobras (the state oil monopoly) for the construction of refineries.

From 1960 onward, moreover, Sao Jose saw a change in the pattern of its population dynamics. In 1960, there were 76,997 inhabitants, a figure which rose to 148,332 by 1970; of the latter, 74,395 were born outside the municipality, and 94.2 percent of these were located in the urban area. Most of the migrants in the local population were of Brazilian nationality, the majority from the states of Sao Paulo (48.94 percent) and Minas Gerais (37.09 percent). There were 2,651 foreigners (2 percent of the population), the same proportion as had been registered for 1920, 1940, and 1950. As regards the urban or rural origins of the migrants, the available data show that around 23,000 persons from the rural area were present in the urban area in 1970; this suggests that the rural area must have had little capacity to absorb workers. In 1940, the rural population represented 63.5 percent of the total population, falling to 11 percent in 1970.

The degree of change undergone by the municipality's productive structure is reflected in its employment structure. There has been a rapid decrease in the economically active population in the primary sector; in 1940, it represented 60.86 percent of the labor force, and by 1973, it had been reduced to 2 percent. At the same time, there was an increase in the secondary sector, which by 1973 comprised 51 percent of the labor force; the remaining 47 percent was distributed among the commercial and service sector (24.5 percent), public administration (11 percent), autonomous workers (11 percent), and others (0.3 percent). Meanwhile, women's participation in the labor force increased considerably: it grew in the tertiary sector to 68.69 percent, where it was concentrated in individual consumer services (39.96 percent) and others, although it lost relative importance in the primary (1.89 percent) and secondary (29.42 percent) sectors.

These data indicate the proportionally greater increase in individual consumer services than in production services for the years after 1950 in Sao Jose. It is true that the collective services sector also grew (education, police, health, etc.); indeed, for the latest intercensal interval, this sector grew more than individual consumer services. Even so, the number of domestic servants, chauffeurs, snack bars, and so on greatly increased along with the so-called "modernization" caused by industrial growth. This shows in turn that Sao Jose is no exception to the occupational pattern created by the prevailing style of dependent capitalist society. In parallel, there was an expansion in tertiary social areas (along with the state bureaucracy), and social consumer services continued to expand.

As regards wage distribution in 1970, in general, white collar employees earned twice as much as workers, although this gap was greater in some industries than in others. There was also a strong average differentiation among wages within the various industries for both white and blue collar workers. Those industries with the highest pay for blue collar workers were chemicals and transportation materials; together, those industries absorbed 37 percent of occupied blue collar workers in Sao Jose, and thus forced the average wage upward. On the other hand, 32 percent of blue collar workers earned less than half the average wage of all workers in the two industries referred to above; the corresponding figure for foodstuffs or metallurgy is 25 percent. Despite these wage differentials, however, the population's living standard did not move beyond a "relative poverty horizon."

As for rural economic activity, until 1960, the "absolute population level" remained steady, although it slowed in some periods. This activity comprised mainly cultivation of rice, Irish potatoes, and sugarcane (especially for fodder). There was also livestock (mainly dairy cattle) and poultry breeding; the latter, along with market gardening, was intensified through use of the low-lying land along the River Parnaiba. Dairy production and livestock breeding were not adversely affected by the industrial boom; on the contrary, they even increased after 1950, despite the loss of rural population. This suggests that resources were used to greater advantage and that production was focused in large-scale agricultural enterprises.

A summary of the main demographic indicators for Sao Jose dos Campos for the period 1940-70 is presented in Table A.3.

CONCEICAO DO ARAGUAIA*

Conceicao do Araguaia was founded in 1897 as a combined catechistic mission and hinterland settlement. Over the

---

*Summary by Maria Lucia Indjaian from Ianni (1978).

TABLE A.3 Dynamics of the Population of Sao Jose dos Campos (municipality), 1940-70: Brazil

Year	Total Population	Rate of Growth (percent)	Decomposition of Increase (percent)		Decomposition of Natural Increase			Decomposition of Birth Rate	
			Migration	Natural Increase	Crude Death Rate (per 1,000)	Crude Birth Rate (per 1,000)		General Fertility Rate (per 1,000)	Proportion of Women Aged 15-49 in Total Population (percent)
1940	32,324		--	--	--	37.9		143.5	26.4
1950	44,804	3.3	--	--	25.8	39.4		154.9	25.4
1960	76,997	5.6	46.9	53.1	14.3	42.1		170.4	24.7
1970	148,332	6.8	48.2	51.8	9.4	34.5		141.8	24.4

Source: Berquo (1975).

years up to 1912, its economy was based on monoextraction of caucho-type rubber, and the town underwent a growing influx of immigrants. These were mainly from the Goias, Maranhao, and the Piaui hinterlands; they arrived looking for industrial and commercial work.

With the beginning of the rubber crisis in 1912, the municipality began to diversify its extractive economy by combining it with agriculture and livestock breeding. This economy, of the peasant type and partially mercantile, prevailed until 1960. Production mainly served the producer's own needs or those of local commerce, as well as trade with Belem; the main products were rice, corn, beans, cassava, cotton, tobacco, sugarcane, and coffee. Livestock breeding was also carried on, mainly of cattle, horses, and pigs.

During the years from 1960 to 1977, the economy and society of Conceicao do Araguaia changed more rapidly, which in turn brought about changes in all social relations and activities. Two events were central to this process. The first was the construction of the Belem-Brasilia highway, completed in 1960, and later connected by another highway to Conceicao do Araguaia. This brought new possibilities for the exchange of goods, people, and information, as well as communication with Goiania, Anapolis, Belem, Brasilia, and other towns. The second major event was the setting up of SUDAM, the Superintendency for Development of the Amazon, in 1966. This official agency was established to provide concessions for investors through tax and credit incentives, thus facilitating the introduction of livestock breeding and agricultural enterprises. Its activities are still being carried on in the region encompassing the municipalities of Conceicao do Araguaia and Santana do Araguaia.

These stimuli led to a rise in population, from 11,283 in 1960 to 28,953 in 1970. Of these, 65.4 percent were not born in the municipality, but had come mainly from Goias (16,610) and Maranhao (2,779). Most were landless peasants looking for land on which to squat and for better working conditions and therefore emigrated to the countryside. In 1970, the great majority (83.41 percent) of the population was engaged in agriculture and livestock breeding, along with extractive activities. The rest (430 persons) were absorbed by activities located in the urban center, but closely linked to rural production.

A comparison of some of the available data shows the changing character of the landowning structure. In 1950, there were 292 occupants (posseiros, or squatters) and one landowner (big farmer) with control of land in the municipality. The occupants were responsible for about 96 percent of rural establishments and occupied over 91 percent of the land involved. In 1970, the 2,136 occupants accounted for over 95 percent of rural establishments, but occupied only 43.64 percent of the land; at the same time, there were 100 landowners, who accounted for 4.46 percent of rural establishments and occupied 56.33 percent of the land.

According to data collected by IBGE (Brazilian Geodesics and Statistics Institute), agricultural and livestock production grew overall in the years from 1960 to 1970, and the number of rural establishments rose from 982 (1960) to 2,242 (1970). The composition of the population engaged in agriculture and livestock breeding in 1972 clearly shows this change. In 1972, INCRA (National Settlement and Agrarian Reform Institute) registered 857 permanent wage workers and 7,011 temporary workers. Of these, the peao, or unskilled wage laborer (mostly of migrant origin, as well as a peasant in the process of proletarianization), was the central figure in the formation and expansion of the large agricultural enterprises. Thus, it is above all in the countryside that the bourgeoisie and proletariat were increasingly taking shape. On the one hand, there were the landowners, the fazendeiros, and the entrepreneurs or their agents; on the other, there were the rural laborers and cowhands. Alongside with these, there were the peasant nuclei of smallholders, squatters, and colonos, all in a critical phase of reorganization or dissolution.

This peasantry, whose economy originally consisted of family labor and was at a very low technological level, and who produced mainly for their own consumption, began to produce for selling on the urban market, where the demand for agricultural and extractive products was constantly rising. Together with this growing articulation between the peasant economy and the market, the peasant was increasingly dependent on a supply of merchandise (both essential and superfluous) generated by industrial capital. This dependency developed and led to a dissolution of the peasant economy. A large number of the peasants were transformed into disguised wage-earner, or simply proletarianized; others, longstanding or recent squatters, managed to have their legal situation redefined and thus received permission to occupy or even own the land, becoming colonos. According to INCRA, in 1971, 90 percent of all rural establishments were in the hands of squatters (posseiros), who occupied 39 percent of the land; about 9 percent consisted of rural real estate with title deeds, comprising 60 percent of the land.

These data help clarify how the area's formation and expansion of agricultural enterprises has taken place. The crisis undergone by the peasantry is a specific aspect of this expansion, involving the struggle for possession or ownership and control of the land, the expulsion and proletarianization of the autonomous producer, and the expropriation of the most important means of production and subsistence--the land.

The antagonism between landowners and squatters took many different forms, from legal negotiations to armed struggle. Despite legislation designed to protect the squatters, the significant laws supported the policies implemented by SUDAM, Banco da Amazonia S/A (BASA), and other federal and state government agencies to protect the formation and expansion of medium and large agricultural enterprises. In short, the process underway in Conceicao do Araguaia--one which helps to clarify the social and economic relations in the municipality--is private appropriation of the land under the control of big capital, with the political and economic protection of the state.

SERTAOZINHO*

Sertaozinho was shaped by the expansion of capitalism in the agrarian world, and serves as a good example of the society and economy constructed by the coffee trade in the west of Sao Paulo state in the late nineteenth and early twentieth centuries (1880-1930). This period was characterized by the strong influence of coffee, planted as a commercial crop mainly in compliance with international demand. This dominated all other activities, such as sugarcane and cotton planting, foodstuffs, crafts and manufacturing, transportation, and commerce. As it progressed, the monoculture of coffee brought about a reorganization of the productive forces. While a free labor system was being set up, a local market was created in connection with the regional one and with the country's most dynamic centers. This in turn involved the transformation of unoccupied public land into private property

---

*Summary by Maria Lucia Indjaian from Ianni (1976).

and the occupation and concentration of landed property. This period also saw increased immigration, mainly of Italians, into the coffee plantations.

The expansion of coffee created local and regional economic subsystems. With these came a more dynamic society and economy, even with the advent of the coffee crisis. Crops were then combined--some perennial, such as coffee, and others temporary, such as beans, corn, and cotton. From 1918 onward this process became more intense and structurally significant, for in that year Sertaozinho suffered a serious frost. In 1924 and 1926, there was drought. All this, added to the 1929 economic slump, led to severe unemployment, with a steep upsurge in the reserve force of agricultural laborers. Some of these laborers attempted to adjust to other agricultural activities, while others went to the towns.

Sugarcane was cultivated in Sertaozinho from the end of the nineteenth century onward, and in the 1930s began gradually to increase in importance; by 1944, the land area devoted to sugarcane had overtaken that of coffee, and by 1953 that of coffee and cotton together. The municipality continued to produce coffee, cotton, corn, peanuts, rice, and other products for local consumption and for trading outside the region. However, the main product remained sugarcane. In 1968, it accounted for 90 percent of the value of agricultural production. This result was repeated in 1970, but increased in 1974, when the figure was 92.6 percent; there were then five sugar mills producing for the regional and foreign markets, in accordance with policies coordinated by the IAA (Sugar and Alcohol Institute).

The organization of productive activities to meet the demands of the sugar industry led to a restructuring of the municipality's productive forces. From 1940 to 1972, there was a significant reorganization of Sertaozinho's landowning structure. The number of rural units fell from 780 to 515, and the sugar mill, understood as a productive complex including the mill itself and the surrounding plantations, became the dominant agro-industrial nucleus. The population working at a mill now comprises rural laborers and industrial workers, supervisors, inspectors, foremen, administrative employees, technicians, and owners. At harvest time (June to December), this population is joined by temporary hired laborers (known as boias-frias or volantes) from the outskirts of Sertaozinho, or from other towns or states, mainly Minas Gerais, Bahia, and Pernambuco.

The growth of the sugar industry has led to the expulsion of some workers and to the redefinition of working conditions for those who remain. This change has occurred not only because of an interest in increasing and improving production, but also because of the formalization of production relations according to the legal, political, and economic requirements imposed by the state or the IAA. The social division of labor during and between harvests has developed so that the production relations are distinct for different segments of the proletariat. The colonos* have tended to become permanent or temporary laborers on a daily or monthly wage, and the colonato system in agriculture has thus been dissolved. This process has also tended to reduce the number of permanent laborers employed and increase the contingent of temporary laborers. According to INCRA, in 1972 only 11 rural properties were being worked by sharecroppers, 21 in number, only 10 of whom had a written contract.

With this modification in production relations in the countryside, the sugar industry has indirectly imparted new energy to the town, to which a significant part of the rural population has migrated. It has thus contributed to a gradual increase in the urban population, which by 1960 had become larger than its rural counterpart: in 1940, 25 percent of the population was concentrated in the urban area and 75 percent in the countryside; the figures for 1970 show an inversion of this composition. This change was accompanied by the influence of migration from other municipalities and states, which was mainly concentrated in the urban area. The rural population fell, became progressively urbanized, and became consumers of the urban world's production.

The continuous expansion of the sugar industry and the resulting change in the organization of production also led to corresponding changes in other agricultural activities (soybeans, corn, rice, peanuts, and other crops). In addition, industrial production grew and diversified,

---

*Colono/Colonato: In Sertaozinho, these terms do not refer to squatters or owners of land, but rather to a system whereby the owners of the big estates granted a cottage and small plot for subsistence to those working on their lands or at the mills. With the dissolution of this system, these workers lose such rights and are evicted from the land.

absorbing 60 percent of the municipality's economically
active population; in certain cases, this involved the
primary sector. Industrial establishments increased in
number from 33 in 1940 to 172 in 1973. In the same year,
metallurgical and mechanical firms, mainly engaged in
production and repair of machinery and equipment for the
sugar industry, employed 50 percent of all persons occupied in the industrial sector. New capitalist production
patterns became generalized through the influence of the
sugar market; the relations of mutual dependence and
antagonism between town and country, agriculture and
industry, workers and bourgeoisie all changed as a result.

A summary of the main demographic indicators for Sertaozinho for the period 1940-70 is presented in Table A.4.

SANTA CRUZ DO SUL*

The lands in the settlement of Santa Cruz do Sul were
occupied from 1849 onward. In that year, 77-hectare plots
were distributed as an incentive to foreign immigration,
which was needed to make up for the scarcity of manpower,
especially in the field of agricultural exports, and to
promote the free land system. The migratory influx to
Santa Cruz do Sul steadily increased until the end of the
nineteenth century and was mostly made up of German
settlers.

The economy of Santa Cruz was based from the start on
family agricultural production for export. Its main product was tobacco, but there were also lard, Paraguay tea,
beans, and corn. Together with these activities, this
development of an export trade in agricultural products
led to an accumulation of capital, which in turn facilitated the installation of production units along capitalist lines. From 1918 on, most of the firms in the town
were engaged in processing agricultural products (drying
tobacco, refining lard) and preparing them for export as
raw materials. This led to an expansion of tobacco-
related activities and a decline in those related to products sold on the home market, subsistence, or pig breeding, thus making the municipality's economy more and more
dependent on a single product.

---

*Summary by Maria Lucia Indjaian, from Lima (n.d.) and
Oliveira (1975).

TABLE A.4 Dynamics of the Population of Sertaozinho (municipality), 1940-70

Year	Total Population	Rate of Growth (percent)	Decomposition of Increase (percent)		Decomposition of Natural Increase			Decomposition of Birth Rate	
			Natural	Migratory	Crude Death Rate (per 1,000)	Crude Birth Rate (per 1,000)		General Fertility Rate (per 1,000)	Proportion of Women Aged 15-49 in Total Population (percent)
1940	21,290	-0.45	--	--	19.34	39.88		179.08	22.27
1950	20,357	4.87	--	--	9.53	40.28		173.14	23.26
1960	32,753	1.89	58.5	41.5	8.65	34.78		152.07	22.87
1970	39,496		135.7	-35.7	7.70	29.57		124.95	23.67

Source: Berquo and Jose (1976).

There was also a greater fragmentation of rural property, reaching a peak between 1920 and 1940. Over this period, the average area of properties fell from 40 to 26.93 hectares, while the number of establishments with between 1 and 20 hectares grew. This considerable reduction in the size of properties meant that it was no longer possible to maintain the system of dividing them up according to inheritance; thus some owners' children were forced off the land, to undergo a process of proletarianization in later years when the town's industrialization was under way.

The process of emigration from the rural zone, already intense in the 1940s and 1950s, became more so in later decades as the parceling out of property continued. It was also encouraged by the tobacco crisis since this product dominated the municipality's agricultural and industrial economy. The tobacco crisis was partly caused by the federal government's inflationary policies from 1962 onward, and partly by a failure to update production techniques. As a result, this major export lóst its market competitiveness. This in turn led to the introduction of foreign capital, which was gradually invested in the purchase of the existing tobacco factories.

The landowning structure of Santa Cruz do Sul is characterized by a predominance of small agricultural establishments: in 1970, the Agricultural Census registered 8,226 establishments in the municipality, absorbing 27,423 persons. There are, however, no precise data on the number of people engaged in tobacco planting. The proportion of wage-earners is small (around 10 percent of the economically active population), as is the share of tenant farmers, squatters, and occupants (around 8 percent). The majority consists of smallholders (colonos) and members of their families (82 percent), who are engaged in subsistence production, along with tobacco and soybean planting and pig breeding.

These activities are carried on in the area where German settlers predominate, which is also the richest. The northern part of the municipality, occupied mainly by Italians, has different features. Here, properties are relatively larger, the ground is less even, and livestock breeding thus predominates, along with Paraguay tea extraction. Wage labor is also common in this area.

Industrial activities are an extension of agriculture, especially tobacco processing and cigarette manufacturing. The 1970 Industrial Census registered 5,287 persons occupied in industry, of whom 3,899 were in production.

Among these, the tobacco industry (including cigarette factories and tobacco-processing plants) employed 1,141 persons as permanent workers. The processing plants are directly linked to the planters; they render technical assistance, supplying fertilizers and insecticides, and finance the construction of curing barns. Thus, the planters are distinctly dependent on these processing firms: although there is no formal contract, any planter who fails to sell his production to the firm that financed him will stand little chance of receiving financial aid in the future.

The tobacco-processing firms employ few permanent workers since their demand for labor increases 3-5 times at the harvest peak (March-April). Souza Cruz has 200 permanent employees, but at harvest time this rises to 1,000. No preference is shown to either sex in the employment of harvest workers (usually it is 50 percent for each), and workers may be either single or married. They work for the processors around 3-4 months every year. The rest of the year they are employed in civil construction or do odd jobs. A few emigrate to Rio Pardo or Cachoeira do Sul, where they work on the rice or wheat harvest, while some remain unemployed. The women usually work as domestic servants in private residences.

Of the large enterprises outside the tobacco industry, the most important are a meat packing plant and a rubber goods factory. The remaining enterprises—mainly lumbering and the manufacture of furniture, perfume, and beverages—employ relatively few workers. In fact, there are many small firms with few or no employees; on the basis of the census data, it can be assumed that most industrial establishments employ on average less than 10 persons.

Along with industrial activities, Santa Cruz has small and medium-sized commerce that serves the needs of the municipality and its neighbors. Most of the larger tradesmen are former tobacco entrepreneurs who, in the late 1960s and early 1970s, were brought up by international groups. It is impossible to obtain a clear picture of the occupational categories in commercial activities from the 1970 Commercial Census since it also includes information on industry. The 1960 census, however, clearly shows a predominance of proprietors and their families in commerce, mainly in the retail sector (39 percent wage-earners); in contrast, wage-earners predominated in wholesale commerce (76.7 percent). The service sector also remained small, absorbing around 7 percent of the municipality's economically active population; of these, 71 percent were proprietors and their families, and 29 percent were wage earners.

Although urban activities were consolidated and absorbed a growing share of the number of occupied persons between 1940 and 1970, the agricultural sector retained the largest share of the municipality's labor force (63 percent), a share that was permanently threatened by the pressure of big capital.

A summary of the main demographic indicators for Santa Cruz do Sul for the period 1940-70 is presented in Table A.5.

TABLE A.5 Dynamics of the Population of Santa Cruz do Sul (municipality), 1940-70: Brazil

			Decomposition of Natural Increase	
Year	Total Population	Rate of Growth (percent)	Crude Death Rate (per 1,000)	Crude Birth Rate (per 1,000)
1940	55,041		12.50	36.55
		2.38		
1950	69,605		18.49	35.96
		2.16		
1960	86,147		7.44	36.57
		1.33		
1970	98,714		7.94	31.39

[a]These population figures also include Vera Cruz, because until 1959 it was part of the municipality of Santa Cruz do Sul.

Source: Godinho (1980).

RECIFE*

In the earliest years following its foundation, Recife expanded into the hinterland occupied by the first primitive sugar mills of the colonial period. The town was also linked with the sugar economy through migration since it was the natural channel through which the rural exodus passed on its way from the Zona da Mata. In the 1950s,

---

*Summary by Sales (1980).

when the population of the town of Recife most increased, the proportion of the migratory increase to the total population growth was nearly 50 percent. The few data available point to the fact that these migrants came above all from the Zona da Mata, a hinterland region which in turn receives migratory currents of a temporary or permanent nature (the so-called corumbas from the Agreste region) coming from regions even farther inland in the same state.

The Zona da Mata therefore forms a green belt around Recife, as happens with other regional metropolises. However, it does not supply the town with foodstuffs--only with migrant population. Apparently, the structural conditions associated with changes in the sugar economy led to this emigration from the sugar-producing region, most of which empties into Recife. The urban problems generated by this sizable influx of migrants can be seen above all in the proliferation of shanty-towns (locally known as mocambos) in the waterlogged outskirts of the town.

The dynamics of interregional integration under the hegemony of the Center-South and its process of industrialization resulted both in the intensification of commerce and migration between regions and in the growth of Recife after 1950. The integration of the Northeast into the model of capital accumulation (whose hegemonic pole was located outside the region) led to the disorganization of the agrarian and productive structure of the Recife hinterland and thus further encouraged migration into the town. Recife's urban problems therefore became linked to those of the region, which centered on the decline of local productive activities.

The same factors which account for migrations at the macro-structural level also account for the disorganization of certain industries. The introduction of manufactured goods from the Center-South was the main reason for the closing down of certain branches of Recife's industry, in particular the textile industry. This helps to explain the creation of SUDENE (Superintendency for Development of the Northeast) in 1959, with headquarters in Recife. The primary objective of this agency was to resolve these problems by revitalizing industry, creating jobs, and diversifying production.

The appearance of SUDENE marked a new era in the life of the town of Recife, primarily because of the new dynamics of urban employment resulting from the industrial projects implemented in the Northeast through tax incentives. In the 1960s, industry in the metropolitan area received a new injection of resources. However, this in fact led to an increase in manufacturing production rather than in the number of jobs, indicating the importance of the technological component in the industrialization of the Northeast under the auspices of SUDENE. The effect of the reorganization of industry in the area on the labor force can be seen in a drop in employment in the secondary sector in municipalities that traditionally housed a major portion of the state's textile industry (Paulista and Moreno).

The greatest growth was in the tertiary sector, especially in those branches where urban underemployment had been heaviest. If the various census data are combined with the findings of anthropological investigations carried out in Greater Recife, the most salient recent feature of the occupational structure in Recife's metropolitan area that emerges is intense fluctuation in the labor force between employment, unemployment, odd jobs, and various kinds of underemployment. Attention must also be paid to the increasing importance of the so-called informal sector in the economy as a whole, particularly during the post-SUDENE period; one example would be small commercial establishments, whose initial capital often depends on the small trader's position in the regular labor market.

The conflicts between the intense population growth, the poor living conditions in the marshland shantytowns, and the rising value of urban land after 1960 led to a new kind of migratory movement—intrametropolitan migration. This movement led to considerable population increases in the 1960s in the municipalities of Olinda, Jaboatao, and Sao Lourenco da Mata, which underwent a process of urban expansion as if they were outlying districts of Recife itself.

A summary of the main demographic indicators for Recife for the period 1940-70 is presented in Table A.6.

TABLE A.6 Dynamics of the Population of Recife (municipality), 1940-70: Brazil

Year	Total Population	Rate of Growth (percent)	Decomposition of Absolute Decennial Increase (percent)		Decomposition of Natural Increase			Decomposition of Birth Rate	
			Natural	Migratory	Crude Death Rate (per 1,000)	Crude Birth Rate (per 1,000)	General Fertility Rate (per 1,000)	Proportion of Women Aged 15-49 in Total Population (percent)
1940	348,424				22.83	44.34	143.70	30.86
		4.18	38.71	61.29				
1950	524,682				18.58	45.58	148.90	30.61
		4.16	58.57	41.43				
1960	788,336				13.41	46.99	166.25	28.27
		3.01	96.76	3.24				
1970	1,060,701				10.12	46.00	166.29	27.66

Source: Jose (1981).

REFERENCES

Almeida, A. L. O. de (1977) Fecundidade e tamanho da familia no Nordeste Brasileiro. <u>Pesquisa e Planejamento Economico</u> 7:291-332.

Altmann, A. M. G., and C. E. Ferreira (1979) Evolucao do censo demografico e registro civil como fontes de dados para a analise da fecundidade e mortalidade no Brasil. <u>Boletim Demografico</u> 10:1-85.

Altmann, A. M. G., and L. L. R. Wong (1981a) Estimativas de Fecundidade para o Brasil e suas Regioes a partir de Informacoes sobre Nupcialidade e Fecundidade Marital. Working Paper, GEADE/SEADE, Sao Paulo.

Altmann, A. M. G., and L. L. R. Wong (1981b) Padroes e tendencias da nupialidade no Brasil. Pp. 343-415 in <u>Anais: Segundo Encontro Nacional</u>. Sao Paulo: Associacao Brasileira de Estudos Populacionais (ABEP).

Anderson, J. E., M. Thome, and W. Rodrigues (1981) Survey of Maternal and Child Health and Family Planning in Northeastern Brazil: Measurement of the Duration of Breastfeeding and Postpartum Amenorrhea. Draft Working Paper, Center for Disease Control, Atlanta.

Berquo, E. S. (1973) Algumas Consideracoes Sobre a Variavel Idade das Mulheres nos Estudos de Fecundidade. Unpublished paper, Centro Brasileiro de Analise e Planejamento (CEBRAP), Sao Paulo.

Berquo, E. S. (1975) Some considerations on the population dynamics of Sao Jose dos Campos. <u>Estudos de Populacao</u>, 1. Sao Paulo: Centro Brasileiro de Analise e Planejamento (CEBRAP).

Berquo, E. S. (1976) A Pesquisa Sobre Reproducao Humana no Brasil. Paper presented at CLACSO Seminario

Teorico-Metodologico sobre las Investigaciones en Poblacion, Mexico.

Berquo, E. S. (1980) Algumas Indagacoes sobre a Recente Queda da Fecundidade no Brasil. Teresopolis: VI Reuniao do Grupo de Trabalho sobre o Processo de Reproducao da Populacao, CLACSO.

Berquo, E. S., and L. Jose (1976) The dynamics of the population of Sertaozinho. Estudos de Populacao 4. Sao Paulo: Centro Brasileiro de Analise e Planejamento (CEBRAP).

Berquo, E. S., and L. Jose (1978) The population dynamics of Parnaiba. Estudos de Populacao 3. Sao Paulo: Centro Brasileiro de Analise e Planejamento (CEBRAP).

Berquo, E. S., and V. da M. Leite (1979) O Metodo de Coale e Colaboradores para Estimar a Natalidade e a Fecundidade. Unpublished paper, Centro Brasileiro de Analise e Planejamento (CEBRAP), Sao Paulo.

Berquo, E. S., and M. C. Quintero (1979) The dynamics of the population of Cachoeiro do Itapemirim. Estudos de Populacao 5. Sao Paulo: Centro Brasileiro de Analise e Planejamento (CEBRAP).

Berquo, E. S., M. C. A. F. Oliveira, and C. P. Camargo, eds. (1977a) A Fecundidade em Sao Paulo. Sao Paulo: Editoria Brasileira de Ciencias.

Berquo, E. S., M. L. Milanesi, and J. R. Prandi (1977b) Estudo da influencia da idade dos pais, do uso de meios anticoncepcionais e do numero de gestacoes anteriores no resultado de uma gestacao. In E. Berquo et al., eds., A Fecundidade em Sao Paulo. Sao Paulo: Editoria Brasileira de Ciencias.

Berquo, E. S. et al. (1981) Estudo do Aleitamento Maternal na Grande Sao Paulo e na Grande Recife, em 1981. Relatorio Final. Sao Paulo: Centro Brasileiro de Analise e Planejamento (CEBRAP); UNICEF; and Instituto Nacional de Alimentacao e Nutricao (INAN).

Boletin de la Oficina Sanitaria Panamerican (1978) Padroes de atendimento ao parto no municipio de ribeirao preto, Sao Paulo, Brasil. Vol LXXV, No. 3.

Bongaarts, J. (1980) The Fertility-Inhibiting Effects of the Intermediate Fertility Variables. Working Paper, No. 57. Center for Policy Studies. New York: Population Council.

Bongaarts, J. (1983) The proximate determinants of natural marital fertility. In Determinants of Fertility in Developing Countries: A Summary of Knowledge. New York: Academic Press.

Brazil, Fundacao IBGE (1971-1980) Anuario Estatistical do Brasil. Rio de Janeiro: Fundacao IBGE.

Cardoso, F. H. (1975) Populacao e crescimento economico: notas sobre a estrutura socio-economica de Sao Jose dos Campos. Estudos de Populacao 1. Sao Paulo: Centro Brasileiro de Analise e Planejamento (CEBRAP).

Carvalho, J. A. M. de (1973) Analysis of Regional Trends in Fertility, Mortality, and Migration in Brazil: 1940-1970. Unpublished doctoral dissertation, London School of Economics, London.

Carvalho, J. A. M. de, and P. de T. A. Paiva (1976) Estrutura de renda e padroes de fecundidade no Brasil. In M. A. Costa, ed., Fecundidade: Padroes Brasileros. Rio de Janeiro: Altiva Grafica e Editora Ltda.

Carvalho, J. A. M. de, and C. Wood (1978) Mortality income distribution and rural-urban residence in Brazil. Population and Development Review 4:405-420.

Carvalho, J. A. M. de, P. de T. A. Paiva, and D. R. Sawyer (1981) The Recent Sharp Decline in Fertility in Brazil: Economic Boom, Social Inequality, and Baby Bust. Working Paper No. 8. Latin American and Caribbean Regional Office. Mexico City: Population Council.

CELADE, Centro Latinoamericano de Demografia, and CFSC, Community and Family Study Center (1972) Fertility and Family Planning in Metropolitan Latin America. Chicago: Community and Family Study Center, University of Chicago.

Coale, A. J. (1971) Age patterns of marriage. Population Studies 25(2):193-214.

Costa, M. A., ed. (1976) Fecundidade: Padroes Brasileiros. Rio de Janeiro: Altiva Grafica e Editora Ltda.

Davis, K., and J. Blake (1956) Social structure and fertility. Economic Development and Cultural Change 4:211-235.

Etges, N. J. (1975) Fecundidade Humana no Rio Grande do Sul. Sao Leopoldo: Universidade do Vale do Rio dos Sinos.

Etges, N. J. (1976) A fecundidade no Rio Grande do Sul. In M. A. Costa, ed., Fecundidade: Padroes Brasileiros. Rio de Janeiro: Altiva Grafica e Editora Ltda.

Faria, V. E. (1975) Uma Tipologia Empirica das Cidades Brasileiras. Unpublished paper, Centro Brasileiro de Analise e Planejamento (CEBRAP), Sao Paulo.

FIDEPE (1980) <u>Indicadores Sociais de Pernambuco</u>. Recife: State Government of Pernambuco.

Gaisie, S. (1981) Mediating mechanisms of fertility change in Africa -- The role of the post-partum variables in the process of change: The case of Ghana. In <u>International Population Conference Manila 1981</u> 1:95-114. Liege: International Union for the Scientific Study of Population (IUSSP).

Godinho, R. E. (1980) The dynamics of Santa Cruz do Sul. <u>Estudos de Populacao</u> 6. Sao Paulo: Centro Brasileiro de Analise e Planejamento (CEBRAP).

Hajnal, J. (1953) The marriage boom. <u>Population Index</u> 19(2):80-101.

Henriques, M. H. F. T. (1980) Unioes legais e consensuais: incidencia e fecundidade na America Latina. <u>Boletim Demografico</u> 10(3):23-62.

Hutchinson, B. (1964) Induced abortion in Brazilian married women. <u>America Latina</u> 7:21-34.

Ianni, O. (1978) A luta pela terra. <u>Estudos de Populacao</u> 2. Sao Paulo: Centro Brasileiro de Analise e Planejamento (CEBRAP).

Ianni, O. (1976) As relacoes de producao na agricultura. <u>Estudos de Populacao</u> 4. Sao Paulo: Centro Brasileiro de Analise e Planejamento (CEBRAP).

Jain, A. K., and J. Bongaarts (1981) Breastfeeding: patterns, correlates, and fertility effects. <u>Studies in Family Planning</u> 12(2):79-99.

Jose, L. (1981) The dynamics of the population of Recife. <u>Estudos de Populacao</u> 7. Sao Paulo: Centro Brasileiro de Analise e Planejamento (CEBRAP).

Kent, M. M. (1981) <u>Breast-feeding in the Developing World: Current Patterns and Implications for Futrue Trends</u>. Washington, D.C.: Population Reference Bureau.

Leibenstein, H. (1974) An interpretation of the economic theory of fertility. <u>Journal of Economic Literature</u> 12:457-479.

Leite, V. da M. (1981) Niveis e tendencias da mortalidade e da fecundidade no Brasil a partir de 1940. Pp. 581-609 in <u>Anais: Segundo Encontro Nacional</u>. Sao Paulo: Associacao Brasileira de Estudos Populacionais (ABEP).

Lesthaeghe, R. et al. (1981) Compensating changes in intermediate fertility variables and the onset of marital fertility transition. In *International Population Conference Manila 1981* 1:71-94. Liege: International Union for the Scientific Study of Population (IUSSP).

Lima, L. M. R. de (n.d.) Notas para o Estudo da Expansao do Capitalismo em Santa Cruz do Sul. Unpublished paper, Centro Brasileiro de Analise e Planejamento (CEBRAP), Sao Paulo.

Lima, O. R. (1967) O controle de natalidade no Brasil. *Revista Vozes* 61:989-991.

Lluch, C. (1981) Income Distribution and Family Characteristics in Brazil. Unpublished working paper, World Bank, Washington, D.C.

Lopes, J. B. (1975) Tipos de Areas Rurais no Brasil. Unpublished paper, Centro Brasileiro de Analise e Planejamento (CEBRAP).

Lopes, J. B., and V. C. Brandt (1978) Extrativismo e decadencia: Cidade e campo em Parnaiba. *Estudos de Populacao* 3. Sao Paulo: Centro Brasileiro de Analise e Planejamento (CEBRAP).

Loyola, M. A. (1978) Reproducao e estagnacao: Estudo das instituicoes sociais e comportamento reproductivo em Parnaiba. *Estudos de Populacao* 3. Sao Paulo: Centro Brasileira de Analise e Planejamento (CEBRAP).

Loyola, M. A., and M. C. Quinteiro (1982) *Estudos de Populacao VIII -- Instituicoes e Reproducao: Estudo da Atuacao das Instituicoes Sociais no Processo de Reproducao Humana.* Sao Paulo: Centro Brasileiro de Analise e Planejamento (CEBRAP).

Martine, G. (1975) *Formacion de la Familia y Marginalidad en Rio de Janeiro.* Santiago de Chile: Centro Latinamericano de Demografia.

Merrick, T. W. (1974) Interregional differences in fertility in Brazil. *Demography* 11:423-440.

Merrick, T. W. (1978) Fertility and land availability in rural Brazil. *Demography* 15:321-336.

Merrick, T. W. (1981) Land availability and rural fertility in Northern Brazil. Pp. 93-122 in J. L. Simon and P. H. Lindert, eds., *Research in Population Economics*, Vol. 3. Greenwich, Conn.: JAI Press.

Merrick T. W., and D. H. Graham (1979) *Population and Economic Development in Brazil.* Baltimore, Md.: Johns Hopkins University Press.

Milanesi, M. L. (1970) *Aborto Provocado.* Sao Paulo: Pioneira.

Nakamura, M. S. et al. (1979) *Sao Paulo Contraceptive Prevalence Survey: Final Report.* Campinas: Pontificia Universidade Catolica de Campinas, offset.

National Academy of Sciences (1979) Preliminary Report of the Panel on Brazil. Committee on Population and Demography. National Academy of Sciences, Washington, D.C.

National Research Council (1983) <u>Levels and Recent Trends in Fertility and Mortality in Brazil</u>. Washington, D.C.: National Academy Press.

Oliveira, E. M. de (n.d.) Santa Cruz do Sul. Unpublished paper, Centro Brasileiro de Analise e Planejamento (CEBRAP), Sao Paulo.

Oliveira, E. M. (1975) Santa Cruz do Sul: Sinteses de Informacoes Historico-Economicos Baseadas em Entrevistas e Leituras, Unpublished manuscript, CEBRAP.

Paiva, P. de T. A. (1982) O Processo de Proletarizacao como Fator de Desestabilizacao dos Niveis de Fecundidade no Brasil. Paper presented at VII meeting of CLACSO Working Group on Processes of Reproduction of the Population, Cuernavaca, Mexico.

Patarra, N. L. (1976) <u>O Estudo sobre Reproducao Humana no Distrito do Sao Paulo</u>. Sao Paulo: Universidade de Sao Paulo.

Puffer, R. R., and C. V. Serrano (1973) <u>Patterns of Mortality in Childhood</u>. Scientific Publication No. 262. Washington, D.C.: Pan American Health Organization.

Rea, M. F. (1981) Aleitamento Materno em Nucleos Rurais do Vale do Ribeira, Sao Paulo. Master's dissertation, University of Sao Paulo.

Rodrigues, W. et al. (1975) <u>Law and Population in Brazil</u>. Medford, Mass.: Law and Populatio Program, Fletcher School of Law and Diplomacy.

Rodrigues, W. et al. (1981a) Contraceptive Practice and Community-Based Distribution Program Impact in Northeast Brazil. Paper presented at annual meeting of American Public Health Association, Los Angeles.

Rodrigues, W. et al. (1981b) General Presentation of Maternal-Child Health and Family Planning Surveys. Paper contributed to IUSSP/ABEP meeting on Family Types and Fertility, Sao Paulo.

Rodrigues, W. et al. (1981c) <u>Pesquisa sobre Saude Materno Infantil e Planejamento Familiar: Piaui 1979</u>. Rio de Janeiro: Sociedade Civil Bem Estar Familiare no Brasil e Secretaria de Saude do Estado do Piaui.

Sales, M. T. (1979) Evolucao socioeconomia de Cachoeiro de Itapemirim. <u>Estudos de Populacao</u> 5. Sao Paulo: Centro Brasileiro de Analise e Planejamento (CEBRAP).

Sales, M. T. (1980) O Recife Se Mudou. *Estudo de Populacao* 6. Sao Paulo: Centro Brasileiro de Analise e Planejamento (CEBRAP).

Schultz, T. P. (1976) Determinants of fertility: a micro-economic model of choice. Pp. 89-124 in A. J. Coale, ed., *Economic Factors in Population Growth*. New York: John Wiley & Sons.

Silva, N. do V. (1979) Papdroes de nupcialiadade no Brasil: 1940-1970. *Boletim Demografico* 9:5-25.

Singer, P. (1975) Notas sobre a Tipologia. Unpublished paper, Centro Brasileiro de Analise e Planejamento, (CEBRAP), Sao Paulo.

Tilly, C. T. (1978) The historical study of vital processes. Pp. 13-56 in C. T. Tilly, ed., *Historical Studies of Changing Fertility*. Princeton: Princeton University Press.

United Nations (1979) *The Methodology of Measuring the Impact of Family Planning Programmes on Fertility*, Manual IX. New York: United Nations.

United Nations (1983) *Indirect Techniques for Demographic Estimation*, Manual X. New York: United Nations.

World Bank (1979) *Brazil: Human Resources Special Report*. Washington, D.C.: World Bank.

World Bank (1981) *World Development Report 1981*. New York: Oxford University Press.